DATE DUE

SAVING THE
SOUL OF
MEDICINE

Margaret A. Mahony, M.D.

Robert D. Reed Publishers • San Francisco, CA

Robert D. Reed Publishers
750 La Playa, Suite 647
San Francisco, CA 94121
Phone: 650/994-6570 • Fax: 994-6579
E-mail: 4bobreed@msn.com
Website: www.rdrpublishers.com

Co-publisher, Editor, Book Designer: Pamela D. Jacobs, M.A.
Book Cover: Julia Gaskill at Graphics Plus, Pacifica, CA

ISBN 1-885003-35-8

Library of Congress Catalog Card No. 99-067841

Manufactured, Typeset, and Printed in the United States of America

10 9 8 7 6 5 4 3 2 1

This book is dedicated with much gratitude to all those persons whose stories grace the following pages.

Contents

Notes to the Reader

The stories presented in this book are taken from actual events. The names have been changed to protect confidentiality. All patients interviewed during the course of the year in which their stories were collected gave their consent for their voices to be heard.

For the purpose of illustrating a point, there are occasional references to events that have occurred in the past. In these circumstances, the stories are taken from actual events but identifying details have been obscured in order to protect privacy.

This book is sold with the understanding that the subject matter covered herein is of a general nature and does not constitute medical, legal, or other professional advice for any specific individual or situation. Readers planning to take action in any of the areas that this book describes should seek professional advice from their doctors, specialists, and other advisers, as would be prudent and advisable under their given circumstances.

Prologue

I. A physician shall be dedicated to providing competent medical service with compassion and respect for human dignity.*

It is 4:00 a.m. I am awakened suddenly, abruptly, from a restless, irritable charade called sleep. I am certain only that my eyes were closed for some unspecified period of time. Perhaps I dreamt something. Something action packed, frenetic, and anxiety provoking—much like my days have been lately.

II. A physician shall deal honestly with patients and colleagues, and strive to expose those physicians deficient in character or competence. Or who engage in fraud or deception.

My soul is talking. It is claiming responsibility for this interrupted and unpleasant night. It does not apologize. It is demanding and unrelenting. *Pay attention!* it screams at me.

To what? I scream back in silent, miserable reply as my eyes start wide open to stare into the darkened, silent room.

Pay attention to what is going on. To what all of you are doing!

Or what?

Or it will destroy you.

III. A physician shall respect the law and also recognize a responsibility to seek changes in those requirements which are contrary to the best interests of the patient.

I am fully awake and aware that any possibility of sleep is futile. This is a chronic recurring event.

I have had far too many of these long, dark nights of the soul. Yes, far, far too many lately. And work awaits at dawn.

My soul will not acquiesce. I am supposed to start thinking. Again!

---

* American Medical Association Principles of Medical Ethics

IV. A physician shall respect the rights of patients, of colleagues, and of other health professionals, and shall safeguard patient confidences within the constraints of the law.

I leave the bed quietly, don my nightrobe, and leave my sleeping husband undisturbed. I pass by two other sleeping persons—my small son and daughter. Sleeping like angels. How I envy them as I tread quietly down the stairs. I am lost in reverie—about many things. My life, my agony, the torture of my soul. It is a physician's soul. A more tormented soul on earth there could not possibly be. I stand before its imperative call. In the kitchen, blinking dazedly as the fluorescent lights come to life.

Flipping halfheartedly through the tea basket, I reminisce on the most recent past. The most recent two to three years. Years of tumultuous change, years of sorrow, and years of disappointment accompanied by a sense of increasing disbelief. Years notable for increasingly disruptive and unbidden long, dark, agonizing nights of the soul.

V. A physician shall continue to study, apply and advance scientific knowledge, make relevant information available to patients, colleagues, and the public, obtain consultation, and use the talents of other health professionals when indicated.

I hold the hot cup of tea in my hands. In the rising steam I can see the faces of my patients before me, with bits of conversation and sometimes entire dialogue replayed verbatim. In this review I attempt in vain to find something positive in the present situation, this situation known as managed health care, but I cannot. I am haunted by the looks of disappointment, the furrowed brows of anger, the tears of sorrow, and the sprouting seeds of distrust—all wrapped in the cloak of impotence.

I tell them that I am unable to change this new system. This is the way it is. I cannot change the rules. It is their health plan that they have signed up for, after all. Why didn't they check into the details sooner than now? This is how their plan works. These words are comforting to say. These words of abdication. As if my hands are clean.

VI. A physician shall, in the provision of appropriate medical care, except in emergencies, be free to choose whom to serve, with whom to associate, and the environment in which to provide medical services.

I participate, but I am not in control. I make it all happen, but I do not write the rules. And if by my participation the patients appear unhappy, well, my hands are clean because that is the way the present system operates. My hands may think they are clean, but my soul is tainted. This will no longer do. I have agonized far too long during these endless nights. I have distracted myself with God knows how many books to pass the time away. What else can I do? I am pleading now. I am exhausted. Answer me! I am begging my soul for mercy. . . .

Just before the sun's rays pierce the leafy sycamore of my neighbor's yard that predawn morning, it finally occurs to me what is necessary.

VII. A physician shall recognize a responsibility to participate in activities contributing to an improved community.

To tell a story. (To tell these stories?) I shudder involuntarily at this thought, which has now been invited for consideration, as it pushes itself—as if by compulsion—to the center of my consciousness. A simple idea, really. I stare out over the mist rising from the lawn, and I can see the words and the pages unfolding before me, as if already finished.

Why me? I ask.

A silent, judgmental reply resounds.

I am bargaining and maneuvering now. This situation is futile. There is so much disappointment, sorrow, and disillusionment. What good will it do?

Expectant silence.

And if I do not?

More of the same as tonight.

And if I do?

Then you shall sleep. Peacefully.

I see. Nodding in bleak acquiescence, I stare unfocused across the lawn. For I can see them all clearly. Hear their stories and feel their distress. I have until today been a silent witness to it all. All of it! Dear God! How has this come to pass?

Do not despair, Physician! For hope is firmly anchored among those faces and interwoven faithfully into the fabric of their lives. A powerful restorative is within your reach! It is yours, but for the asking, in the end.

Preface

Prepare yourself to enter the intimate world of a physician. Witness an entire year of experiences, thoughts, and reflections. You will see that a physician's life is unpredictable, intense, an admixture of surprise and suspense, and full of the awareness of the powerful unknown force beyond.

By necessity, there will be reminiscence and explanation in order to achieve understanding. By virtue of the subject matter, there will be complexity.

One purpose of this book is to highlight the contemptible consequences of managed health care. This intimate view may arouse some unpleasant and negative visceral feelings. It is very important not to direct any of these feelings at any particular physician, hospital, or other entity. I believe that the human beings involved are doing the best they can under extremely adverse circumstances.

Rather, direct these feelings at the real culprit—that invisible, intangible, *seemingly* omnipotent force known as managed care.

Patient Stories

Give us your tired, your poor (and rich and in-between),
Your huddled masses yearning to seek medical care.

I can visualize an elaborate game, with someone dividing up all of the "covered lives" in this valley and devising all sorts of strategies and devices by which to attract and "capture" them. What actually happens to them after they are "captured" seems less important.

In Search of . . . Hope

This was a hectic day. It started off with an illusion of calmness that lasted until midday. It was much like the spring days in this valley. They begin with a blanket of fog that covers all with a calm, soothing shroud until midday. The fog then burns off to reveal everything under the unrelenting glare of the sun. Such a metaphor describes my day.

I began the afternoon forty-five minutes behind schedule. This was a rarity for me, as I do my level best to adhere as closely as possible to the schedule. I am respectful of my patients' time and aware that they have other commitments. I dislike running behind for many reasons, but the most particular reason is that I am then obliged to start off every conversation with an apology: "I am sorry, I am running behind today. . . ." (Over and over again. . . . throughout the seemingly endless afternoon.)

However, this particular afternoon, had I been able to explain it to them, I am sure the patients would not have minded. I was delayed because I was listening to another patient's heartbreaking story. Helen needed my assistance at that moment; no other time would do. She had dropped by near the end of the lunch hour to talk. She had been through some tough times recently and found herself at a crossroads. My role was to listen.

Helen had been diagnosed with breast cancer approximately two years earlier. After completing the initial treatment and having dealt successfully with the inevitable emotional fallout, she believed that she was "safe." She was faithful to her follow-up appointment schedule and had had no evidence of recurrence. So far, so good. That is, until last July.

That is when the intense back pain started and she made an appointment with her oncologist. Diagnostic studies were ordered, and after waiting one agonizing week she learned that the cancer had indeed spread to involve her spine. She was devastated by this news. She was acutely aware of the seriousness of this situation and was greatly concerned. She had come face-to-face with her mortality. It was at this point that she began to feel uncomfortable with the manner of the treatment received at her oncologist's office.

Helen began to notice that the office appeared very busy. She noticed that it appeared to take quite a long time to obtain test results. The information was given only during office appointments, and sometimes there was a wait of two to three weeks before receiving the information. She was increasingly dissatisfied with the manner in which her messages were dealt with. Out of all the messages left with the nurse, she could recall only about one or two being returned in a timely manner. She began to notice a particular and perhaps unwelcome tone in the receptionists' voices when she called. She received the distinct impression that she was calling "too much" and "too often." She wondered: Was she trying to receive more services than perhaps she was entitled to under her "health maintenance organization"—her "HMO"? This was particularly evident when she sought a second opinion from a specialist at a university hospital. She received the impression that this was a service that *perhaps* was outside of her entitlement. She had to fight for it, and the request was granted.

She began to wonder if the office or the physician actually cared about her as a person. Do they actually have enough time? Does the doctor ever look at my messages? She began to doubt this, as she could not recall receiving any return calls from the doctor. Rather, only the nurse returned her calls, and only after a minimal delay of forty-eight hours. Her final question: Do they really believe my case is so hopeless that I am not even worthy of their time?

The result of this indifference was that she stopped calling. Helen was left by herself to wonder about this or that symptom. . . . Is "this" important? Is "this" a potentially serious side effect from chemotherapy? Could "this" new pain signify that my cancer is spreading? Important and agonizing questions. She needed someone to talk to.

Her periodic chemotherapy appointments at her physician's office left much to be desired. After checking in and receiving the cursory and customary greeting, she was led into a large room with several other persons who were also receiving chemotherapy. It was cold, impersonal, and dehumanizing. She felt that she was being a nuisance when she requested the use of a pillow and a blanket. This was because the treatment lasted four hours and the sedative that she received often resulted in fulfilling its intention—she fell asleep. Since she was a "regular," why did she have to ask each and every time for the use of a pillow and a blanket? It was a simple courtesy. Couldn't they remember?

It was the culmination of all of this that caused her to begin to wish for a different doctor. She knew that her physician was well respected, and she had no doubt of medical competency. This was not enough to dispel uneasiness and disquiet. Something was missing. Helen began her inquiries among her network of friends.

She was given a recommendation and placed a telephone call to a different oncologist's office. It was a very positive and encouraging conversation. She requested information to be sent in the mail. She received the literature a short time later. Upon opening the packet, the first item she noticed was an article about *hope*. That was *it*! The missing ingredient. She was aware of this immediately and became determined to transfer her care to this physician. Only one stumbling block remained. She had to make an appointment with her primary care physician in order to request a referral. She used the term "beg."

Helen made an appointment with her primary care physician later in the week. She was dreading it because of the energy expenditure required. She had already spent a great deal of energy collecting her medical records and reviewing them in order to present her case. She was already so very, very tired, as she was still in the midst of periodic chemotherapy treatments. She suspected that she had actually remained much longer in the care of her present oncologist because of the deterrent that requesting a referral represented. Time was of the essence. Her time. Hope was in reach and was so absolutely essential. Her appointment was in two days.

I made a note of it and promised that I would personally intervene on her behalf in order to see that her wish and desire were realized. She had been through enough already. It was the very least that I could do.

In loving memory of Helen, who found hope in time.

Pap Smears and HMO Contracting

Connie is a young, hard-working Silicon Valley employee. Typical of her peers, she puts in long hours at work. There is an intensity in the workplace that cannot be escaped. This desire to work, to push, to excel drives the workers in this valley. It is their pulse, and it is full and bounding. At this speed there is little tolerance for detours, especially if they carry an emotional price.

She asked me yesterday what my opinion was regarding the pap smear lab that held the contract for her HMO. Was it a good one? She was concerned because the results had returned. Her initial pap smear was *not* within normal limits. She was in the office for the purpose of obtaining a repeat test. It is very disturbing when women learn that their pap smear results are not normal. One of the reasons they faithfully visit the gynecologist every year is to hear "Everything is fine." It is good to hear this, perhaps because they know deep down inside that quite possibly someday things may not be "fine." So receiving news about an abnormal pap smear is not welcome. It causes them to ponder and worry and fret.

Connie wanted to know if the pap smear lab was reliable. In particular, she wanted to know if the result was valid. This concern quite possibly is encouraged by the occasional coverage in the media regarding large commercial pap smear labs. The bulk of this commentary is unfavorable. Her question caught me off guard.

I rendered a careful reply. I stated that it was my understanding that the pap smear lab in question was surely adequate and satisfactory. I was also reasonably certain that the HMO had set performance and quality-assurance guidelines and that the laboratory would most certainly have met these standards. In addition, a state regulating board was most likely involved as well. Generally speaking, I felt the results could be trusted to be accurate. This answer was not good enough for the earnest, concerned twenty-eight-year-old who sat before me. Her eyes did not leave my face.

She persisted. Was it the best lab? What was my specific answer to this question? Was there actually another laboratory that I preferred?

Direct questions require honest and complete answers. No, I replied. I did not think that this was the "best" lab. Realize, I elaborated, that the designation "best" carries a significant subjective component. My concerns regarding the lab were few, but not insignificant. First of all, it was a larger, more "commercial" operation compared to the one that I prefer. Second, I have some reservations regarding the financial arrangements that may exist between the two parties. I am not privy to the specifics, and I cautioned her on my speculation in this matter. However, it is generally known that the HMOs are perpetually negotiating for their contracted services, and the bottom line seems to be the overriding concern. Shop talk among physicians reveals that it is not unheard of for HMOs to actually contract with labs at a price set *below* the cost of performing the test. This is all wrapped up in some complicated package deal, with high-volume inducements seeming to be the primary consideration. This makes me uneasy.

It is not possible for me to render an unqualified endorsement of the lab. An additional subjective factor in my decision is that I happen to know the physicians of my preferred lab. I know them to be conscientious and to possess the highest integrity. This is not to say that the directors of the nonpreferred lab are not; it's just that I do not know who they are.

Connie then informed me that she wanted me to send her pap smear to the "best" lab. She was willing to bear the expense herself. Before the proliferation of HMOs, I was able to send all of my patients' pap smears to the "best" lab. Now, I can perform this service only for my non-HMO patients and, of course, the occasional savvy consumer.

I honored her request.

This is, of course, the type of treatment that I expect when I make my annual visit to the gynecologist. In fact, it was the topic of my first visit: What lab would she use, and did she think it was the best? Not being hindered in any way by insurance or contracting stipulations, she was free to use her judgment and select what was, in her opinion, the "best." That suited me just fine. What else would I want her to do? Nothing less than to operate with only my best interests at heart.

What is a "covered life"?

I would like to fantasize that "covered lives" is a term that refers to those few individuals we all know who are so well organized that they have all of their bases covered. The term might also refer to those extremely efficient individuals who seem always to have their loose ends "wrapped up." Alternatively, it could be used to describe the several hundred thousand individuals who make this valley their home, referring to that time during our rainy season when they exit their houses in the morning appropriately garbed in raincoats and boots, with umbrella in hand, thus being "all covered up."

As much as this fantasy is pleasing to me as a source of reflection and escape, such is not the case. The term "covered lives" refers to all of the individuals in this valley who have health insurance. Rather than view these covered lives as important tokens to collect as a means of obtaining power and prestige, I feel otherwise. (The number of covered lives that an organization can lay claim to is useful as bargaining power in negotiations with major health insurers and hospitals, for example.)

Insensitivity

I was well under way, working in the office through the bulk of an unusually busy afternoon schedule, when I received a telephone call that would add a twenty-minute delay into an already twenty minutes behind schedule. At the completion of the telephone call, I would be running forty minutes behind.

It was an important call. Theresa called me directly from her hospital bed. She was worried about her HMO not covering her hospital stay. I thought that she already had enough to worry about without needing more problems.

Theresa had delivered a baby yesterday that was seven weeks premature. She was still in that state of confusion, shock, and disbelief that is the normal accompaniment of this type of event. Her baby was doing well in the intensive-care unit, and Theresa was ready to go home this evening—approximately thirty-six hours after giving birth. One could make an argument for prolonging her stay; unfortunately there would be no "medical necessity" to back it up.

Her particular problem started earlier this morning. The decision regarding her discharge plan was finalized on morning rounds. Theresa then performed her duty of contacting the insurance company to notify them that her post-maternity stay would exceed twenty-four hours. It was at this point that she spoke to a utilization review coordinator who informed her that maternity coverage was only guaranteed at twenty-four hours, and who went on to elaborate that the likelihood existed that the additional twelve hours might not be covered. The coordinator kindly informed Theresa that this cost would be approximately $1,200. This only added to Theresa's anxiety at a time when it would not have been thought possible to do so.

In between visits to the NICU, trying to recover from birth, and adjusting to the reality of being a new mother, Theresa found herself involved in conversations with the hospital utilization review coordinator, her nurses, and her HMO. Unable to clarify this issue, she finally called me.

As I listened to this tale, I was overcome with a variety of emotions: disbelief, irritation, and disgust. I could not quite isolate the precise nature of the disturbance, but I felt that somehow I was implicated in this affair. My name printed in plain black-and-white in the provider directory has somehow given tacit approval for this entire scenario to exist and continue. While I am quite capable of rectifying this situation, I also feel deeply that I am to be held accountable for its existence. At times like these, when I am experiencing a sinking, queasy, unsettling feeling in the pit of my stomach, I realize that I cannot get out of here fast enough.

I promised Theresa that I would contact the appropriate persons involved and explain the details of the case to ensure that coverage for the entire hospital stay would be guaranteed.

I suggested to her that she concentrate on taking good care of herself and her precious little baby girl, who at this most important time deserved her mother's undivided attention.

The Dawning of Realization

I was enjoying a rare smoothly running afternoon in the office today. The type of afternoon that my assistant and myself are grateful for, because we have been given the gift of time. Time to breathe, time to make a joke, time to notice that my office manager appears tired, and time to return messages from those most patient patients. It is a fleeting gift and for that reason appreciated all the more. It is a little-known secret that physicians actually experience a thrill when they are running on time and according to schedule. It was in this state of professional euphoria that I entered the room to interview Isabelle, the last patient of the day. She was scheduled for a routine annual exam. I was in for a surprise. Euphoria would soon dissipate.

As I reviewed her medical records, I realized that she had not been in the office for two and a half years. I asked her where she had been. I also wanted to know how she was doing.

With a resigned look on her face, she replied that things were not going well. My curiosity was immediately aroused. I asked for an explanation.

She mentioned that since her last visit she had changed her insurance plan and had been enrolled in an HMO of which I was not a member. She had been seeking medical care among the physicians on that medical plan. She had been enjoying excellent health up until and including the time of her last visit in my office. She then began to have problems that became apparent shortly after she had changed insurance plans.

She had been plagued for two years by the development of chronic back pain and progressive immobility of her spine. At the present time, the immobility had progressed to the point that she had difficulty in attempting simply to twist her upper body and she had trouble bending over to pick up an item off the floor. I remarked on the fact that she was a young woman and this type of problem was most unusual for someone her age. I inquired as to whether or not she had been seeking medical attention and what the result had been.

She replied that she had been seeing physicians through her HMO. Specifically, she had been seen by and had had consultations with five physicians and two physical therapists. It appeared to Isabelle that not one of these physicians had been able to establish a correct diagnosis for her disabling condition. Consequently, a suitable treatment regimen had not been rendered. She had the distinct feeling that she did not fit into a "standard" clinical profile. The physicians did not seem able or willing to pursue evaluation of this problem adequately from her point of view. They seemed "apathetic" to her concerns. Her concern regarding her chronic pain increased and was exacerbated when she first began to notice the problem of limited movement. She became even more concerned when she began to have trouble bending over.

She felt that assistance in the management of her pain was woefully inadequate. It was Isabelle herself who suggested to the physicians that physical therapy might prove useful. It was the lack of direction on the physicians' part that prompted Isabelle to do her own medical research. Through a med-line search (a review of the medical literature which is usually topic specific), she was able to learn about all of the possible diagnoses that might apply to herself. From this type of research, she also learned about all of the appropriate remedies. She found herself bringing this up for discussion at the time of her physician appointments.

At the completion of her two years of evaluation, she had only increasing pain, progressive immobility, and no diagnosis or any idea as to what might be wrong with her. She felt disgusted and disappointed with the quality of medical attention she had received. Why couldn't they find out what was wrong with her? Why didn't they believe the intensity of the pain that she was experiencing? She was growing increasingly concerned and anxious about the progressive immobility. This was not good. Wasn't there something that could be done to help her? She expected her physicians to perform better. She expected them to demonstrate greater concern. She expected them to act in a more proactive manner.

At the end of two years she felt as if she had come to the end of the road—with nowhere to go. She felt as if there was no hope for her. In the midst of these most desperate of ruminations, it finally dawned upon Isabelle to consider switching health plans.

She established a relationship with a new physician and was most relieved when the doctor actually appeared to take her problem seriously. When the physician expressed the wish to get to the root of the problem and stated "We ought to be able to determine what is going on," Isabelle felt as though she were being given a most priceless gift—that of true compassion backed up by professional expertise. A sign of hope at last. Perhaps she would be able to recover, after all.

She was given an appointment with a specialist and was looking forward to that day. Since she was in my office for her annual checkup, she solicited my opinion as well. I gave her a recommendation of a physician who also specialized in treating this type of problem. I expressed my opinion that, between the two of them, something ought to be discovered soon.

However, I cautioned her that the person I had referred her to might not be on her present medical plan. She replied, "At this point it does not matter. I have finally realized that I may have to go 'out of plan' and pay 'out of pocket' to find someone who can really help me."

Year-end summary statements outlining goals and objectives from HMOs and other insurance entities focus on proud statements regarding the number of "covered lives" each can claim for itself. I was recently at a meeting where the subject of discussion was a particular medical group and the number of covered lives that it had acquired. It appears that the name of this game is how many "covered lives" each of these competing entities can acquire. The greater the number of "covered lives," the greater the sense of power.

That I am also known as a "covered life" is a disconcerting thought.

Dana

We were working at the typical frenzied pace often associated with an "on-call" day when the request from the general surgeon's office was made. Their receptionist was on the telephone asking for an immediate authorization number so that Dana, one of our patients, could be seen in their office. Dana had made an appointment for a follow-up visit with the surgeon. She had undergone a breast biopsy a few months ago and had been advised to make the follow-up appointment. She had dutifully done this and was sitting in the waiting room. However, under the rules of her HMO, she could not be seen in the office without permission (authorization) from her primary care physician. The receptionist mistakenly called our office, believing that we possessed the authority to grant such permission. She had good reason to do so. This highlights one of the peculiarities of Dana's HMO.

A few months ago, I had seen her for her routine annual exam. As is the case with most women, she only sees her gynecologist for the annual health visits. She had completed the required selection of a primary care physician. As is typical of many women, she could see little reason to actually see him (or her). Patients often bring all of their problems to us, believing that we can assist them. At the time of the exam, I found a breast lump and was relieved to be able to send Dana directly to a surgeon. This particular plan allows me to take this single most important step. This was done. She underwent biopsy of a benign lump.

Dana was reminded while in my office recently that she was due for her postoperative checkup with her surgeon. She forgot, however, to obtain permission from the primary care physician—thus precipitating the urgent phone call on Friday afternoon.

While I am allowed to send Dana initially for evaluation, I am not allowed to authorize the follow-up visits. The receptionist was informed of this disappointing news. She then was required to place a telephone call to the primary care physician's office in order to obtain permission—which adds consideration of another interesting facet of this saga.

Since I was the referring physician, I received all of the pertinent details, that is, copies of the operative report, biopsy result, recommended treatment plan, and follow-up schedule. It is entirely likely that the primary care physician did not receive any of this information. This would have happened only if Dana had explicitly informed the surgeon. It is typical for the specialist to ask the patient for the name of the referring physician. This is done to ensure that pertinent medical information will be sent back. I suspect that Dana replied that I was her doctor (true), and it is likely that the conversation did not extend further along those lines. Fast-forward to the present.

The receptionist now places a telephone call to the patient's designated primary care physician. Has the patient ever actually seen the doctor? Is this physician even aware that the biopsy was performed and of what the results were? Would urgent permission be granted under such circumstances? It would certainly require a *lengthy* explanation over the telephone.

My assistant and I sadly shook our heads over this episode. Would Dana actually be seen today? How much effort would be exerted on the part of all concerned to make sure this would happen? It was regrettably out of our hands. Was all of this necessary? What is the point, really?

What Seems to Be Missing?

One of the most interesting aspects of my profession concerns the wide variety of patients that are seen daily—along with their unique stories and viewpoints. It is truly a privilege to be a part of such a daily walk with humanity. It is an enlightening, humbling, and sometimes astonishing ramble. It is a constant reminder that we (physicians) are not on an island. The connection to the patients and their perspective is critical to achieving the goal of practicing good medicine. I am always being surprised by what the patients will say. Their insights are at times so perfectly lucid and to the point that it cannot be stated any better. Such would be the case today as I entered the room to examine Tammy, who was scheduled for a routine annual exam.

I commented that it had been one and a half years since she was last in the office. She concurred, stating that it had been a very busy year. She relayed some news regarding an illness that involved a member of the family. She then mentioned that she herself had been suffering from a medical problem of a chronic nature. She had recently learned the underlying cause. She concluded this past history with the remark that her personal health was improving. She was looking forward to a better year.

I finished taking the recent history and completed the physical exam. I then advised that she proceed with an endometrial biopsy. This was necessary to make sure that she did not have any precancerous changes in the lining tissue of the uterus. She was in the menopausal change, and her symptoms mandated that this precautionary step be taken. It was at this point that she mentioned her concerns and frustrations with her HMO.

She had recently become a member and was learning "the ropes." She had received the provider directory and had been relieved to find my name listed. Accordingly, she made an appointment in the office for her annual checkup.

Upon arrival, Tammy had dutifully presented her insurance card. It was then that she learned the discouraging news that I was *not* a member of the plan. Coming to my office to receive medical care actually constituted "going out of network." Different rules were applicable to this type of situation. She was confused and felt very foolish. She had assumed that if my name was listed in the provider directory, I must be included in the network. Our office staff had the thankless job of explaining to her that they did not know why I was listed. They apologized. It was explained to her that the content of the directories was out of our hands. They speculated that it was possible that she had received an outdated directory. There had been many changes lately, and some shifting of the provider networks had occurred. Tammy was left with the decision to remain in our care or to switch to a physician on the panel. She decided to remain with our office, as she had been a patient for many years.

I listened to this rendition of events with a mixture of concern and speculation. I felt the need to caution her.

"Additional follow-up is needed in order to address your needs completely. I would be happy to take care of this situation," I said. I also explained that some effort was required on her part to continue her care in this office. She would be required to contact her primary care physician and request an exemption. Specifically, it was necessary to request "out of network" permission to continue her care with me.

Tammy replied that she was certainly quite motivated to take these steps. She mentioned that she was tired of switching doctors. She stated that she would take care of the required details immediately. She would obtain the necessary referral to return here for treatment.

We have an office policy to be explicit with patients when they endeavor to make these "out of network" decisions. This policy is in existence because of the widespread confusion that we have witnessed to be prevalent—confusion instigated by the seemingly endless changes that have occurred and continue to occur with respect to patients' health insurance coverage.

Tammy was advised that an out-of-network exemption would cover only about eighty percent of the office charges. She said that it was definitely worth it. She did not want to start all over again and establish a relationship with a new physician. "It is scary [to contemplate taking such a big step]. The issue of trust is so important."

"Besides," she concluded. "I may have other deficiencies, but common sense is not one of them."

Where will all of these covered lives receive their medical care? In what manner will it be delivered? This HMO-model system is already overloaded. There is not enough time in the day to really "take care" of these lives when they seek medical attention. Of course, that is what they really desire—to be taken care of, to be listened to, and to become well. It feels as if there are too many patients trying to obtain care from too few physicians.

Participating in HMO medicine brings to mind a paraphrase of the poem displayed in the Statue of Liberty:

Give us your tired, your poor (and rich and in-between),
Your huddled masses yearning to seek medical care.

A Long-Distance Plea for Help

I received a telephone call late this evening from Barbara. She is one of my relatives, and she lives in the Midwest. She was experiencing a significant amount of pelvic pain. She called specifically to request my advice. These types of requests are fielded frequently by "physicians in the family"—as family members seem to possess the desire to double-check rendered medical advice. I have the distinct feeling that there has been an exponential increase lately in this type of long-distance advice.

Barbara was experiencing a flare-up of a chronic problem that was well known to her previous gynecologist. She had moved, and she had not been bothered by any symptoms until recently. Her primary concern this evening was the fact that she was experiencing pain, and none of the prescribed medications was working. She was worried about making it through the weekend, since the pain was debilitating enough to awaken her several times during the night.

I asked her whether she had seen a physician for this. She replied that she had been seen in the urgent care clinic of her HMO. An ultrasound had been performed. She believed that something was found on the ultrasound exam that could account for her pain. However, she was required to wait five days until her appointment with her primary care physician. At that time, she would be able to learn what the next step would be. I asked her whether she had made an appointment with a gynecologist. She replied that it was not allowed under the rules of her HMO. The decision of whether or not she would be sent to a gynecologist was at the discretion of the primary care physician.

I asked her how she was feeling. She said that she was unhappy about waiting such a long time before being seen by her physician. She also wanted to be able to go directly to her gynecologist for evaluation. This is what she was accustomed to doing under her previous insurance plan. She was uneasy about the referral process. What if she was not sent? She also expressed her opinion regarding the entire HMO system of medicine.

"I am concerned that someone is not going to be taken care of in a system like this." She felt very uncomfortable as to her own immediate outlook. Her primary concern was the pain that she was experiencing. She did not think it was possible to make it through the weekend without a change in treatment.

My advice to her was that it was absolutely important that she remain adamant and vocal. "The squeaky wheel gets the grease," I reminded her. I told her to call first thing in the morning and insist upon receiving an appointment with a physician—before the weekend. This would ensure at the very least that appropriate pain medication could be prescribed. This was followed by my trump card.

"When you see your primary care physician on Monday, tell him that you have already spoken to the gynecologist in the family. She is wondering why you have not yet been given a referral to see a gynecologist."

That is a sad commentary on the present state of affairs, but at least it should ensure that Barbara receives appropriate medical care.

I am virtually certain that I am not the only "MD in the family" who has been dispensing this type of advice lately.

Why?

On average, a pregnant woman sees her obstetrician approximately fourteen times during a nine-month period. Add to this the number of "in-between" visits and in most circumstances a second pregnancy, and it is easy to see why a strong and unique bond is developed. Once formed, such a bond usually lasts for the entire period of time that the obstetrician is in practice. The level of trust and comfort that the woman has with her obstetrician is unequaled in her relationships with any other physician—however much the insurance industry would try to convince us otherwise.

Emma was in the office this morning for a routine obstetrical visit. All was going well. This was her second pregnancy, and as she was comfortable with the various changes and symptoms, she had no questions in that regard. She did come with a particular request. She had noticed an unusual growth on the skin of her face. She had been bothered by this problem during her first pregnancy. She recalled that she had seen a dermatologist for treatment. With this in mind, she asked me to authorize a referral for a visit. She mentioned that during her last pregnancy I had been able to perform this task.

It is hard to describe the feeling that settles over me when I am about to tell someone news that she is not going to like. Knowing that the recipient of the news is going to become crestfallen precipitates a temporary feeling of dread. This is followed quickly by the erection of "barriers" to prevent being drawn into the undertow of disappointment. Doctors do not like being the bearers of bad news. Some of us have learned to do this very well, others have not. It is one circumstance to be the bearer of bad news when it involves an unavoidable serious medical problem, such as a problem with the baby or a complication of labor. It is quite another circumstance altogether when one plays an assigned role and is obligated to be the bearer of news that is "bad" only by virtue of the fact that the patient is a participant in an HMO plan. It was in the latter of these two situations that I now found myself. As I rewound the usual and standard reply, it occurred to me that I have been placed in this situation far too many times as of late and for no good reason.

I inspected Emma's area of concern and agreed with her that a dermatologist was the appropriate physician to treat such a condition. I then told her that I was not able to refer her to a dermatologist. I did not possess this authority under the rules of her HMO. She was disappointed. I have perceived that it is often difficult for patients to be confident and make specific requests of their physicians—even when they are right. I believed that in this particular case this was so, which meant that the disappointment would be felt all the more acutely by her—and secondarily by myself. She ventured another question.

"Why can't you issue the referral? You were able to do so during my last pregnancy."

I replied that the rules had changed since then. I remained perfectly able and willing to do so. However, her HMO had decided that all such requests and authorizations must go through her primary care physician. I am only allowed to make referrals for specific problems related to her pregnancy.

She was not very happy. "It is a waste of time and money to be obligated to make an appointment with the primary care physician. Why should I have to make an office visit for the sole purpose of requesting a referral to a dermatologist?" She thought that I should be able to make the referral.

I thought silently, It is hard to argue with pure logic. I nodded in acquiescence.

What else could I say? I discussed with her the possibility that a referral might not be such an automatic expectation. She was aware of this. She then commented that she had seen her primary care physician for a similar skin condition and he had proceeded to treat it himself. She was not pleased with the result. I then suspected that this formed much of the basis for our entire conversation. I felt a most pressing need to administer a short course in assertiveness training.

"Listen carefully. If you were not pleased with your service, be insistent upon your request for a referral. You do know what is best for yourself. You are entitled to see a dermatologist under your health plan. Do not let the arbitrary rules of your HMO stand in the way if you feel so strongly about it, particularly with your previous experience taken into account!"

Emma agreed with me and stated that she would do as I advised. However, I remained doubtful. Most patients, particularly women, remain far too passive regarding their own health issues. It is hard to confront such an entrenched and monolithic entity.

As I observed her leaving the office, I surmised that the chances were fifty-fifty at best that she would actually make it to the dermatologist's office.

Discounted high-volume medicine has replaced the traditional model of medical care-giving. The emphasis is on providing the service and taking care of and "servicing" as many patients as possible during office hours. The time spent with the patient has so little value at present that it is not unheard of for the length of a typical interaction to vary from six to ten minutes. In many ways, this brings to mind an analogy to Jiffy Lube. I have in the past been a very well satisfied customer of this business establishment. I have been pleased with the quick and efficient service I have received there. However, I would venture to say that even the directors of Jiffy Lube would hesitate to recommend that this model of business practice be adapted and modified to suit the physician's office. And yet, sadly, this is what seems to have occurred. Too many patients to be seen, too little time in which to see them.

Musical Primary Care Physicians

"My health insurance plan has changed again. It is becoming such a frustrating experience."

Thus did a routine well-woman visit start off this morning. I know Rosalinda well. I managed her care a few years ago, when she required a hysterectomy for endometriosis, a serious gynecological problem. I reflected upon that time while commiserating with her.

"Yes, I realize how frustrating it is for you. I am growing tired of hearing about it all day long. There is an alarming degree of unhappiness that exists. You are lucky that you had your problem diagnosed a few years ago—before all of this rigmarole became entrenched."

At that time, the nature of Rosalinda's surgery required an expert in female surgery. Fortunately for her, I had the luxury of selecting the best person. This selection ensured that her surgery, which was of a complex and difficult nature, was able to be performed without incident or complication. I shuddered to think of what might happen to her at this time if we were to relive the same sequence of events. I would not now have the freedom to choose as well as I chose then.

Rosalinda then elaborated on her health insurance woes. This is the fifth time that her health insurance plan has changed at work. Again, the plan requires that she choose a primary care physician. Thus, she is faced with trying to select the fourth or fifth primary care physician—she has lost count—in the same number of years. The primary care physicians are aligned with particular specialists in certain networks. Therefore, it is important for the woman subscribers to make certain that their gynecologist belongs to the same network as the primary care physician. This is due to the gatekeeper and permission aspect. These women learn that they cannot come to my office for evaluation of a gynecological problem without first obtaining permission from the primary care physician. A prerequisite to obtaining permission is, of course, to make certain that I am in the same network. So the astute patients usually have to make several telephone calls to verify this information.

As it turned out in this particular case, Rosalinda's present primary care physician is not on her new plan. Thus, after completing the behind-the-scenes investigating of the pertinent relationships last year, she now has to do it all over again. The single constant in her mind is to make certain that she retains the ability to receive her gynecological care in my office. In a gesture of fatigue and resignation, she mentioned, "I just picked a random name off the list."

She feels that it is entirely likely that she will never see her primary care physician, as she likes to come to our office to receive her care. It is necessary for her to go through the charade of selecting her primary care physician prior to being allowed to come to our office. Under a capitated method of reimbursement, she is an ideal patient from the point of view of the primary care physician (PCP): a patient who is signed up with the PCP, but will likely never make a single visit to see him or her during the year. Since the PCP receives payment whether or not Rosalinda is seen, there is little incentive to change the present system.

Rosalinda ended the interview by sharing with me a new angle on providing health care services. The employees at her place of work were required to attend a recent meeting that addressed the new changes in their health benefits. Apparently, they were informed that, contingent upon accepting coverage under one of the health plans, they would be required to report to a special clinic for their annual exams. The identity of the physicians who were going to be performing these exams was not made clear to the employees. This is assuming that they are, in fact, physicians. It was made clear that it was a separate group of providers, as distinguished from their designated primary care physicians. My ears pricked up at this interesting bit of news. Was this a health care version of "outsourcing"?

Leave it to those MBAs . . . and bless their creativity!

Who exactly are the people performing these exams? Are they physicians? Physician assistants? Nurse practitioners?

Since they were clearly not the primary care physicians, what would happen to the relay of medical information, already in an extremely tenuous and somewhat unreliable state? If these persons actually found something on these routine exams that required medical attention, to whom would this information be relayed? Would I ever receive any information regarding any of this? I, in whom the patient has the greatest degree of trust?

The most fundamental elements involved in receiving good medical care have to do with continuity, careful attention to detail, and long-term follow-up (the longer the better). Changing PCPs as if one is playing musical chairs is undesirable enough. Being required to obtain your annual exam with an unknown and unproven entity is remarkably unwise and quite likely to prove to be extremely hazardous to your health.

This practice should qualify for a warning label from the Surgeon General himself, at the very least.

Friday Morning: There Is a First Time for Everything

In the unpredictability factor, Fridays rank second, being exceeded as a general rule only by Mondays. One heads to the office on Friday morning wondering what will occur during the day. I find Fridays as predictable as the wind and as stable in nature as a sand castle at the beach. On this particular Friday morning, I was on the way to the hospital to make rounds, looking forward to sending a grateful patient home. The day of discharge from the hospital is a day that is looked forward to and appreciated by patients and their physicians to an equal degree. It is the day the coveted answer is finally given to that most important question:

"When am I going *home*?"

"Today."

"Thank you."

I was planning to send JoAnne home. She had undergone surgery the previous night. She had been bothered by abdominal pain for many months. After pursuing all of the various treatment regimens, the decision was reached that surgery would most likely help her. In this instance, the preoperative assessment proved to be correct. There were findings made at the time of surgery that were believed to be the source of her pain. Surgical treatment was undertaken, and I was eager to see how she was doing this morning. Was she better? I most certainly wanted to know.

JoAnne smiled when I walked into the room and remarked, without prompting, how much better she felt. The pain that she had been living with for the last several months was gone. She expressed her gratitude. I was very relieved.

This is, of course, what happens when surgery is done for all the right reasons—that is, with the intention of correcting a troubling problem affecting the body, thus accomplishing the result of making the patient feel better. It induces a warm, fuzzy feeling, precipitated by the gratitude of the patient and augmented by the relief that the anticipated surgery is over, no complications were sustained, and the pain is gone. The magnitude of this feeling of gratitude is such that it engulfs the patient and the physician in its generous, unabashed presence. I was aware of it. It was a good way to start off the day. I finished by completing the necessary chart notes. She could go home.

As I noticed that I had been given the generous gift of a few minutes to spare before starting office hours, I realized that I was feeling hungry. The cafeteria was still open for breakfast. If I hurried, I would make it just before they closed the doors.

I had learned several years ago that a physician cannot rely on those regularly scheduled intervals of repast, also known as breakfast, lunch, and dinner, to automatically appear on the daily schedule. The work is too unpredictable and demanding to allow for this luxury. The time slots necessary for these mealtimes actually exist only as potential spaces. That is, it is likely that time will be available for obtaining periodic nourishment, but it is the responsibility of each physician to make certain that it actually occurs.

I was feeling all of this sense of responsibility and obligation as I headed toward the cafeteria. My pursuit of necessary sustenance was interrupted when I heard my name on the overhead paging system. I was being asked to call the nursing station on the ward.

It seemed very strange. I had just left. What could this be about? It was not an emergency page, and I had arrived in the cafeteria. I was accosted by the wondrous smells that made me appreciate the fact that I was *really* hungry. I made the decision to quickly obtain a tray prior to answering the page. I still had to work the remainder of the day, and without food it would certainly be less enjoyable. Having procured my tray expeditiously, I dialed the floor, curious to learn what routine matter had been neglected.

The charge nurse answered the telephone, and I could sense the uneasiness in her tone of voice.

"I am notifying you that your patient, JoAnne, was given a medication erroneously this morning."

Confused and momentarily taken aback, I found myself clarifying that she was actually correct in her patient identification. The same patient that I had just finished speaking with? My only patient on the ward? She confirmed it to be so.

A sinking feeling settled over me as I requested additional details. A temporary nurse (referred to as a "registry nurse") was working today. She had given JoAnne a medication intended for the patient in the adjacent bed. She was apparently a very nice person and was mortified at having made the error. Appropriate notification protocols were being followed. I released a heavy sigh as the ramifications started to become apparent. I had never in all my years of practice encountered this situation before. I had no idea of what proper procedural steps to follow. I was incredulous.

"Have you notified JoAnne?" I asked.

"No. We do not do that. We notify you."

"Oh, I see." *The ball is in my court.*

After satisfying myself that the routine incident report was being completed, I sat down to eat breakfast and think quietly, in the corner of the cafeteria, about what to do next. I began eating, but what had looked so appetizing a few minutes ago had lost a substantial element of appeal.

Well, well, well. What to do? How to handle it? I began to feel annoyed. My thoughts centered on this business of hiring registry nurses, which lately is becoming a common occurrence in hospitals. It is somehow linked to the reduction in full-time and part-time regular staff.

Apparently, with the core of regular staff pared down to achieve targeted goals of profitability, there is no longer any buffer to allow for adequate staffing when illness or vacations are factored into the equation. In these circumstances, registry nurses are hired for the day.

They are not familiar with the hospital. They are not familiar with the procedures, the charting, the equipment, the medication trays, or the computer system. They are most certainly not familiar with the physicians, the regular nursing staff, or the *patients*. It is not difficult to see that under these circumstances mistakes can easily be made. I found myself appreciating the fact that it had not happened previously. Which guardian angel does one evoke to look after patients in the hospital?

My first inclination was that I must tell JoAnne. How could I not do so? However, there were other factors to consider. An uneasy argument was played out in my mind, with the debate centered on the pros and cons. The medication was a hormone tablet. Chances were very good that she would not notice anything. I was concerned as to the impression this incident would register on her mind, particularly after I recalled part of the conversation that we had had early on in the visit today. That conversation revolved around a previous hospitalization that had occurred a few weeks ago.

She had also discussed that experience while in the office for a routine appointment, shortly after she had been discharged. She had described that hospitalization as the worst time of her life.

At that time, she had had only one prior hospitalization with which to compare her experience. It had occurred four or five years previously and had been a wonderful experience. She recalled the superior nursing care and recalled that the entire experience had left her with a good feeling—a feeling that comes from being well taken care of. That was in the era I refer to as "BMC" (before managed care).

Her more recent hospitalization stood out in such sharp and unfavorable contrast that JoAnne could not actually believe she was in a hospital. That hospitalization lasted several days, and she required almost continuous IV treatment with antibiotics. She recalled approximately a half dozen instances when she felt completely abandoned by the nursing staff for several hours at a stretch.

She was left to notice when her IV line became empty and found herself in the position of reminding the nurses to replace it. She had a particularly distasteful recollection of the instance when she was identified as having acquired an infectious complication of her treatment. For this reason, she found herself being moved to an isolation room in the middle of the night. She wondered what was now so terribly wrong with her that all this had to be carried out in the wee hours of the night. As she watched the nurses install the ominous warning sign that limited the access of visitors to her room, she asked for an explanation. It was not given to her. With increasing anxiety, she requested that at least a telephone call be placed to her physician. This request was denied. She became increasingly anxious. At this point, the charge nurse was called to make an assessment. She told the patient that she was "hysterical" and promptly administered a strong sedative. JoAnne went to sleep. This night was capped when she was awakened by the housekeeper—who apparently possessed the urgent need to turn on the lights and clean her room at 5:00 a.m. Eventually, contact was made with her physician, she recovered from her complication, and she received the coveted and longed-for discharge order.

We had discussed JoAnne's present hospitalization this morning. Being cognizant of the last experience, I had been hopeful that this was a better one. She assured me that things were going much better this time. She thought that the nursing staff had improved, and it was beginning to erase some of the previously formed negative associations. Knowing this made it difficult to admit that I had to dissolve the pleasant association and remind her of something that she would rather forget.

I found myself in the unenviable position of throwing cold water on a warm, glowing fire. The bucket was being handed to me against my wishes and desires. However, duty and obligation mandated that I accept the bucket and release its contents. Resolved to undertake this most unpleasant task, I stood up from the table not really noticing that my meal lay only partially consumed—a reminder of unfinished business ahead. I now glanced at the time and realized that I would again be starting very late today. I was thinking that the entire morning would pass in excruciating slowness, with every single visit being laced with disappointment. Why would I be running late today? The answer was not for my patients' ears. They would not want to hear the reason. I could hardly believe it myself.

I was in a state of deep contemplation during the elevator ride to the floor. How to begin such a conversation? Certainly with hesitancy. Certainly with reluctance. Certainly accompanied by a small prayer asking for the ability to convey such information in a manner that would be able to relay the truth without precipitating much aggravation or, even worse, anger.

Still not certain of how to proceed, I entered the room. JoAnne was surprised to see me. It was apparent by the look on her face. It has been my experience that patients know instantly when the physician has news that is unfavorable. How it is that they know this, I am not certain. Something in our manner, the angle of the lines on our face, the slant of our posture, or perhaps a combination of all this nonverbal communication gives us away immediately. So it was in this case.

After exchanging the usual and customary greetings, I paused. She waited, uncomfortable expectation clearly etched on her face.

"Listen . . . uh. . . . The nurse this morning inadvertently gave you a medication that was not meant for you. It was intended for her. [I gestured to her neighbor, unseen on the other side of the curtain.] It was a hormone tablet. I am not anticipating any serious side effects, fortunately."

The silence that followed was momentous and pregnant with personal reflection on both sides.

She said, "I am already aware of this. The nurse has been in to tell me. She was feeling very bad about the whole episode."

I replied, "Well, I suspect that it is likely that you will not experience any side effects. As it was a hormone tablet, it would be like adding a half cup of coffee to an existing double mocha. Whether or not you will notice anything different will depend upon your sensitivities."

I felt the need to temper this unfortunate news with something positive. "I wanted to reassure you that I am not aware that any other mistakes have been made during your hospitalization. I mean to say that I am as certain as I can be that all of your previously administered medications were correct and were given as they should have been."

She nodded and grimaced a little. "Thank you for being honest with me."

"I could not have done otherwise."

We were both lost in thought again, appreciating the uncomfortable silence that lay between us—a manifestation of reveries of an unpleasant nature.

Our eyes then reconnected, and a moment of additional silence and reflection intervened. I then found myself verbalizing what I suspected was on both of our minds.

"Let us hope that this is your last hospitalization for a long time to come."

She nodded. "It's a deal."

Friday Afternoon: Welcome to "Night Gallery" (Or So It Seems)

By the time I had finished seeing all of the scheduled office patients, I was longing for a nice quiet lunch. Someplace that would allow recuperation and reconciliation from the disruption sustained by the soul from the morning's events. Lunch hours of late often serve as a refueling time for me, not only in the literal sense, as in eating and drinking, but also in the philosophical sense, as in needing a break from the stresses and strains and allowing internal repairs and reorientation to take place. All of this seems to be necessary to prepare for what might lie ahead, the unknown and increasingly unbelievable events that are waiting to present themselves and demand to be dealt with.

The afternoon began innocently with a busy but not unreasonable schedule. One could begin to imagine at two o'clock that it might be possible to arrive home in time for dinner at seven o'clock—that is, if all went according to schedule.

I was in the midst of the afternoon schedule when I was interrupted by the nurse practitioner.

"Doctor, I have a patient that you must see right away."

Louise had booked an appointment on the nurse's schedule for what, over the telephone, was believed to involve a relatively straightforward problem. The nurse realized immediately that this was not the case. My assistance and expertise were required.

As I entered the room, I received a tense greeting.

"Hello, Doctor, I hope that you can help me."

I inquired as to the pertinent details and recent history. She was more than eager to fill me in.

Louise had first noticed a small bump on her groin area three days ago. With the passage of the first twenty-four hours, the bump had enlarged at an alarming rate. It was accompanied by painful swelling. She then began to experience some difficulty when walking. After the passage of an additional day and after home remedies proved entirely unsatisfactory, she began to feel extremely concerned. She knew that she needed to see a doctor, and she suspected that she ought to see a gynecologist. However, she was enrolled in an HMO plan that would not allow her to visit our office without prior authorization. She had previously enjoyed a good relationship with a primary care physician, but that physician had recently terminated participation in her HMO plan. At the moment, she had a designated primary care physician "on paper" but had not yet been seen in the office.

She called the office. She felt strongly that the problem could not wait until the weekend. Louise was told that the primary care physician was gone for the day. She was not given the name of any backup physician. She urgently stressed to the receptionist that her problem required attention soon. The receptionist offered an appointment for the following Monday.

What followed next caused Louise to experience some confusion. When the receptionist questioned her in detail and determined the precise nature of her insurance plan, the Monday-morning slot was no longer available. Louise would have to wait until Tuesday. This relay of information was accompanied by the development of a more aloof and businesslike tone in the receptionist's voice. Louise perceived the change and did not like it. (*Was this due to her status as an HMO patient?* she wondered.)

She became upset and repeated her earlier assertions regarding the perceived seriousness of the situation. She explained that waiting through the weekend would not be in her best interests. She asked the receptionist a question.

"Would the doctor be responsible for her case if her condition worsened over the weekend?"

The receptionist rendered a curt reply and placed her on hold. After a few minutes, the phone line went dead. She was left with the dial tone from which to seek consolation.

Louise began to feel desperate and realized that she was left with two choices. She would most certainly forget about the authorization business; she was already resigned to paying out of pocket for her care. At this point, that was irrelevant. She just wanted to see a physician. She was left with the decision of whether to try to make an appointment with her previous primary care physician or to make an appointment in our office. She recalled that her primary care physician's office always seemed very busy. The chances of being seen on less than one day's notice did not seem very good. Her recollection of our office was that it was less busy. She had been coming here a long time—as she thought about it, much longer than for any of her primary care physicians. The decision was made. She would call our office.

In this anxious state, she telephoned our office and spoke to three different individuals. It was necessary to remind her that technically we were not supposed to see patients without prior authorization. She explained the entire situation and was granted an appointment.

When I examined the area in question, I had to withhold my astonishment and dismay. I had never seen such a serious infection in such a location. Louise required admission to the hospital and immediate treatment with antibiotics. She was relieved, at last, to finally find someone to take care of what she already suspected was a serious problem.

She was exhausted from the strain and energy that were expended to obtain this result. Why did it seem so difficult to obtain what should have been easy and relatively straight-forward? It was to the credit of her own savvy, intuition, and persistence that she landed in our office. What would have happened to someone less determined?

The sense of relief at finally finding someone to address her concern properly was quickly replaced by the need to vent quite eloquently her feelings regarding her treatment during the past week. She was distraught and highly irritated by the entire sequence of events. She went on to say that this entire HMO business was very disturbing. She had had to change primary care physicians three times in the past three years. She did not think that this was a very good idea.

"I have no established relationship with these doctors. They do not know who I am when I call. There is no level of trust in these relationships. No rapport. There does not seem to be any meaning either."

She recalled that one of her former primary care physicians had expressed to her his feelings of the most extreme dislike regarding his participation in HMO medicine. He relayed to her the fact that he felt overworked and underpaid. She had felt the greatest sympathy for him and his plight. He seemed like such a nice doctor. She did not think that physicians deserved this type of treatment from the HMOs.

"They should be treated better. Particularly when you consider all of the years spent on education and hard work."

Louise feels that all of the intimately involved individuals, that is, the physicians *and* patients, are being pushed around. She feels it is likely that people may become hurt in such a system.

I listened with the greatest patience to this monologue, realizing it was serving a therapeutic purpose. I then expended extra effort aimed at calming and reassuring Louise, who had just gone through a harrowing week. I explained the diagnosis and gave much calm, confident reassurance that with proper treatment she would recover. She was admitted directly to the hospital. She admitted to feeling much better upon leaving the office. She was beginning to allow herself to relax. All would be better now.

I redirected my attention to seeing the rest of the scheduled patients and doing my best to play catchup. At least in this circumstance I could safely tell the patients that I was running behind due to an emergency. This goes a long way toward soothing ruffled feathers. Just as I was anticipating obtaining a firm grip on the schedule, I was paged by the receptionist. She told me that Louise was on the telephone urgently asking to speak with me.

"She seems upset."

I could not have imagined what happened next.

"Hello, Louise? What is going on?"

"Please tell the nurses who I am!" she pleaded. "I have checked into the hospital, and they have addressed me by the wrong name. They have told me that they were getting ready to start my treatment. *I am refusing any treatment until you tell them who I am.*"

Shocked, stunned, and speechless, it was all I could do to hold on to the receiver. After what seemed like aeons, I regained my composure.

"What do you mean they do not know who you are?"

"They have called me by the wrong name. Please tell them who I am!"

At this point, after such a day, I fantasized that perhaps Rod Serling himself would appear in the hallway and announce, "And this concludes tonight's segment of 'Night Gallery,' ladies and gentlemen."

However, such was not the case. This was not fiction; it was reality—mine and Louise's. Sensing panic and desperation in her voice, I emitted an extra-large dose of calm reassurance and soothing confidence.

"Do not worry. I do not know what has happened; however, I will straighten it out. I promise. As soon as we finish speaking, I will telephone the charge nurse. OK?"

"No, Doctor, that is not good enough. I have a pen and paper in hand. I want you to tell me the name of the medication that I will be receiving. I would like you to spell it for me. I want to make sure that it is the right one when they give it to me."

I released a long, slow exhalation and complied with her request.

"Thank you, Doctor. If there is one thing that I have learned this week, it is that I have to take care of myself."

After additional soothing remarks, I ended the conversation, telephoned the charge nurse, and straightened out the mess. Apparently they had confused her with another Asian patient.

It took supreme effort and concentration to complete the remainder of the schedule. My heart was not in it. Once my office visits were completed, I visited Louise.

She was glad to see me. I extended additional confidence and reassurance. She would be fine, I said. She would get better. Before I left, we both checked the identity of the medication hanging in the IV tubing. In the interest of both of our good night's rest, I wanted to see for myself that it was correct.

Who was this woman? A self-employed businesswoman of a very successful enterprise—used to deadlines, used to delivering "quality goods" on time, used to pressure, hard-working, and possessing ethics, honesty, great strength, and integrity. She had just been living the worst nightmare of her life. Compliments of managed care.

No, this was not a script for an episode of "Night Gallery." But with only a little bit of editing, it very well could be.

The practice of the art of medicine was never meant to be carried out in such a manner. It seems as though we have dropped our standards and are now providing this "service" with the lowest common denominator in mind.

Amy

Life holds few surprises that have not been revealed in the physician's office.

The message was marked "personal." It arrived late yesterday afternoon. This meant that only I could help Amy. It was not meant for the nurse. These messages induce a great deal of curiosity when they come in marked this way.

They also necessitate careful preparation as the contents of the message can vary considerably. It may be a question regarding treatment, or it may be that I need to provide intensive counseling regarding a crisis situation. Fortunately for Amy, the content of her message fell in between the two extremes, identifying with the former rather than the latter.

I had seen her in the office earlier this year for an annual exam. She had recently returned to the area after spending some time living out of state. She was happy to be back and was anticipating becoming pregnant in the near future. She expressed the sentiment that, with so many recent changes in her life, it was a good feeling to become a patient again in our office. It was reassuring to come back to a physician whom she knew well and with whom she felt comfortable.

Her telephone call today was a plea for assistance and guidance. In the time that had passed since her annual exam, the company that she worked for had changed health insurance plans. My name was not included on the list of providers. Amy was discouraged by this news as she was now pregnant and had the undesired task of trying to find a new obstetrician.

With the assistance of her child's pediatrician, she was given a referral to a physician practicing out of a large clinic. She called at four weeks into her pregnancy hoping for an early appointment. She was eager to met the new obstetrician. She was told that all first appointments for pregnant women occurred after three months had passed. No exceptions to this policy were granted.

But what if I do not like the doctor? she wondered. *By the time of my appointment, I will already be three months along. If I do not like the doctor, I will be switching doctors fairly late in the pregnancy.*

This reflection caused Amy to ask the receptionist, "Can I meet the doctor sooner for a consultation appointment?"

"No," was the reply. "We do not make these types of appointments because we do not have the time available."

Amy wondered silently, *If they do not have the time to meet with and talk to me, how are they going to find the time to take care of me during my pregnancy?*

She was unsatisfied with the arrangements. However, not knowing what else to do, she accepted the appointment. Her uneasiness persisted.

After going on a vacation, Amy returned home to find a message on her answering machine. It was the clinic asking to change her appointment. The doctor was unavailable for the day in question, and they wanted to postpone her appointment.

Amy felt unsettled by their request and she wanted some advice. She felt the need to at least speak to the physician with whom she had scheduled this appointment, so she left a message with the clinic nurse. She wanted some reassurance at this point. She wondered if they really cared about her.

The prevailing uneasiness accompanied her as an unwelcome shadow—she could not shake free of it. She found herself at work explaining this sequence of events to her boss, as well as her feelings of anxiety and apprehension. He recommended that she consider using his wife's obstetrician. She called that office and explained the entire situation to them. She expressed her sense of urgency and repeated her request to at least be granted permission to meet the doctor. She had experienced complications with her first pregnancy. It was increasingly important to her to become settled in a new office and feel comfortable with the new obstetrician.

Amy was immediately impressed with how pleasant and thoughtful the new receptionist seemed. It was such a contrast to the curt and seemingly uncaring manner in which she had been treated at the clinic. She was granted a timely appointment; however, she was still feeling rattled and called me seeking advice.

I found it interesting that even though she had left a message with the physician in the large clinic—with whom she had an upcoming appointment—she had not yet heard back from that physician when I returned her call. I had not even been able to return it on the same day it was received.

What did I think about all of this? Is it usual to ask a pregnant woman to wait a standard period of time (e.g., three months), even if she expresses a desire to the contrary? Is it usual for the doctor not to make consult appointments? It seemed to her that things had changed considerably since her first pregnancy.

I explained to Amy that her experience at the clinic was typical of medical practices that are geared to provide service to large numbers of persons. The volume of persons receiving care in this manner requires that most care be delivered according to impersonal protocols.

"Well," she replied. "I did not like being treated that way."

I could not find fault with her feelings. She then requested my advice regarding the new physician with whom she had just made an appointment. Unfortunately, I did not know the physician, so I could not offer an opinion.

"I do not know who the doctor is, but if your boss's wife was pleased with the experience, that is an important recommendation. I am also reassured by your perception regarding the office staff. You thought the receptionist was pleasant and caring. The office staff often serves as a mirror that reflects the personality of the physician. You also were able to obtain an appointment within three days, which speaks of availability."

I ended our conversation with this final advice: "Use and rely upon your intuition. Make sure that you feel comfortable with the office and the physician. Make certain that you perceive that they want to make the effort to get to know you and are interested in taking good care of you. If you are sensing that all of these elements are present, then you may rest assured that you have found the right place."

Contemplating the Meaning of
the Term "Managed Care"

What is often not appreciated in the practice of medicine is that many medical challenges tend to unfold gradually over a period of several weeks. Much like an unripe tomato on the vine, the problem gradually changes color, hue by hue, day by day, until it eventually reaches the full ripe appearance and consistency that identify the process as being complete. One can then step back and appreciate the complexities involved in the entire process.

Following someone for a slowly developing medical condition is similar in that the process can be quite subtle in the beginning and progress slowly at first until it begins to progress at quickening speed to present itself fully developed and complete. At some point during the maturation process, it may become desirable to step in and intervene, not because one does not want the fruit to ripen, but rather because one does not wish it to ripen too soon. Such is the case with preterm labor—where early intervention can make a tremendous difference.

I had been following Mary in the office for several weeks. She had received her initial care from another HMO before changing to her present one. She then came to our office. She was a little leery of her experience at her previous HMO and brought her concern with her. This dissipated over the subsequent visits. She had just begun to feel comfortable when she was involved in an automobile accident. Fortunately, no one was seriously injured, and Mary, aside from sustaining some neck and shoulder strain, was only concerned in regard to the welfare of the baby—who did not appear to have suffered any problems related to the accident. Mary required an overnight stay in the hospital to be sure that all was well. She was discharged with much reassuring information the following morning. She was seven and a half months pregnant at this time, and her problems began shortly after discharge.

She was seen frequently in the office and soon began to complain of experiencing abdominal and pelvic cramping pain. These symptoms occurred primarily at home and were noticeable any time that she tried to walk. In addition, she began to notice increasing pain, discomfort, and limited mobility involving her back and neck.

I was concerned with two problems. The first had to do with the very real possibility of preterm labor. The second had to do with Mary's muscle and back pain. In my mind, there had to be a link between these two problems, as their appearance coincided so strongly—both seemingly associated with the accident. Mary would clearly benefit from physical therapy, but I was not allowed to authorize it. She had to obtain this permission through her primary care physician, a person whom she had not yet met. An introduction was carried out expeditiously, and the primary care physician's office then set to work on obtaining authorization. I was unable to assist in that area. However, due to persistent symptoms suggesting a problem with preterm labor, Mary was readmitted to the hospital.

While at rest in the hospital, she exhibited no signs of preterm labor. This did not surprise her, because she primarily had them only while at home. Without solid evidence upon which to justify medication, and hoping that the physical therapy might help, I sent Mary home, with careful and close follow-up scheduled. As I watched her and examined her closely during the next few days, it was apparent that her symptoms were getting worse. She had not received approval from the HMO regarding the physical therapy. For some reason this was not approved in a timely manner.

Ten days had elapsed since the accident, ten days full of pain and tension involving her entire spine and ten days full of persistent and increasing pelvic cramping. At this point I was concerned about the possibility of preterm labor. I did not want to miss it; otherwise, the consequences would be dire. I asked our authorization person in the office to request approval for home uterine activity monitoring. (This is a monitoring system designed to detect the signs of preterm labor that is utilized directly in the patient's home.) It seemed to make the most sense to me—especially considering that she experienced her symptoms while at *home*. In addition, she had demonstrated physical signs in the office that made the diagnosis almost certain in my mind. I was confident that the HMO would approve this request. I felt that the evidence was clearly seen and I recalled that they had previously been quite pliable in this area, knowing full well how valuable preventive strategies are in this situation. My confidence was such that I mentioned to Mary that approval would be imminent. We could then clearly identify the problem and initiate treatment.

Our authorization person relayed all of the information to the HMO. She spoke to the Utilization Review (UR) High-Risk Coordinator. Apparently she was new on the job and not helpful. My staff person made six telephone calls during a two-day period trying to obtain authorization. After the entire story had been reiterated several times, the UR coordinator stated that she needed to speak with me. I was then obliged to take time out of my busy schedule to explain to this person exactly what my staff person had already explained. I impressed upon the UR coordinator what it must feel like to have constant back and neck pain, to experience discomfort when walking, to have a nagging worry regarding the baby, and to have no relief in sight. I also inquired as to why the physical therapy had not been authorized. Wasn't the link between these two problems clearly seen?

Surely, she could see how treating one could help the other. She replied that she did not know anything about the authorization regarding the physical therapy. That was a different department. Her concern was only with the home uterine activity monitoring. Since Mary did not meet the strict criteria to justify its use, the UR coordinator would be required to speak to the physician reviewer. She would get back to me.

My staff person felt extremely frustrated, particularly considering all of the time that was spent repeating the same information over and over again. The UR person at the HMO obviously did not grasp the medical importance and the implications for the patient. My staff person wondered, "Why does this person possess the power to refuse the medical necessity of a treatment that the physician feels is essential?"

Forty-eight hours later, I was able to speak directly with the medical reviewer. I repeated all of the same information again. The dialogue was typical in that it did not contribute favorably to the disposition of either party concerned. It possessed a terseness that signified that neither person was content with the "assigned roles." We could not fool each other. Decent and caring physicians both, we each knew better. We continued on, carrying out our assigned roles with equal parts reluctance and resignation. The conversation ended with the hope that the treatment would start soon. I had stated my case well and felt that the reviewer had completely understood my concerns.

In the end, however, despite my considerable powers of persuasion, my request was denied. Mary was not "critical" enough. She fell outside the standard protocols.

The practice of the art of medicine and the practice of medicine by protocols are mutually exclusive concerns.

Two weeks after the accident, Mary did receive approval for physical therapy. She continued exhibiting symptoms related to preterm labor and required two additional hospitalizations. She was placed on strict bed rest, and the trips to physical therapy were curtailed. She had attended two sessions before the strict bed rest restrictions were imposed. The primary care physician's office was then requested to obtain approval for home physical therapy treatments. For reasons unknown to anyone, this request was not processed in a speedy manner. On the fourth hospitalization following the accident, the full-blown manifestations of preterm labor were apparent. This last hospitalization required treatment with intravenous medication and lasted four days.

Once the distraction provided by the hospitalization and preterm labor problem dissipated, Mary began to feel irritated and annoyed. Add to this the continued neck and back discomfort, along with the nagging concern that this was all related to the preterm labor issue, and one can well imagine the state in which she decided to personally call the HMO and vent her feelings. She spoke directly to the person at the HMO who had, in the end, denied the home physical therapy. Mary wanted to know the reason why. She explained the entire complicated sequence of events to this person. The UR person replied with great astonishment that she had had no idea of all that had transpired. This was followed by Mary's expressing her most extreme dissatisfaction with her entire treatment. Finally, home physical therapy was approved—six weeks after the accident.

The physical therapist's first comment to Mary was "Boy, you really have a problem here. We have a lot of work to do."

In the final analysis, Mary and her husband, extended family, friends, and neighbors all find themselves pondering the definition of "managed care."

Is it about managing how to take care of someone . . . or is it about managing how not to?

It seems to have been forgotten that these "covered lives" are actually human beings possessing mind, body, and soul. Why did anyone think that these human beings would fail to notice the changes? It has likewise been forgotten that physicians are also human beings possessing (if increasing numbers of physicians would allow this consideration) mind, body, and soul. The physician–patient relationship is one of privilege, mutual respect, and responsibility. It has been distorted almost beyond recognition under the guise of managed care.

A Matter of Professional Ethics

That there is a rising sense of distrust exhibited on patients' behalf seems evident from reading various newspapers and journals and listening to other sources of commentary. Patients' distrust seems to be aimed at this business of managed care and their perceptions of the motivations at work. Some of these persons have formed their opinions based upon their own personal experience. Others have heard stories from relatives, friends, neighbors, and immediate family members. Generally speaking, the physician is shielded from witnessing any significant expression of this sentiment, as the majority of patients do not directly confront their physicians with a rendering of their honest opinions. Recently, however, I became the recipient of an unfiltered, gritty, honest expression of one patient's regard for this recently changed health care delivery system. The surprising factor to consider, after I had had enough time to analyze and ruminate on the exchange, was not that my patient would confront me in such a manner but rather why more patients did not.

We were working late in the office that day. Karen was the last person on the schedule. It was supposed to be a routine visit. A note scribbled in pencil next to her computer-generated time and reason for appointment suggested something different. She was requesting a letter. For what? I could not guess after reviewing her chart. I shrugged my shoulders. I would learn soon enough.

I had been following her for several weeks for a problem with pain, and her surgery was scheduled with another physician. I had thought that all of the details were taken care of, and I was a little surprised at the visit this evening.

Entering the room, I could sense that Karen was tense. I braced myself before cautiously asking the standard physician's opening query, "So, how can I help you tonight?" She proceeded directly to the point.

"We have to change health insurance plans. In order to qualify for the new plan, I am requesting that you write a letter explaining that I am in good health and have no preexisting condition. It is also necessary for you to write that no further treatment is necessary. Then I am guaranteed of being accepted."

Write a letter that is completely false? I knew I had heard correctly, but I did not want to believe it.

"This is the only affordable coverage that we can qualify for and be granted admission into the plan. I need it for myself as well as my family."

I could tell that she actually expected that I would comply with her request. I slowly exhaled and found myself explaining in a deliberate, painstaking reply.

"I cannot write this. It is not truthful. It is unethical. I simply cannot do this."

As she listened to these unexpected and unwelcome words, pent-up outrage, anger, and intense desperation were unleashed into the room—extending to the ceiling, to the walls, and into my heart. I was rendered momentarily speechless as I was waylaid by these powerful emotions. It was as if I were in a little boat at sea suddenly knocked loose from its moorings. It was all I could do to hold on for dear life as the boat was battered by each new wave of discontent. For what seemed to be the longest time, I was unable to perceive the ultimate direction of the boat—only that it was rocking precipitously back and forth.

After a time she composed herself and asked, "Why are you not going to do this?" With sarcasm she continued. She wanted to know how I could actually maintain the pretense of claiming to be an ethical person in a system that to her eyes was full of unethical types only.

"I cannot believe that you are not going to write this letter. I know how this system works." Through a work-related experience, she had had the opportunity to observe the business practices of one HMO at a very intimate level.

"They are business types. They are very different from you medical types. You, perhaps, are still guided by ethics, but they are guided only by avarice.

"They [her insurance company] started raising our rates just after my husband and I turned forty. Now they are so high—in spite of our being in good health—that we cannot afford it any longer. Not only are they charging several hundred dollars a month for premiums, we are also required to first satisfy a twenty-five-hundred-dollar deductible. And we have just received a notice that the premiums have been raised again."

I sat lost in a stunned, silent haze, feeling all of it, not really knowing what to say. As I began to recover my wits, I could see her point.

She continued. "This is supposed to be a system about human beings. Nobody cares about the human beings any longer." Then a change in tone, followed by "Do you have any children?"

"Yes." *Why does she want to know?*

"Well, what type of health coverage do you have, if you do not mind my asking?"

I answered, still lost in a fog. The direction of the conversation was still a mystery to me.

"Well, your failure to grant my request will come back to haunt you. You will see. Someday you may find yourself in a similar situation. It could happen to you, you know."

Clear crystalline light pierced the fog and I could see it. My failure to cooperate was being seen as an obstruction to obtaining health care coverage.

Desperation sat embodied before me, caught in a nasty system, trying to do everything in her power to try to take care of herself.

I could not find fault with her motives; neither, however, could I grant her request.

It seems to have come down to this: my ethical principles versus affordable health care coverage. How can this be?

Sarah

"Can you please give me a recommendation for a new family doctor? I am no longer comfortable with the one I have."

"Really," I replied. "What seems to be the problem?"

"I have been a patient in that office for four years now. I have witnessed such a deterioration in the quality of care. I am just not comfortable. It is really a shame. When I first started seeing the doctor four years ago, I was impressed with her level of commitment and thoroughness. She seemed genuinely interested in my health. She conveyed a great deal of confidence. I felt secure there."

Sarah continued. "But now everything is changed. The office is too busy. It is packed all of the time. It doesn't matter whether I have a scheduled appointment or not. I still wait over an hour to be seen. I have also noticed that the newly hired assistants just seem to be rushed, harried, and unprofessional.

"The office used to be 'comfortable' busy—now it is just 'crazy' busy. You expect a good doctor's office to be busy, but it has gotten out of hand.

"I never really know which of the doctors I am going to see. I would like to be able to see the same one every visit, but it doesn't work that way. You end up seeing whoever is available. I am worried about this skin condition affecting my hand. I have been seen in the office for over one year. I have been given different treatments but nothing has worked. I keep asking about a referral to a dermatologist, but in response I hear, 'This is something that we can take care of.'

"It used to be that I could easily obtain a referral to a specialist, but it has changed over the past year. The doctor does not seem to want to grant this. I just wish that I could get better.

"My husband and I always used to have indemnity insurance. We had a choice earlier to receive treatment under an HMO plan, but we did not want to be treated like an 'HMO family.'

"Due to financial considerations, we changed to this HMO last year, and we are beginning to have second thoughts."

I listened to all of this in silence. I was thinking about two things. I was divided between addressing the request at hand—trying to generate a name which I could in all honesty give to Sarah in the hopes that it would lead to an experience different from the present reality—and the underlying realization that this scene was increasing, as if a broken record had been left on the turntable. My fatigue was growing as each repetitive dialogue began anew.

"Well, I will try. Bring in your list of participating doctors, and I will do my best to select a physician. I will try to select the one who is most likely to grant your referral to a dermatologist. Waiting an entire year for a specialist appointment seems long enough."

June

As patients have become more sophisticated in their knowledge of the present state of health insurance, there has been a tendency for the particularly astute and wary to become extra vigilant. They know from listening to stories from friends and neighbors that this is a prudent state of being. It is seemingly necessary to double-check almost every statement issued from the insurance company to verify accuracy. The business personnel in physicians' offices, whose job it is to deal exclusively with this area, know even more intimately how treacherous a task and how arduous an ordeal it can become—depending upon the plan. June is an RN and recently had a dilatation and curettage (D & C), a procedure to correct irregularities of the menstrual cycle.

On her postsurgery checkup visit, she enlightened me on her most recent experience. She was extremely grateful, she said, for having stayed right on top of the situation.

Her first call came right after the surgery. A request was made about the name of the surgeon. This information was needed to ensure that the surgeon would be paid. June thought that this was very strange, as the surgery had been preapproved. They should have had this information on file. The representative then checked the file and apparently found the information. June received a letter from the company one week later that indicated that it had paid the physician. However, it had issued the check to a different doctor. She became concerned and called the insurance company again. In order to address this confusing point, it was necessary for her to become explicit and inform them exactly who I was. At this point our office was required to rebill. What happened to the paperwork sent in the first billing could not be determined. June then received a statement explaining that my payment was being denied because they had already paid—*that the payment was to a different doctor seemed to escape their notice.*

Eventually, persistence on June's part and that of our billing office paid off. After additional time spent on the telephone, the problem was finally resolved.

June then received a letter addressing her bill at the surgery center. It stated that the cost was going to be covered only at seventy percent, instead of the anticipated ninety percent, because the facility "was not a preferred center."

Again, this did not make sense, because the surgery had been preapproved—the merits of this process were coming into increasing question. June had understood that it *was* a preferred center.

She had to insist that the clerk double-check this assessment. With some reluctance, the clerk did double-check. It was with surprise that she informed June that it was a preferred facility, after all. It seemed that an adjustment would be made, all things considered. One could almost make the point here that perhaps patients should be allowed to pay their own bills. Payment would proceed much more quickly and with fewer hardships.

As with most medical snafus, it seems as if once a patient has caught one of these insurance-billing viruses, he or she just cannot shake it. It seems to linger on a bit, as June shortly experienced.

A few days after the surgery, she began to experience symptoms of an allergic reaction. Since she was an RN, she was well versed in recognizing the signs of the life-threatening allergic reaction known as anaphylactic shock. She began to notice swelling in her throat and tongue. Because she was close to a hospital and no one was at home to help her, she drove herself to the emergency room. June knew what her preferred hospital was—most patients in this area know this very well. With this in mind, she dutifully headed for it.

However, on the way she began developing trouble breathing, and she knew that she needed help immediately. She pulled into the parking lot of a hospital on the way. She arrived in the emergency room gasping for air and was able to just barely blurt out her history. The problem was immediately recognized and lifesaving treatment was initiated.

June recovered from the incident without any adverse sequelae, except for that attributed to her pesky insurance virus. It seems that the insurance company initiated some type of dispute over payment after reviewing the claims submitted for this emergency admission. The dispute revolved around the fact that June had received her lifesaving care at a nonpreferred hospital.

Time is what is missing. Time to get to know one another. Time to listen. Time to reflect. Time to think. Time to observe. Time to do research. Time to communicate fully to the mutual satisfaction of both parties concerned.

Little wonder, then, that widespread unhappiness exists.

Nancy

"How are things going, Nancy?" Thus began the routine visit.

"I am thinking of changing my primary care physician. I am just not happy with mine. The office is too busy. I am never able to reach the physician on the telephone. The physician never personally calls me—even when I request it. We are not in an HMO plan and are paying good money for our health coverage. The service should be better than this. I was out of town recently and had a serious medical problem. I called my doctor and requested a return telephone call. I waited in vain for several days. I wanted medical records to be sent, to help the doctor who was taking care of me, and this did not happen.

"When I returned, I was sent to a specialist for my problem. What a wonderful doctor he is! I was so impressed with his manner, his professionalism, and his caring attitude. He evaluated my condition and specified particular laboratory studies that were to be ordered by my primary care physician. I went to the office and had the required laboratory tests done. When I returned to the specialist's office for consultation he discovered that the correct laboratory tests had not been ordered. The specialist was very surprised that this had not occurred, especially after he had been so explicit in his instructions."

After this laboratory mix-up, she requested a referral for a primary care physician directly from the specialist. He obliged, and she is in the process of transferring her care.

I explained to Nancy that this is, of course, how the referral process works best. Once you find a doctor you like and feel comfortable with, you can count on the fact that you will be referred to someone who practices in a similar manner. This physician to whom you would be referred would most likely be the physician of choice for your physician, as well as for his or her family and friends.

Nancy mulled this over and continued. "I want a doctor to make me feel as though I am his or her only patient—even though I am well aware that I am not. I also want to know or to feel that the doctor genuinely wants me to do well. To become better. That he or she cares about me. Finally . . . I want to know that if something awful happens to me, the doctor will be there for me."

First Impressions

Maria was in the office three weeks ago. It was her first visit, yet this new beginning was unfavorable. She had to wait in the waiting room for some time as she was not able to be seen immediately—she was not yet an officially approved entity in her HMO computer system. Maria found this disclosure irritating as she had been paying premiums on this health plan for the previous six months.

Nonetheless, our office staff was required to contact the insurance company directly to obtain authorization so that she could be seen as scheduled. After a minor delay, we were granted permission to see her—one single visit was approved.

As I entered the room to meet her, I recognized the all-too-familiar tentative, inquiring glance that women invariably give to their gynecologist. They want to establish trust and rapport. They most certainly want to feel comfortable. They are looking for reassurance and wanting to feel that they are in good hands. Finally, what they want to hear eventually, at the end of the visit, is "Everything is fine."

At the end of the visit, I recommended that Maria undergo two additional procedures. These would have to be performed in follow-up visits, as authorization was required. One of these procedures would have to be approved by the primary care physician. The second procedure needed authorization that would be obtained by my nurse, working directly with the HMO. As I discussed this with her and asked her to schedule a follow-up appointment, she surprised me with the following question.

"Can you recommend a new primary care physician? I am not happy with the one that I am presently assigned to."

As the year progresses, this request is now second only to "Where are the rest rooms?" What my response should honestly be is "You do not need a new primary care physician. What you need is a new health plan." Sometimes honesty prevails. Other times I try to work with the system as it is presently. This is definitely a mood-dependent response. Today I am in a good mood. I will try to help.

"Oh, really," I replied. "What seems to be the problem?"

"Well, I thought that the communication skills could be improved upon, and my first impression was not favorable. I was in the office for my annual checkup and it was the first time that I had ever met the physician. The physician spent the entire time complaining to me about HMO medicine. While I can sympathize with the situation and viewpoint, I did not feel it was appropriate to spend the entire length of the visit dedicated to this topic."

"I see." *What does one say? I have run out of any constructive commentary. Rules of etiquette advise me that in these situations it is best to remain silent.*

I then sat down to think carefully of possible names for referrals. My most recent favorites had closed their practice to this type of HMO patient. I suggested two names whom I had heard of recently and kept my fingers crossed. *What the covered lives do not realize is that this system that has been created is an albatross around all of the participating providers' necks. It is unfortunate that it is most painfully visible around the neck of the primary care physician. Nobody seems to have a good idea as to how it can be removed. That the desire exists to remove it is the understatement of the century.*

With this new referral, I reiterated the caution that she not change her primary care physician now, as we were in need of obtaining permission to complete the evaluation. If she changed now, a delay in treatment could be predicted.

She returned to the office three weeks later. It had taken that long to obtain permission from the primary care physician. In the meantime, Maria had logged considerable time with our local telephone company trying to straighten out the administrative error that had left her off the list of "Approved Subscribers." In this endeavor her efforts were rewarded. She was granted permission to return to our office.

I was able to complete one procedure that day. We were then left with only one task. That was to obtain permission regarding the next procedure. My assistant was very reluctant.

"I understand that the phone lines at the administrative offices are very busy lately. The time spent on hold has increased considerably. I do not know how I am going to find the time in the day to do this."

"Well, do your best."

I feel sorry for the medical assistants. I have heard my assistant mention that sometimes she is awakened in her sleep by a momentary panic, thinking about all of the details and procedures. In the middle of the night, she is beset by insomnia, hoping that she has not forgotten anything— whether it be an important detail, a phone call, authorization, labeling a specimen, or the salient points of a conversation with a distraught patient.

"There are so many important things to keep track of. Sometimes I cannot go back to sleep."

From a friend:

Her husband has a chronic problem with allergies and is frustrated by the following:

He requires many specialist visits to ensure proper treatment, yet each time he must obtain approval via his primary care physician. Each time he is allotted three visits, each given with an expiration date so that if he does not make his appointments within the specified time frame, the authorization becomes invalid. He must start all over again.

The time he spends on the telephone trying to work this out— hours and hours each year—is mind-boggling.

Worth Waiting For

Paul, a neighbor, shared this story with me.

The entire family receives medical care from a group of family practitioners. Over the years, they have met and have received treatment from all of the physicians in the group.

Sheila and the kids are content with whomever they happen to see. This is because they are basically healthy and require only the occasional antibiotic treatment.

Paul, however, has had a few medical problems and has learned to be more selective.

Recently, he became increasingly bothered by a moderate amount of intense back pain. When he called and requested an urgent appointment on Thursday, he learned that his favorite physician was unavailable until Monday. He was offered the option of seeing one of the other physicians on Friday. Thus, he found himself in this dilemma: Wait until Monday to see his preferred physician, or see one of the other physicians on Friday.

As he thought about this, he weighed the possibility of achieving pain relief before the weekend versus the manner in which the pain relief would be achieved—requiring a visit with the alternate physician.

The decision was easily made. In spite of the likelihood that he would pass the weekend in pain, he decided to wait until the 5:00 p.m. appointment on Monday. That physician was the only one in the group that was satisfactory to him. Why?

"He is the only one who will spend more than five minutes with me during a visit. He is the only one who really gives me the idea that he cares about my health. He is the only one who really listens to me and expresses interest in me as a real person.

"It is definitely worth waiting for. No one else will do."

From a Registered Nurse:

"We, the consumers, have become accustomed to not paying for our medical care. Now we are beginning to realize that in order to obtain good care we are going to have to change our thinking."

Tammy

I initially examined Tammy in March. At that time, I recommended that she return for an endometrial biopsy, to evaluate her irregular menstruation. It has been *five months* since that visit. She returned today. I wondered what had happened.

During her visit in March, it was determined that she needed to obtain out-of-network permission in order to return to our office.

She had approached her primary care physician (PCP) at that time. However, the request was flatly denied.

She then had to change insurance networks in order to select a PCP who could refer her back to our office (in-network).

She interviewed two PCPs she did not like before finding a physician she did. It was by the good grace of this third physician that she was allowed to return.

This business of selecting a new physician took three entire months.

She had her appointment with the new PCP in July. She explained the entire situation to him. He was very helpful, and his office immediately started the referral process.

She received the referral in the mail. As is typical for our patient population, these changes have made them extremely wary. Many are on their guard with respect to their dealings with their HMOs. Consequently, nothing escapes their scrutiny. They look at every notice received, scan every bit of correspondence, and take full names for every person with whom they speak.

I suppose the next step is for them to request copies of their charts. This might give them comfort. It might be nice to have them, just in case. Increasingly, it seems, you never know. Many patients have already begun keeping their own files at home with their operative reports, biopsy reports, laboratory tests, and so on.

In this instance, Tammy noticed that the letter was dated July 10 but postmarked July 20. Since all of these referrals have an expiration date, she found this a curious discrepancy.

However, she was happy to finally receive it, as it had been four months since she had been seen in our office.

She called for an appointment. On the day of the appointment, she was contacted by the HMO. She was informed that she could not keep her appointment that day as scheduled. The authorization number had not been granted. She had no option but to cancel.

The following day she received a call notifying her that she did have the authorization number, after all. She was allowed to proceed and make another appointment.

Tammy thought to herself that she would not want to have an emergency. What would happen then? Since she suffers from other medical problems, she has given her husband strict instructions regarding the issue of any potential hospitalizations.

Apparently, they were reminded at a recent benefits meeting that a call must be made to the HMO by the second day of hospitalization at the latest. This call is supposed to originate from the "manager at work." If this is not done, the hospital is paid only fifty percent of the cost. Tammy has rehearsed the scenario with her husband countless times— since she is so worried that he may forget.

"If I am hospitalized and incapacitated, I will not be able to make this call. I hope that he remembers this."

She also worries: What if the manager is too busy or does not call? Or is on vacation? So much to worry about. She doesn't even want to think of the red tape involved if one of them ends up at a nonpreferred hospital.

I listened to this commentary with solemnity. It is hard to know what to say . . . "Good luck"?

In any case, attention was then directed to completing the procedure. *A procedure that was performed five months after it was initially recommended.*

Uneasiness

Carol was in today for a routine annual visit. She handed me a copy of her most recent laboratory work as I entered the room. I noted that her cholesterol was elevated.

She replied that it had been much higher in the past. She began taking cholesterol-lowering medication two years ago. Initially, she had had to try a couple of brands before finding the one that worked the best. Then she described the following.

Under the terms of her present HMO, she is required to use a mail-away pharmacy. When she sent for a refill of her medication earlier this year, one of the staff members at the mail-away pharmacy telephoned her at home. She was asked to switch to a different brand of cholesterol-lowering medication because her present medication, which *had* been on the formulary, was no longer on it.

She was quite reluctant to do this considering her past difficulty with actually finding the right medication that worked. Besides, she thought it was strange that they would call her directly.

She replied, "No. I want you to call my doctor and discuss this change with him. I am not qualified to make this decision."

Apparently they did so. After contacting her doctor, the pharmacy changed the medication.

Carol now finds herself in a trial period to determine whether this medication actually works as well as the previous medication. Apparently, as she understands it, if proof can be obtained after the three-month trial period that it is not as effective as the previous medication, then a case can be made for her primary care physician to request an exemption to the formulary. This *might* allow her to return to the prior medication. However, even at that point, Carol understands that there is no guarantee that she would be able to do so. It might be a different medication instead. She is wary because this is exactly what she did under the direction of her primary care physician two years ago, before they settled on the medication that worked best.

However, at the present time, she finds herself more concerned with her husband's medication. He has high blood pressure and had been taking a medication that worked well to control it.

Earlier this year he also received a telephone call from the mail-away pharmacy staff person. She requested that he consider a change in his blood pressure medication because his present medication was no longer on the formulary. He was very unhappy with this request.

Why should he change if the present medication was working so well?

He replied that the staff person should call his doctor. He, like Carol, did not feel comfortable with the responsibility of making such a decision.

The pharmacy called the physician, and the medication was changed. He first became aware of this when the new medication arrived in the mail, along with a note of explanation.

Now he also finds himself in a trial period to determine whether this new medication is as effective as the previous one. He finds himself practicing increased diligence, because he perceives a distinct uneasiness underlying the entire transaction—something bothersome that he cannot quite put his finger on.

He is astute, well educated, and understands the importance of monitoring his blood pressure at home. Which he does now at a much greater frequency than ever before.

And from another concerned patient:

"*The insurance companies have become really good at putting things off. Can't anyone see that by delaying early treatment the problem only gets worse? Instead of a small problem, they end up with a huge problem and a huge bill.*"

Marissa

("Marissa" is an alias. This story was told by her mother.)

When Marissa was about three and a half years old, her preschool teacher mentioned to me that she had noticed tremors in Marissa's hands when she attempted to cut paper, and so on. She suggested that I talk to the doctor, as there had been another student with tremors in the past who had been helped with medication. I immediately called Marissa's pediatrician and spoke to the advice nurse. I was worried that it could be epilepsy, muscular dystrophy, or something worse. She told me that it was probably nothing, to watch for the tremors and mention it at the next visit. Up until that point, I had not noticed any tremors myself.

At her four-year-old checkup in August, I mentioned the tremors to the associate pediatrician (who often sees the pediatrician's patients because he is rarely there). She examined Marissa and was unable to see the tremors herself. She felt that if we did not see them it was not a problem to worry about.

In September Marissa started a new preschool. During the next several months, the teacher kept seeing the tremors and repeatedly mentioned them to me. The teacher finally told me that she was really concerned because the tremors were affecting Marissa's fine-motor development. She was considering recommending that we hold her back from kindergarten.

Concerned, I asked my family and friends if they had noticed the tremors. Two of them said they had but had not wanted to alarm me. I noticed them now occasionally, but they were slight. Additionally, the doctor had seemed to think it wasn't a problem, so I hadn't worried too much. I had been back to the pediatrician's office for other reasons and had brought the tremors to their attention. Finally, in the early months of the following year, I took Marissa to the pediatrician for a cold or something. I asked that he please have her examined for this problem. He agreed to refer her to a neurologist.

The neurologist gave her a physical examination and announced that he did not see the tremors and she seemed perfectly healthy. However, to put our minds at ease, he ordered an EEG and an MRI. We tried to have the EEG performed one day in the office when she was premedicated in an attempt to relax her. She was too scared, however, to lie still. The examiner was impatient. After this highly upsetting experience, and without having the EEG performed, we went home.

The following week we went to the local hospital for the MRI. Since Marissa is very afraid of needles, the physician ordered suppositories that would relax her. Needless to say, this was not pleasant. She was so disturbed by the proceedings that it took several hours for her to fall asleep. She was almost asleep, and because we were running out of time for the MRI we were obliged to place her on the table. The noise awakened her. She was extremely upset. I held her in my arms until she fell asleep. They were finally able to perform the MRI.

The next day my husband brought her to the neurologist's office for the EEG, as I was exhausted from all the events of the day before. Somehow they were able to obtain the EEG reading. The neurologist also ordered another test. He told my husband that the radiologist had found what looked like a cyst in the brain stem and this was very serious. Although it did not look like cancer, it was in the worst possible location in the brain. This occurred the Thursday before Memorial Day weekend. I called the doctor requesting additional information as I was becoming really worried. I wanted some bit of explanation before the weekend. He mentioned that he was sorry but he was going away for the long weekend and would not be able to give us any more information until he returned on Tuesday. Then he would personally review the MRI and render his assessment. I asked specifically, "Was it in the brain stem?"

He replied, "Yes, that is what the radiologist report had indicated."

The anxious weekend passed. On Tuesday morning we called the office and were told that we would have to wait until the afternoon to learn of the neurologist's reading of the MRI. When he finally telephoned, he informed us that the cyst was on the outside of the brain stem. Whew! This was better news.

It did not look like cancer and was probably an arachnoid cyst (an accumulation of spinal fluid that had formed a cyst). It was necessary to remove it to prevent damage to her hearing, facial muscles, and ability to swallow. He suggested that we find a neurosurgeon. We asked him for recommendations, and he gave us the names of two who worked at local hospitals and one who worked at a university teaching hospital.

We knew that choosing the best surgeon for such a delicate operation would be crucial, so we discussed this with my husband's godfather, who is a pediatric surgeon at a teaching hospital.

After hearing the neurologist's recommendation, he mentioned that he would never advise operating on a small child with anyone other than a pediatric neurosurgeon. In addition, he felt that it was important that we use a pediatric anesthesiologist. Regular neurosurgeons, he said, often operate on backs or other similar cases. Since this was a very delicate surgery on a small child, it was going to require the best surgeon that we could find. Also, he suggested that we use a teaching hospital where they had access to the newest equipment, and so on. He referred us to a pediatric neurosurgeon at a nearby teaching hospital, explaining that this was the best pediatric neurosurgeon west of the Mississippi.

When I called the office, they were reassuring. They said they would make an appointment available as soon as possible. Our next step was to call our primary care physician for a referral for an appointment. I was then informed via the pediatrician's nurse that, rather than using the pediatric neurosurgeon, we would have to use a neurosurgeon on our plan and use the hospital on our plan. I was frantic! I was so upset that my husband would not let me speak to the pediatrician. I felt that the pediatrician was standing in the way of providing good care for my daughter. I knew now that if the surgery was not done appropriately she could be permanently harmed by it. I was so disturbed that I could not speak to the office without yelling at the staff or threatening a lawsuit. I did not want to do this at this stage, as I thought it would make matters worse. My husband did all of the talking. I was incensed that they were actually suggesting a course of treatment that I had every reason to believe would be detrimental to my daughter.

I telephoned the pediatric neurosurgeon's office and told them of this problem. They reassured me that they would work on it and said not to worry about it. I made the decision then and there that we would pay the three-hundred-dollar office visit out of pocket. If necessary, we would borrow the money to have Marissa's surgery done by the pediatric neurosurgeon. He had come so highly recommended. It was very important to have the right doctor. If necessary, we would ignore the HMO guidelines.

When we arrived at the pediatric neurosurgeon's office two days later, we were informed that they still had not received approval. We kept our appointment, though, and awaited the opinion of the doctor. After he had examined Marissa, he explained that he thought that it was an epidermoid cyst. It was not fast growing, which was reassuring news. However, it was his opinion that surgery should be scheduled for the summer. We explained our insurance problem to him and he told us not to worry. This was not the time to waste our energies on insurance issues. It was time to take care of our daughter.

He appeared disturbed that the authorization had not been obtained. He then went into his office and called the pediatrician personally to explain the intricate nature of the surgery and why it was so very important to use a seasoned neurosurgeon and an experienced pediatric anesthesiologist. He also explained that, in this city of 250 miles' distance, an entire wing of the hospital was set up solely for cases just like these. Because of the special care that Marissa would receive, she would most likely be able to go home sooner.

I speculate that what ultimately convinced the pediatrician to grant permission had something to do with the fact that he and his colleagues had failed to diagnose her condition for well over a year. It helped that he received a call from this world-renowned surgeon, to whom the pediatrician had in the past referred patients (*before managed care*). He said in the end that he would approve the request. I am convinced that if I had not been so assertive and if the pediatric neurosurgeon had not personally called, the approval would not have been given. I shudder to think what the consequences would have been.

A couple of weeks before the surgery, the neurosurgeon set up an appointment for Marissa to be evaluated by an educational psychologist so that we would have a "before" picture of her fine and gross motor skills prior to surgery. The day before that appointment, the doctor called and said that the HMO had turned down the approval. The pediatric neurosurgeon was furious. The pediatrician was of no help. He said that there was nothing he could do. The testing cost hundreds of dollars that we did not have at the time. So we canceled the appointment.

We proceeded with the surgery at the out-of-town hospital. The care taken to prepare Marissa emotionally for surgery was tremendous. The surgery was a success. The cyst turned out to be an arachnoid cyst after all. Marissa remained in intensive care for two days and in the hospital for a total of four days.

Six months later we were advised to schedule an MRI to check on the cyst. I knew that Marissa would have to be asleep in order for an accurate study to be obtained. By now she was terrified of doctors despite everyone's best intentions. Again I had to hassle with the pediatrician to have the MRI performed near the office of the pediatric neurosurgeon. This was in order for her to be under the care of the pediatric anesthesiologist during the test.

After having been through so much hassle and red tape, I have been transformed. I am like a dog to a bone, and nothing will stop me from insisting that my daughter receive the care that she needs. I was successful in this instance.

The MRI demonstrated that there was a small amount of fluid in the cyst but it had regressed significantly. The doctor was pleased, but we were disappointed. The story was not finished yet.

We have now arrived at the ten-month marker after surgery, and we are about to schedule another MRI. I find myself distracted by the stacks of bills that have not yet been paid by the HMO. One was sent to collection, so we are being hounded by the agency. I called the office, and they had not even billed the HMO. I am particularly miffed that the neurologist billed us for a five-minute call at fifty dollars. The insurance refuses to pay it. I have called the HMO so many times that I have lost track. They keep saying that they will get back to me, but they do not. My husband has suggested that I create a paper trail to log each of these phone calls. This is all so very time consuming and frustrating. All I want is for my daughter to get better.

I have a deep desire to switch primary care physicians for my daughter because obviously I have lost faith in him. However, the HMO will not allow this because she is still under the care of the pediatric neurosurgeon and it was the pediatrician who obtained the original approval.

I am frustrated because, if she becomes ill, I do not know if I can trust this pediatrician again.

The whole experience has been frightening and frustrating. I often shudder to think what would have happened if we had not had the experience of my husband's godfather to rely upon. He was the one who recommended the excellent pediatric neurosurgeon.

Deep down inside, I feel that the pediatrician pitted my daughter's health against saving the HMO their almighty dollar.

Maggie

"Please call! I'm having a serious allergic reaction to my hormone medication!"

Thus started our day, with this 8:30 a.m. message.

Associating the message with Maggie's history, I remembered that she had called a few weeks earlier. At that time she had requested advice. Although she was doing quite well on her present hormone medication, she had just discovered that the HMO formulary had changed. Her present medication was no longer preferred. We had discussed options, and we agreed to change the medication to another product that was similar but not identical.

Maggie used the new medication—a hormone patch— once and did not have any problem. The trouble started after the second application when she noticed that the entire area covered by the patch was bright red, hot to the touch, and swollen. She tried one more application. After the same problem developed, she called our office.

I diagnosed an allergic reaction and prescribed cortisone cream, as well as a tablet to control the itching.

Obviously, she could no longer take this medication. We were now in the position of needing to ask for an exemption to the formulary.

When my assistant called to clarify the issue, it appeared that Maggie could resume her prior medication at a $20-per-month co-pay. The financial incentive to use the other brand was in place.

Maggie found all of these recent developments curious. She had been taking this medication for many months. It had previously been listed as a preferred medication; that is, she had been able to pick it up at the usual co-pay until this spring. So something must have occurred recently in order for the HMO to initiate the preferential treatment and obvious incentive for patients to use one brand over the other. Was one more expensive than the other?

She took it upon herself to call a pharmacist and inquire about pricing. She found that her prior medication cost $72.65 for a three-month supply. The present medication—the source of the allergic reaction—would cost $71.75. Only a ninety-cent difference. Surely this was not enough to justify a $20 financial penalty for continued use. She also reasoned that the HMO could probably obtain better prices than she could. With all of this in mind, she sent a letter to the HMO asking for consideration of an exemption. She explained her previous satisfaction with the first medication and explained in detail the extent of her allergic reaction, which took six weeks to finally resolve. She then asked candidly: If the prices were so similar, why did the difference exist? She wondered about the reasoning behind this. She specifically requested that an exemption be granted to allow her to receive the other medication at the usual co-pay.

Four weeks later she received the news that an exemption would be granted. She could return to her prior medication, the one that had worked well. The one that she had had no problem with, after all. As a sign of goodwill, she was given a three-month supply at no cost.

What is the nature of the financial relationship between HMOs, formulary decisions, and drug companies?

Musing Upon Our Canine Companions

A routine well-woman exam started off uneventfully today—until it snowballed into a blizzard. Thank goodness these women are allowed to come to their gynecologist of choice. As in the case that follows, I do not know what would happen to them if they were not allowed this saving grace.

After starting out with a discussion about menopause and hormone replacement therapy, Susan discovered that she had many questions now that she had found a serious listener.

"You know, I have never had a complete physical exam since we came out to California. I go to the PCP, but I have never had an exam that included lab work. I have never been offered any preventive health information or advised to attend classes. What do you think?"

"I would think that you are supposed to be receiving some type of care along these lines. That is what your insurance is supposed to provide for you."

"Well, here's another thing. I have had this chronic ear problem for two years. It is a very annoying pain. The PCP keeps prescribing the same medications, but it is not getting better. I wish that I could see a specialist. I am never sent. Just the same prescription keeps being renewed. I had an X ray once; it did not help. I really would like to see a specialist. I think that I need to see an ear, nose, and throat doctor."

She continued with increasing animation and conviction, as she was grateful to release four years of pent-up frustrations. "And my knuckles. Look at them! I have a history of arthritis, as does my mother. Hers is so bad that she just had to have a joint replaced. My hands hurt so much now, they are constantly sore. The knuckles are getting swollen. I visited my PCP recently and asked, 'Can't something be done? Are there any other medications that I could take?' He told me that there were no other medications.

"I went there to see him with a referral to a specialist in mind, but this was denied. It has now progressed so that I have difficulty writing. It's getting worse with each passing week. The PCP recommended an exercise class. This was a step in the right direction, but I feel that I need something else. I am afraid to think what it is going to end up like."

A pause here, followed by a heavy sigh. "And my mother receives such good care from her doctor.

"Recently, I have begun to be bothered by this searing, hot pain in the bottom of my foot. It feels as though it is burning on the inside. At certain times, just crossing my legs brings it on. I visited my PCP for this and was told not to worry, exercise would help. No referral was given to any specialist. This pain really bothers me. I am unable to walk on it when it happens. The fact that it is new really concerns me.

"I had excellent care in the Midwest. The doctors were wonderful and the preventive health education was superb. I felt as though I was really well taken care of. Every year we had a physical, and you could tell that the doctors really cared about you. The wellness program was outstanding. Frankly speaking, we have been in California for four years, and the medical care stinks!

"There is no effort directed at prevention. I have to be really sick before anyone will pay attention to me. I know better than this. I know enough that I should be doing things to stay healthy, but I don't know how that happens with this health plan.

"I have to tell you about my dogs, because I have been thinking a lot about this. Recently they became very ill, and we had to deal with a variety of vets—including specialists. They have been outstanding! They are so caring, so committed. They took such good care of my dogs!

"It has occurred to me lately that my dogs are receiving better health care than I am."

After listening to all of this, I recommended a new PCP. I suggested that at least two specialist visits were in order—if not three. I also generated a permission slip that she could present to her new PCP in order to increase the chances that a specialist visit would actually be approved. Her knuckles, her increasing pain, her deteriorating health, and the new disturbing pain in her foot were all I could think about.

A California Steeplechase

Donna is a well-educated, forty-something health care professional. She described the following experience last week while in the office.

During a routine self breast exam she was shocked when she found a breast lump. It was certainly new. It did not belong there. It was unwelcome, and immediate action was imperative to hold off anxiety and dread.

She knew that she should obtain a mammogram. She called the facility. She had been going there for many years. It could not be scheduled outright. Apparently, it needed to be ordered by a physician first.

Donna found this really strange and questioned the receptionist further. It turned out that there were no immediate openings—they would, however, place her on the cancellation list.

Since it now seemed that a degree of waiting was in order, she asked if it was possible to schedule a routine mammogram in a few weeks' time. This would coincide with the time for her annual mammogram. She had always been able in the past to schedule her mammogram without any difficulty. *Like many other health care centers, this facility had undergone changes in management and organization dictated by the force of managed health care.* This present difficulty was strange, and Donna had no frame of reference that was appropriate. It had always worked so well before. Even the dialogue was puzzling.

"We cannot allow you to schedule a routine mammogram because you have a problem."

To which Donna replied, "Let me get this straight. You won't or don't have a spot for me since I have a problem, and you will not let me schedule a routine mammogram because I have a problem."

This was affirmed, and she was told that she should make an appointment with the doctor. She then asked to be placed on a waiting list and decided to obtain consultation in our office.

She first needed permission from her PCP. She called that office for a referral and spoke to the receptionist. She described her situation, as well as her concerns and worries regarding the breast mass. To which the receptionist replied, "Please call the referral line for that request. I can't spend any more time on the phone with you. I have five people waiting on hold. They might have something *really important* that is wrong with them."

Frustrated and taken aback, Donna then left a message on the referral line. She asked specifically to be notified, as soon as possible, when the visit was approved.

A few days passed, and she did not hear back. She called again and listened to a recording. *It's impossible to get a real person on the phone anymore.*

She was able to speak briefly again with the receptionist, who stated that she knew nothing about her request. She suggested that the patient call the HMO directly to determine if authorization had been granted.

She called the HMO authorization line and found a person who was helpful. However, he reluctantly explained, there was little that he could do without information from the PCP's office.

She called the PCP's office and had the unanticipated pleasure of speaking with the bookkeeper. She was very kind and promised to help. However, there was little that she could do because the UR person was not in the office at the time.

Finally, she was able to speak to the UR person and relayed this entire sequence of phone tag, to which the UR person replied, "Sorry it took so long. It looks like you fell through the cracks."

She had never in the past encountered such difficulty. It made her wonder. If she were ever in an emergency situation, she would be in trouble.

She eventually obtained permission to be seen and came to our office. I verified that she had a breast lump and ordered a mammogram. Permission was also needed from the PCP's office, so that she could be seen by the general surgeon. We would start the paperwork involved.

Armed with this "official order" she again called for a mammogram appointment and was again disappointed at the lack of availability. A few more days would pass before she could be granted an appointment.

She asked why she had not been called before this. After all, she had been placed on the cancellation list. In checking the list, it was discovered that her name had not been added. Somehow it had been left off.

With extreme agitation she mentioned that she was a health care professional and was very unhappy with the entire nature of her interaction. Suddenly, a curtain parted and two appointments were then available the next day.

All of this left Donna with no choice but to compare this experience with the past. This year's ordeal was distressing. In years past she recalled receiving a consultation directly with the radiologist. This year, only the technician reported back, relaying the reading from the radiologist.

The technician shared with her that patients were very unhappy with the declining level of service. She had unfortunately been the recipient of many patients' venting of feelings.

The technician also mentioned that the employees feel "like a number now." The personal attention to their needs and desires, as well as those of their patients, has diminished considerably.

A patient's description of trying to make an appointment with a primary care physician:

"I had to make six telephone calls to differing primary care physicians' offices before finding one that would accept me. The very first question they ask is 'What is your health insurance plan?' Every time I mentioned my HMO, the reply was the same. 'We are no longer accepting patients with your plan.' I was so desperate one night that I broke down, cried, and called my parents. I finally found one office who agreed to accept me."

An Earnest Search for a Second Opinion

The nights are very long and incredibly exhausting. Vickie is up most of the night—gripped by the labored, raspy breathing of her two-and-a-half-year-old son. It is a short, noisy intake followed by a long, labored outflow. In and out. Rasp and wheeze. All night long. Then a pause, and she holds her breath. Her breath is thankfully released with resumption of her son's rhythmic, spasmodic breaths. But the spasmodic breaths are not what concerns her. It is the silence that causes fear. It is the silence—*that pause*—that induces the insomnia. Sometimes she sits still by his crib, staring, fixated on his small chest wall. Waiting for the movement of those small ribs, the reassuring movement, all the while keeping track of the silences. They have not changed. They have an established pattern. To her relief, she discerns that there has been no variation. She cannot sleep with this. She is only able to intermittently doze off while sitting and maintaining her vigil. She will hold out for a few days longer. Surgery has been recommended. She only has to wait until all is approved and authorized. She is reflecting upon it, in the dark recesses of the night. The light from the exterior reflects on the blankets, on her son's pinched face. Why does it have to be so difficult?

Vickie does not have a good feeling about the specialist who is taking care of her son. Paul is suffering from sleep apnea due to an unusually severe case of swollen tonsils that are blocking his airway. This was recently confirmed by an official sleep study. She wondered why that was necessary. The overnight monitor, the technician who slept in the house, she could have told them as much. She is the one who knows, after all. This problem had been ongoing but had worsened lately. They had seen the specialist last year, and she had liked him then. She had formed a favorable impression. But this year the impressions were different and disturbing.

It is the time to think. This time. Everyone else is asleep, and she can think a great deal and rehash every comment, every nuance. She is rehashing it because she is looking for some sign of reassurance, some comfort. This doctor, who is going to operate on her small son. She wants to know that he actually wants to do so. That he cares about her and Paul. He seemed to care last year, when it was not so bad. Since Paul was so young, the decision had been made to postpone surgery until he was older, when the risk of complications would decrease. Now it appears that it can no longer be postponed. Surgery will be scheduled. She wishes the doctor had given her a greater sense of confidence. She recalls the conversation in the office regarding surgery.

"When will it be scheduled?"

He replied, matter-of-factly, "It is out of my hands. It depends upon your HMO. It could take a few weeks or it could take a month before it is approved."

Weeks or even a month more of these endless nights! Distraught by this nonchalance, Vickie spoke to her pediatrician. She requested a second opinion. "I know that he is supposed to be a good doctor, but I want him to care about my son. To notice what I am suffering through."

To which her pediatrician replied, while shaking her head slowly, "You are not the only one who is requesting a second opinion. All of my patients are requesting second, and some even third, opinions. They do not like the way that they are being treated at their doctors' offices. It is very disturbing. I just don't know what to do."

Vickie is becoming very nervous. She just wants her son to get better. She wants the surgery to go well. She wonders how she can turn her son's life over into the hands of someone who does not appear to really care. However, she knows from past experience that he did express the capacity to demonstrate concern and compassion. So perhaps it was just some temporary circumstance. *Or the cumulative effects of HMO-induced physician burnout. Now beginning to rear its ugly head in our valley.*

She came to my office asking advice. What could she do? What should she do? Where could she find consolation and encouragement?

My advice: Make an appointment and be prepared to pay out-of-pocket to see a physician who does not participate in HMO plans. You will find what you are seeking there.

In her state of distress, she did this. She and her husband, Christopher, had a wonderful visit with this doctor. He gave them so much comfort and consideration and spent so much time with them. He made certain that all of their questions were answered. They had found peace and consolation. He concurred with the other specialist's recommendation and agreed that surgery was in order. He reassured them all would go well. They could worry less. They could begin to relax. The last benefit he gave them was peace of mind. He reassured them that the doctor who was doing the surgery was indeed top-notch; they need not worry about his technical expertise. Their son would be in good hands.

As to why the bedside manner had changed over the course of the year, this final question could not be answered. It was the only answer that had to be left unsaid. The physician knew why. All of the physicians know, but these things are not yet being shared with the nonphysician world. Perhaps because no one yet has any great idea how to change the present onerous system. That it should be changed dramatically is beyond question. But how to do it? Until this question is answered, no one is willing to address the tremendous price being extracted from all of the human beings involved. A price so steep that even to acknowledge it would induce unfathomable and perhaps unpredictable and possibly even violent repercussions.

Erosion of Autonomy

The pathology report lay before me. As I read it, a frown pursed my lips.

Early dysplasia (the earliest precancerous changes that can be identified on biopsy).

It was present on all of the biopsy specimens taken. That implied widespread involvement. Christina would require a LEEP procedure (an electrical cautery procedure designed to remove the precancerous tissue).

I was bothered by this thought: The lab to which the specimen was sent to be analyzed was unknown to me with respect to quality. I was also unaware that the biopsy specimens were going to be sent there until the report came back. It was then that I noticed the unfamiliar letterhead. It is not my preferred lab. I know that lab quality can vary considerably. I am perturbed to realize that my prerogative of sending my patients' biopsy specimens to the "best lab" has been usurped. First mammogram facilities, then clinical labs, then pap smear labs, and now finally pathology labs.

Usurped by a business manager at the lab who has been busy negotiating contract rates—apparently lower than the preferred lab. How else to explain their landing the deal?

I have heard through the grapevine that errors have been made by this lab. I have had no personal experience of this, but this knowledge makes me uneasy.

I call Christina, who flies into a panic learning that she has precancer. I explain in a very reassuring manner that we can take care of this—very soon—in a follow-up office visit. Chances are excellent, I tell her, that treatment will cure it in one visit.

I hear her voice cracking at the other end of the line as she tries to maintain her composure. I send soothing messages of consolation and hope along the connection.

This is typical of the response when women learn about a problem affecting their reproductive organs. The female anatomy is anchored so strongly to the female psyche that the shock waves reverberate from the center out.

In response, Christina wants this fixed tomorrow.

"We can schedule it soon," I say. However, I explain that I will feel better just double-checking the reading. My uneasiness has grown. I want a second opinion before subjecting her to minor surgery. I have never felt the need to double-check a lab report before. This was uncharted territory. But this physician's intuition will not be set at ease until this is checked again.

"OK." She sighs in reluctant agreement.

Meanwhile, authorization needs to be obtained from her PCP, so we could not do it tomorrow even if we had the scheduling capability.

I request and receive the slides after a few days, and I make an appointment for them to be reviewed.

I am flabbergasted by what the reviewing doctors say. *They consider the biopsy to be unequivocally within normal limits.* They would recommend nothing other than a repeat pap smear in six months.

Oh, my God! What will Christina think? Outwardly, "How can this type of mistake occur?"

"It's fairly easy if the lab lacks sufficient expertise."

"Oh." I am at a loss for words.

Unbidden, I think of all the patients who unwittingly, due to enrollment in their HMOs, continue to have specimens sent to that lab.

I return to the office and call Christina.

"I hope you are sitting down. I have just received the reading on the review of your biopsy report. *There is nothing wrong with you.* You do not need surgery. You just need a follow-up pap smear."

Incredulousness is transmitted to me. "How can this be?"

"The lab has made a mistake."

"Well, I am relieved." Silence . . . then "One would think that the HMO would choose more carefully. Think of the expense involved if I had undergone a procedure that I did not need."

I add, "Think about this: Any procedure carries complication rates—even if they are slight. What if you had had a complication resulting from a procedure that you did not need?

"Listen . . . in the future, all of your pap smears and biopsy reports are going to the lab that I am comfortable with. I hope that you are willing to pay for this out-of-pocket—for both your peace of mind and mine.

"I cannot take good care of you if I cannot trust the pathology report."

"OK."

The sad truth is that preventive health care is not expensive. It is critical, however, that it be accurate.

Two hours later, another patient's pathology report is returned bearing the same letterhead.

I groan.

Beam me up, Scotty!

Sarita was in the office today, and she reminded me of a discussion we had held last year. After a little prompting, I immediately called it to mind.

One and a half years ago, I had referred her to an internist. She had returned later to inform me that she did not really appreciate the experience. The doctor seemed too busy, was not particularly friendly, and did not seem to have enough time to spend with her.

She had not been back since and was reluctant to return. Recently, however, a problem arose requiring a return visit.

"What a wonderful experience! The doctor was just great! Everything was what I would have expected, given that you referred me to the office. I don't know what the circumstances were at my first visit that caused the initially unfavorable impressions. Perhaps we both were caught on bad days."

What has occurred is that one and a half years ago the physician was participating in HMO plans; since that visit, the doctor has stopped doing so.

Beatrice

Beatrice sat before me. The passage of time had been kind. Only a few wrinkles were noticeable around the eyes and the angles of her mouth. She emitted the air of someone who had dealt with life's challenges with calm, cool acceptance—especially the difficult ones. There had been a few. She had borne them well, throughout these several decades of living. She simply had not allowed it to be otherwise. She had been taught this a long time ago, how to deal gracefully with life's challenges. She had learned that lesson as a young woman. It had been useful. It had been practical. She had benefited from this. Lately, however, she was running out of grace. Perhaps it was more difficult at sixty-something to deal with these things. But she suspected that perhaps it was not her age at all. Was it something else?

It was her husband's problem that was on her mind today. She explained that he had recently been diagnosed with prostate cancer. The surgery had been performed. Findings at the time of surgery indicated that further treatment should be performed. They understood that he had options. A while ago he had been in the care of a urologist whom both of them had really liked. Her husband had felt comfortable in his care. But recently, due to referral stipulations, he had been obliged to see a different urologist. With this recent finding in mind, they sought consultation regarding treatment options. They began to feel uncomfortable. Something about the manner of this new physician caused uneasiness. They were not the type to question physicians as a rule. However, as they spent more time in consultation with this new physician, they began to think with increasing urgency of the previous one. When it came down to the particular treatment recommended, they were really uncomfortable. They had done some research, and the side effects of radiation were scary.

They went home and thought it over. It was such an important decision. They decided to request to see the previous urologist. They knew him, and they desperately needed to feel comfortable. There was too much at stake.

They made an appointment with their PCP and requested a change to their previous urologist. He was now on the plan, so a referral should be easy to obtain. Except that it was not forthcoming. Something vague emerged regarding the reason why. The PCP would have to check on it. He would do his best and would have to get back to them.

They were not interested in any delays. They wanted an answer that they could trust. On their own, they called the urologist's office and made an appointment for the next week. Thank goodness they did not have to wait long. What a relief! No, they had not gotten a referral. No matter, they explained to the urologist's receptionist, they were going to pay cash for the visit. They had grown weary of this entire permission business. It had made little sense to them previously; they could see no sense in the delay now.

As a courtesy, they informed their PCP.

They busied themselves with some errands and tried to keep their minds occupied. After a less than satisfactory attempt, they went home.

The message machine was blinking. With curiosity they pressed the button. Both listened with weary hands resting on tired hips.

"You cannot go to the urologist next week." They recognized the toneless voice of the medical assistant from the PCP's office. Stunned, they looked at each other in disbelief as the message continued: "Since he is in the network of participating physicians, you cannot pay cash; you cannot go unless we approve it. If you have any questions, please call the office."

Shock and disbelief turned these gracious, usually tender eyes into flashes of burning anger. She turned to look at her husband.

"What kind of system is this? Where are we living? Is this communism? How dare they tell you that you may not go to see a physician when we are willing to pay for it in cash. Who do they think they are?"

His weary eyes echoed her sentiment, and he had to sit down.

He arose a little while later to call the office and express fully and completely their anger, their disgust, and their fatigue, all the while trying to keep frustration and fear at bay.

The message was duly received; no promise was immediately made.

After a long, restless, and unrewarding night's attempt at sleep, a telephone call was received the next day. It appeared that permission would be granted, after all.

He placed the receiver down and informed her of this "good" news. All she could think about was the price paid for this news. The emotions lived. The feelings stirred. The distrust insinuated.

No, she thought to herself, she had not been brought up to deal with people this way.

She shook her head sadly and wondered, *What next?*

Marla

I walked into Marla's room. She looked up and smiled in recognition. She was talking on the telephone.

"Look, can I call you back? My doctor is here."

She hung up the receiver and glanced at me with gratitude.

"It's good to see you. Thanks for stopping by."

I said hello and sat on one of the chairs resting against the wall. I had read the printed notices posted on her door prior to entering the room. She was in an immuno-compromised state. I took care to wash my hands and keep a little distance lest I accidentally pass on any "bugs" that she didn't need. Bugs that could make her deathly ill.

She had been in the hospital ten days, having been diagnosed upon admission with leukemia. She was undergoing chemotherapy and would remain in the hospital a total of three weeks.

"What a summer you have had!" As I waited for her reply to this softly spoken understatement, I followed the IV tubing carrying the chemotherapy into a special vein in her chest. It snaked down from the lofty position on top of the IV pole before it disappeared beneath her hospital gown. I thought that overall she looked pretty good. Perhaps the cheeks were a little gaunt, but the eyes were bright sparks and her mood was upbeat.

"I feel so much better now," she replied. "As for the summer. Yes, it was terrible. In hindsight, I know now that the stomach pains and fatigue were signs of the leukemia, but no one could figure it out."

"The culprit was hiding out in your body—discovered only ten days ago."

"Yes. I knew something was terribly wrong when I was admitted. It took my doctor two days to find out what. Now I am on the chemotherapy, and I am feeling better.

"You know, this is my first experience with any illness—and what an eye-opener it has been for me. My doctors have been excellent, you know. They have worked so hard for me. I had no idea how hard you [doctors] actually work. The rest of us, with our nine-to-five jobs, can leave it at the office and go home. But you, you have to work whenever the patient needs you. Whenever that is. I had no idea.

"I heard your name being paged on the overhead system a few nights ago. Is there only one Doctor Mahony that works here?"

"Only one."

"Well, you were busy that night."

"I was indeed."

"And the nursing staff. Wow! I can tell that they are really under duress. It's so obvious, and I am sorry to see it. In spite of that, they still are able to deliver their compassion and concern. They are working *so hard*. I just had no idea of the capacity of the human-to-human interaction that actually occurs inside the hospital." She shook her head and continued.

"When you are healthy, you do not appreciate this dynamic. The doctors and nurses are so important to me. It has been and continues to be an unbelievable experience."

I nodded in agreement and did not say much—being lost in silent reflection and contemplation.

It is, of course, the action of the doctors and nurses to save her life. That is what they intend to do with their treatment and care. That is what they are trained to do.

I had recently heard that eighty percent of the population are healthy and twenty percent are the ones who actually utilize health care. Marla was previously in the happy-go-lucky eighty percent and suddenly, without warning, finds herself in the twenty percent. In the process, she is amazed at discovering what really goes on inside hospitals. Amazed at the hard work, long hours, dedication, and commitment exhibited by her physicians and her nurses. Amazed because somehow, while lost in the happy-go-lucky eighty percent, she never had the opportunity or desire to even think about this. Now that she has found herself in the twenty percent, it is all she can do not to think about this.

What matters most is the care and attention given to her by her physicians and nurses. Care and attention that only they are trained to deliver. Care and attention that she was only too willing to receive.

It boils down to basic principles of humanity: healers taking care of the sick.

Somehow, lately, the importance of honoring and respecting this most ancient of traditions, this very basic, primitive healing function, seems to have been misplaced.

Unsung Heroes
and Heroines

There is a palpable uneasiness present in the entire medical community. "Entire" meaning all of the persons who work in this vast and complex enterprise. This includes the allied health staff, the nurses, the physicians, the educators, and all others who have daily contact with the human beings who come to them in their hour of need, seeking attention, seeking recovery, seeking healing.

Comments on the Nursing Staff:
Not Just Anyone Will Do

I was involved in a delightful yet sobering conversation yesterday. A retired physician stopped by the office to visit. After we had exchanged the usual pleasantries, the subject turned to the present state of medicine. Although he is officially retired, he remains very much involved with medicine, as it is the love of his life. Truly, a better match between person and profession would be hard to equal. He was and remains such an excellent example of what a physician should strive to embody that his patients still inquire as to his health and well-being eight years following his retirement.

He is presently involved in volunteer work at a local clinic, and he is concerned about the nurses who work there. They have great fear with respect to their job security. I mentioned that I had recently attended a meeting of physicians who had expressed extreme dissatisfaction with both the quality and the quantity of available nurses at hospitals. There appears to exist a chronic shortage of experienced nurses in spite of the contradictory evidence of recent layoffs in the field. Where have they all gone? My colleague and I both agreed that this problem is most distressing to physicians, because maintaining the integrity of the physician-nurse partnership is critical to achieving good patient care. My friend concluded our conversation with this: "The physicians are no longer in charge of medicine." I silently concurred. After he left, I found myself reminiscing.

I recalled my first impressions regarding the nursing staff upon my arrival eight and a half years ago. They were excellent! This stood out in such sharp contrast to the circumstances of the county hospital where I worked as a resident. There the nurses were always in short supply, and staffing was never to be relied upon.

It was a privilege and a relief to be able to work with such a professional and highly committed group of individuals.

They were experienced and reliable and rendered superb patient care. Secure in the knowledge that the nurses would fulfill their role in the physician-nurse partnership, I was then free to concentrate solely on fulfilling my responsibilities. For their part, I observed them to be, on the whole, content. They enjoyed the respect of the patients, physicians, and hospital administration. They were encouraged to pursue additional professional fulfillment by various means—additional education or advancement into administration, for example. As a young physician, I could not have asked for a better environment in which to practice medicine.

Sadly, this has all changed. I remember the unsettling beginning of this transformation. It occurred with the first mention of managed care a few years ago. I cannot recall it precisely, because there have been so many profound changes in medical practice in recent years that it is impossible to remember the precise sequence. This type of remembrance also flies in direct opposition to one of the protecting functions of human memory—that one wants to remember only the happy times. However, I will do my best to recall it.

Managed care was coming, we were told. Things would need to change. Health care costs in general and hospital costs in particular were excessive. A reduction in these costs was necessary. I remember attending a meeting addressing particularly the issue of nursing and associated staff. It was at this meeting that I first became acquainted with the terms FTE (full time equivalent) and PTE (part time equivalent). These terms were to be applied to discussions regarding the nursing staff. Apparently, a formula had been developed that elucidated the most efficient use of the FTEs and PTEs. The hospital administration felt obliged to follow this formula and adapt its tenets to the nursing staff. There was a desired cost-effective ratio to be achieved when the number of patients was compared to the appropriate number of FTEs and PTEs. Compliance with the recommended ratio became the order of the day.

I recall my thoughts at that time. FTEs? PTEs? Are we not discussing individual human beings? Do they not have names like Susan, Joyce, Barbara, and Joanne? Do they not have careers, aspirations, and professional standards? Hospitals complied with the formula, and this type of thinking and management was widespread. The result of all this restructuring is that many of the old familiar faces are gone. Some left the hospital for work in a physician's office. Some have found employment in the ever-growing home health care industry. Some have changed careers altogether, and some have moved away. I miss these comforting faces, their experience and their excellent clinical judgment. To be sure, a few of the old guard remain, surrounded by the young and inexperienced. Where is all of this heading?

As I muse, this concern is only enhanced. Notwithstanding the changes that have already occurred, what can be done to assure quality patient care? What will be the means to retain these young nurses to make certain of lengthy tenure—which is essential to assure development of clinical judgment? The essence of good medical care and of rendering good patient care is the development of clinical judgment. This wisdom comes to the individual chiefly through experience, preferably many, many years of experience. It requires the development of a keen eye to see how the clinical picture is developing. This is important, because in nine times out of ten, when something starts to go wrong, the optimal time for intervention is in the earliest stages, when the clinical signs are subtlest. It takes experience and instruction from other individuals who possess years of experience to pass on this knowledge. This skill is not found in textbooks or training classes. It unfolds gradually, while working with one patient at a time, one clinical situation at a time, preferably over and over again until the knowledge is gained. This has to be recognized as a wisdom possessing the utmost value.

I have been disturbed by the trend in the hospital industry that views the RN as an expense item on the budget analysis, an item that should see a reduction in its column. Consequently, there has been a reduction in the number of RNs at many hospitals. Under the guise of restructuring, individuals possessing a lesser degree of education have been hired to carry out so-called routine nursing functions that were formerly under the domain of the RN. An example of this is the common practice of hiring lesser-skilled individuals to obtain and record the vital signs of the patients.

These lesser-skilled employees now routinely take the vital signs of the hospital patients. They dutifully write this information on clipboards and record it into the medical record. Presumably this is done after checking in with the charge nurse. Vital signs. A remedial task? Let's think again. They carry the designation *vital* because they are so absolutely indicative of the condition of the patient. Whenever I am concerned about the true condition of my patients, the first step in the assessment process is to take their pulse—*myself.* Anyone can count, but who is able to make the determination as to whether the pulse is strong and steady or weak and thready? If the pulse is rapid, who is trained to think of the next most important question: What is the blood pressure and what is the nature of this most revealing relationship? Finally, temperature, pulse, and blood pressure dutifully taken are meaningless numbers without attachment to a sense of clinical judgment regarding the patient.

Physicians have been disturbed about many of these adjustments in nurses' staffing because the nurses have the important job of watching our patients while we are away. Ultimately, the responsibility for the patient's welfare is ours. This is a responsibility that is carried with us all day long, into the night, through the next day and week and month, and on and on. In spite of the concerns of nurses and physicians regarding these staffing changes, they remain because "someone" has done outcome studies that demonstrate that no adverse effect on patient care can be demonstrated. This is true, but the reason why this is so has to do with "boundary crossing."

Having the sole responsibility of the patient's welfare etched indelibly on our psyches during our training, physicians almost subconsciously cross over into areas of patient care that traditionally fall under the realm of nursing, if this becomes necessary. The physician is trained from the earliest moment to carry out whatever duties are needed to ensure a good outcome for the patient. If a deficiency exists in an area of care that falls under the traditional nursing function, the physician will step in and correct the deficiency. It is taken on as another necessary responsibility automatically, without regard to turf considerations. "Boundary crossing" also works from the opposite direction, for example, when the nurse speaks to the physician and mentions "By the way, did you notice that these laboratory tests are not within normal limits?" Likewise, the physician will hear "When I was attending to the patient today, I became aware of this significant clinical sign." This is the trademark of an excellent nurse, and I know many such persons. It also demonstrates the collaborative nature of the physician-nurse partnership. We have the same goal—improving the welfare of the patient.

Many examples exist of boundary crossing as seen from the point of view of the physician. Some are minor, such as simply reviewing the entire chart and double-checking to make certain that all information is current and up-to-date. If the laboratory results have not been recorded in a timely fashion, the physician will pick up the telephone and call the laboratory directly. If the patient has a particular request that has not been attended to properly by the nurse, the physician will attend to it. There are also instances of greater concern.

A patient of mine was in the hospital recovering from surgery. Andrea was doing well with respect to the surgery, but "something else" was wrong. At the end of the day, while visiting her in the hospital, I perceived significant intuitive warning signs but was not able to isolate the source. (This was because the nature of the problem was such that I had no previous experience dealing with it.) I consulted a colleague, ordered laboratory testing, and went home. Distinct uneasiness prevailed throughout the evening, and some time later I felt compelled to call the nurse and inquire about Andrea. Sleep would elude me unless I could determine exactly what the nature of the problem was. She replied that Andrea's condition had not changed considerably since my departure. This gave me a little comfort. I then inquired as to the lab results. It had been some time since samples had been drawn. Were the results back? The nurse replied in the affirmative. I requested that she read them to me. She relayed the results with such a calm and unassuming voice that I almost missed the crucial bit of information. Half a second passed before I realized what she had told me. With increasing urgency and concern I replied, "Read them to me *again!*" She did, and with a shock of recognition I realized that one of these laboratory values was indeed *critical* and Andrea needed immediate expert assistance. A delay into the morning would have been too late. It was apparent that the nurse had no idea of the magnitude of the problem. (It was particularly disturbing because the laboratory test result would have been *highlighted as being within the critical range.*) Andrea was able to be treated, after I requested a consult from the appropriate specialist.

Yesterday, while I was in the elevator with a physician colleague, she remarked on the necessity of staying at a patient's bedside for two hours the previous evening. She had to make sure that all of her orders were carried out by the nursing staff in a timely manner and that her patient received the care that his medical condition required. She was unable to go home and sleep until she was certain that, in fact, this would happen. She knew that maintaining a physical presence on the floor was her only assurance that the orders would be taken care of.

As a physician, I feel that this cannot continue. The nurses are unhappy, the physicians are frustrated, and the patients. . .yes, well, what about the patients? What must they think? They are entitled to more than this. We all are. We need those RNs. More to the point, I would like to see their status elevated. In my opinion, they should be viewed as being among the *most cherished employees in the entire hospital.* I would like their working environment to change so that they will desire to remain on the job for many years. They should again receive encouragement to pursue their professional fulfillment. How can the development of clinical judgment be encouraged? How can long tenure be achieved? How can we ensure that experienced and clinically proficient nursing staff remain in the hospital setting? Who will watch over you when your doctor is away? Not just anyone will do.

The intuitives who reside in this community are very apprehensive. Reports of tragedies are surfacing throughout the network. An investigation has been carried out in an out-of-state hospital regarding an unusual number of patient deaths. Somehow, uncredentialed persons were allowed to masquerade as physicians—with dire consequences. Complaints against HMOs have risen, and nurses and ancillary support staff employed in the industry have been on strike. Academic medical centers are feeling their security rug being yanked from underneath them. The future holds greater uncertainty than anyone can recall ever having been present in the past. So great is their sense of disturbance and urgency that medical centers have begun a public relations campaign to educate the public regarding their importance and their perilous state. Articles in medical journals are appearing that attest to declining patient-care standards, declining quality of the nursing staff, and indirect assertions regarding the true intentions of hospital administrators.

Formulary Snafu

I was in the midst of a solitary reverie today when I was approached by a drug rep bearing the most urgent news. I was actually relaxing in a chair in the hallway of our office and was enjoying a three-minute break when he arrived. He had made a special visit to warn us of an impending formulary snafu that would have negative implications for our patients. My attention was immediately engaged.

He explained that, due to a merger in the HMO industry, a formulary problem was in the works. It appeared that one HMO was about to take over another. Somehow, during this takeover period, his company's products were no longer going to be listed on the formulary. This would have the following effect on our patients: If they were presently taking medications of this particular manufacturer, they could expect over the course of the next few months, when they presented themselves at the pharmacist's for a refill, to be informed that the medication was no longer "on the formulary." At that point they would be instructed to call our office so that we could straighten out the problem.

He was here to inform us that there would be plenty of free samples made available to these patients so that when they began calling we could instruct them to stop by the office to pick them up. This period of disruption in formulary coverage was predicted to last only until the negotiations were completed. At that time, the rep assured me, the products would be reinstated. Curious about the nature of the problem that initiated all of this, I inquired as to the reason for this occurrence. He replied that he did not know precisely, but it appeared to be linked to a negotiation issue. I thanked him for his concern regarding the patients' well-being. I found it interesting that I had received no formal communication regarding this problem. I wondered if I would ever have found out if this kind drug rep had not thought to come by and warn us. Could this really happen? We had no choice but to wait and see.

The fact that this sort of incident could occur was not surprising to me—it was not the first time I had encountered it. It reminded me of a similar incident that had occurred several months ago. Without any warning, an HMO dropped a manufacturer from its formulary. It happened to be a manufacturer of extremely popular medications. Many of our patients were on them. Our attention was first brought to this development by an inundation of telephone calls from the pharmacies, usually on a Friday afternoon, with the message "The medication that you prescribed is no longer on the formulary. Please choose another."

Great consternation and confusion ensued. Many of the patients had recently been seen, were doing well with respect to their medication, and had left the office with a prescription designed to last the entire year.

"Are you certain of this?" we asked the pharmacists.

"Yes," they assured us. "It has been recently changed."

Changed without notifying us or the patients, I concluded, judging from the ensuing confusion. We then spent many minutes on the telephone on Friday afternoon talking to patients and choosing alternative medication. Approximately two weeks after this all began, we eventually had the situation confirmed by contacting the HMO. The reason why this occurred remained a significant source of speculation.

It was highly entertaining during those first several days of confusion to witness the triumphant looks of "competing" drug reps. They entered the office with renewed energy in their stride, no doubt spurred on by the knowledge that their market share was about to be enhanced considerably.

Yes, one by one, they exuded sparkling enthusiasm as they reminded us of the outstanding attributes possessed by their products. (The fact that it had all been heard before—recited previously and dutifully listened to on more than one occasion—seemed to slip their mind.)

As to the fate of our unfortunate drug rep of the "fallen" product (fallen product of an excellent manufacturer, by the way)? He appeared on the scene two weeks later with a long, sad, resigned look, and with his side of the story. His chin was so low it left a telltale scraggly scuff mark all along the carpet. Apparently, all of this was the by-product of some prickly point of negotiation.

We, of course, explained this as well as we could to our patients—giving them the day-by-day updates as we received them ourselves. Their unhappiness increased with their level of understanding. All (physicians and patients) ended up complaining vociferously to the HMO. Record numbers did so, and all of this communication must have paid off. I have stopped receiving those pharmacy calls. At least for the time being.

All of this elucidates the complexity of the present situation—a situation riddled with seemingly isolated occurrences of undesired incidents affecting the human beings who, with trust in their heart, present themselves to this system at the most vulnerable time of their life, when their defenses are down, when they turn themselves and their lives over to those who run the present system.

A Word or Two from Our Friendly Neighborhood Pharmacists

The changes in medicine have not been confined to the doctor's office or the hospital. Changes in the pharmaceutical industry have been widespread and profound.

It is a Saturday morning, and I am on call, fielding what could be as many as ten to fifteen routine and ordinary calls—requests for antibiotics, requests for other medications, and sometimes just general advice. The comforting kind. The kind that people need when they realize that upon waking on Saturday, with the pressures of the hectic week behind them, they have to have an answer. An answer to the question that has been on their mind for a few weeks now and will wait no longer. They must know what it is that is ailing them. So they call on Saturday to talk. To receive soothing advice. The nature of these calls is diverse. I need to be prepared when the pager goes off. It could really be about anything. Fortunately, the first call was purely routine. The patient was bothered by a bladder infection, which is easily treated with a prescription for antibiotics.

I called in the prescription myself and listened to the recorded message while the assistant was putting the pharmacist on the phone. I gave him my name, my office address, and my license number—all of the usual bits of required information. Then came the final question: "And with whom am I speaking ?"

"You *are* speaking with the doctor."

"Oh, what a surprise! I so rarely speak to a physician anymore. It is hard to believe that there are actually any of them left 'out there.'"

"It is sad, isn't it?"

He concurred that this was a rueful commentary on the evolving state of affairs in medicine. "It is this insurance-driven attention to the bottom line," he continued. "My pharmacy has begun to draw a line in the sand with respect to some of the insurance companies' policies. Enough is enough."

I could not agree more.

The intuitives are suffering from bouts of increasing anxiety in many instances, in some cases accompanied by the beginnings of desperation as well. Why can't everyone see it? These are not random, isolated, statistical aberrations. There is an invisible web that binds them together. Cause and effect can be intuited but, alas, not definitely proven. This hardly matters to the intuitives, who see and feel and make connections that are invisible to others.

The intuitives look at the summation of the events to date and, after analyzing the present state of affairs, find themselves looking to the future with alarm accompanied by a deep sense of foreboding.

The RPH Factor

It was quiet in his pharmacy that day. It was a holiday, but never mind. He came in. He was quite a bit behind. He had work to do. He would be open tomorrow, and he knew that some of his patients would come in for their medications. He needed to catch up. It was important to him. He knew it was important to his patients. With no one to talk to and without telephone distractions, he had all day to catch up. To work uninterrupted. He cherished these days. He loved his work.

The RPH factor. Now why was this on his mind? He had learned this acronym long ago. It was self-determined from the accumulated experience of life and living. It was a guide that he had learned to use when faced with difficult decisions. A very useful guide. It comes to his consciousness more and more lately. His subconscious brings this thought forward unbidden. Not that it is unpleasant. No, he has no qualms himself. He has always been a faithful subscriber. He has found it useful on many occasions. He has lived his life that way. He is at peace with himself. But why, then, was it coming to the forefront with increasing urgency?

The RPH factor: Check on the Reality of the problem; research it thoroughly to truly understand its complexities. Investigate the Practicality of the solution; this, again, in his experience, could take hours of careful and meticulous thought. Honesty. How honest have you been in deriving the solution? Of all these, the most important is honesty.

A heavy sigh escapes him, and he adjusts his glasses as he opens his patient index-card file. There it is in the upper-right-hand corner of this well-cared-for three-by-five card: 1A.

This marks the first card for this particular patient, someone he saw for the first time in 1969—over thirty years ago. He pauses to run a puzzled hand through his thick, white shock of hair. Thirty years. Is that possible? He flips through each card, remembering the years and pausing to reflect on the prescription given then. How it had helped. And this time.

A different solution, again helpful. He can still remember the look of gratification—the look that melts your heart. After reliving the satisfaction of that particular day, his fingers rest on the present active card: 21A. The prescription he filled last week. He had been glad to do it—he is always glad to do it. They had talked when the patient came in. Talked about the family. Talked about his job. They had talked about many things. Thirty years' acquaintance. Indeed, there had been a lot to talk about. Much had gone on. Of course, the patient had talked about his medical problem. The reason why he came in. Yes, questions about the medication were reviewed again. He loved this part of it—the talking, the explaining, the soothing reassurance that he could give. It was rewarding in so many ways. That is why he does it. Why he has done it for forty-eight years. He is slowing down now. It's his heart. But the relationship with his patients brings him back every day. He cannot imagine doing anything else. The personal satisfaction. The counseling sessions. He knows that he is assisting in achieving a favorable outcome for the patient. This is a marvelous professional relationship! That was how he was educated. That was the ideal, and he had practiced pharmacy this way for many years. He cannot imagine ever being asked to do otherwise.

He stops in his reminiscence. He must prepare for tomorrow's patients. He carefully lays out their medications, double-checking the prescriptions and trying to predict what questions will be asked. He reviews the medications to make sure all the precautionary advice is ready. He picks up the first package, but . . .

It all comes down to honesty. That RPH factor again! Where did he learn it? He pauses to search his memory.

He was born and raised on a farm in Canada. It was a small community, perhaps three hundred persons. Accountability to the members of the community was taken for granted in such a small, tightly knit group of people. It was impossible to act otherwise. Accountability and honesty. It was an understood underpinning of that community. He had spent his youth there. It was etched into his psyche indelibly. He had carried these values with him when he first stepped off the train in Berkeley in 1946. So many years ago! He will never forget coming to California. What a difference from Alberta! The whole world opened before his eyes. It was an exhilarating time—fabulous, really.

He enrolled in his preparatory courses at the University of California at Berkeley—never having a moment of doubt that it was what he wanted. He graduated in 1950 from the University of California San Francisco with a Bachelor of Science and Pharmacy. He was called to serve in the army and was away for two years. That was a completely different experience. Again, the world widened before his eyes and he reveled in it, that experience of gaining an appreciation of the world's tremendous diversity. It was then that he began to realize, as he often thinks now, that there are six billion persons on this planet and all are different. Each of us is unique. This was his guiding principle, and its seed was planted during his travels in the army. When he returned, he would reenter school and graduate—one of the first six-year graduates of UCSF School of Pharmacy. It was a top-notch school with excellent professors and a research staff second to none! He cherished it all.

He carried the idea of individual uniqueness with him, and it flourished during his education. Of course, we are all biologically unique as well as biochemically unique. This view was perfectly compatible with the true compounding pharmacist that he had been since 1950. He would uphold the time-honored traditions of pharmacy, making unique medications at the request of physicians to fit the unique demands of the patient. Of course, in all these years of practicing pharmacy, he has never met the average patient. He is sure by now that he never will.

It all comes down to honesty.

This thought will not go away today. He recalls a conversation with a physician colleague last week. Poor soul. He could sense in the harried, curt manner on the telephone that this doctor was too busy, too pressured, too rankled. It was not always this way. . . . It's terrible what has happened. He muses as he picks up a package. He looks at the name and smiles. Another long-term patient. Then a thought demands recognition. Hmm. Interesting. Is it a communistic application of theory? This new system that treats all physicians the same. This system that does not allow excellence to thrive. What was all that nonsense about the Cold War, when some of what we were fighting has taken root right here before our very eyes? Why can't anyone else see it? It matters a great deal how the professional relationship develops. The mind is a powerful element to engage in the good of therapy. No two physicians are alike. No two people are alike. He shakes his head, knowing how the excellent physicians must feel. It doesn't take a rocket scientist to predict the future. He wonders where all these excellent physicians will go.

And the pharmacists, what will happen to them? Pharmacy is a time-honored profession. It is his professional expertise, that is, his knowledge, education, training and experience, that is called upon when a physician requests a particular medication for a patient. It is his responsibility to make or dispense that medication. It is a professional responsibility that has *value*. This is being lost. There is an intrinsic value to the professions of both pharmacy and medicine, and this is being run out of town, obliterated by the powerful economic forces now controlling the scene.

When he wants any service, whether it be bricklaying, dry cleaning, or top-notch neurosurgery, he wants the application of knowledge, education, training, and experience that go into making it the best service possible. A pharmacist who doles out twenty prescriptions per hour is not practicing the time-honored profession of pharmacy.

There have always been two aspects of medical practice that have had to be considered: the economic and the professional. But the economic aspect is overpowering the professional aspect. The proliferation of misinformation to the public, with the resulting confusion, has assisted the effort.

The RPH factor. Investigate the Practicality of the solution.

He is glad he is a nonparticipating pharmacist. He couldn't stomach what his colleagues have to put up with in the guise of his profession. Under the auspices of utilization review and compliance, it is now common practice for patients to receive a reminder that their prescription is up for renewal. This is purportedly done to solve the problem of non-compliance with prescriptions. Reminding patients directly will solve this problem. Remind them to go to their pharmacists and pay for their refill. But, he wonders, has no one considered that a patient may not like taking the medication? Perhaps it has produced unacceptable side effects. Perhaps he or she has found a different solution to the ailment. Perhaps a conversation has taken place between the patient and the prescribing physician, and this medication has been discontinued. Why has this important consideration seemingly been left out? He certainly *hopes* it hasn't; however, his gut tells him that it is the monetary gain to be realized from these reminders that is the impetus behind them.

It all comes down to Honesty. Honesty as an integral part of obtaining and drafting the solution.

Formularies, average wholesale pricing, large drug distribution centers, and mail-away pharmacy programs. Chaos . . . and deal making. He wonders about this business-driven mantra. You have to make a deal. It's the secret deal that counts. He understands that deals are being made between hospital administrators, insurance companies, and drug manufacturers. He fears that the ultimate goal is pro-fiteering—at whose expense?

The RPH factor. Check on the Reality of the problem.

Counter prescribing was a common practice up until the 1930s and 1940s. Back then, if a person went to some pharmacists with a particular ailment, he or she might have been led into the back room. After a conversation, he or she might have been told "I have just the thing that will help. I will sell it to you." This practice was frowned upon and strongly discouraged during his training and education. It was not acceptable professionally. The doctor was felt to have the greater expertise in deciding what treatment was best. This idea of physician expertise was vigorously promoted at that time by drug companies as well as the medical profession. It was the impetus for the expression *available only by prescription*. Now, everyone seems to be letting go of this idea of physician expertise. Something so frowned upon sixty years ago now is back in vogue and is backed up by the powers that be: the devaluing of physician expertise. There were good reasons to stop this practice back then. The reasons have not gone away. Some had to do with respect for the profession. Respect for education and learning. He slowly shakes his head.

Honesty.

He wouldn't want to be a patient in a hospital. He feels that in many hospitals the inpatients are being cheated out of pharmacy services. A hospital-based pharmacist should have the responsibility of medical drug chart review so that, when a new medication was ordered, he or she could review and research the interactions and the side effects and then pass judgment—professional judgment—that this new medication would not harm the patient. That was the role of hospital pharmacists. They were proud to have such an indisputably valuable part to play in the hospital drama. They *thought* it was invaluable. He does not understand how hospitals have been allowed to change this. The physician used to have the ability to utilize the expertise of the pharmacist. This oversight and guidance are going by the wayside. In its place, hospitals have pharmacists on staff with the emphasis now on hiring pharmacy technicians to assist the pharmacists with their activities. All that oversight was deemed redundant. Perhaps the physicians and nurses ought to be able to provide the appropriate level of care, or perhaps the technicians could supervise each other. It apparently is not cost-effective to employ a pharmacist in this duplicated and expensive role. He groans out loud to consider how many medication errors could happen. *He cringes involuntarily at the thought.*

Reality. Practicality. Honesty.

He stares now at the computer screen—this high-tech, impersonal substitute for his twenty-one hand-crafted cards. It is the footnote at the bottom that raises the level of his consternation. "The patient is being underdosed." That's a new one on him. Again, someone's idea of improvement. The dosage prescribed by one of Stanford's top neurologists for a seemingly evasive diagnosis does not match the computer protocol. It is glaring at him. He is taken aback. What should he do now? This new conundrum has been created by the computer and the prewritten protocol. You see, he was trained to dispense the medication *as written*. Fifty years ago when he was trained, it was his understanding that he did not possess the knowledge, the education, and the training to second-guess physicians—especially this one. No, he *would* dispense as written. This physician knows better. His fingers tap restlessly on the keyboard. He does not appreciate being handed this medical legal dilemma, this warning on the screen: The dose did not match the protocol. It would be ludicrous in a way, if it were not so serious. He is not privy to the doctor's chart. He does not know the interaction. Why is this message on his screen? Is he supposed to call the physician? He cannot even imagine that conversation. How would he begin? He could expect an earful. He cannot dream of such an obvious assault on the expertise of his physician colleague. Yet there it is on the bottom of his screen. Who has put it there, and just what in the world is he supposed to do?

The RPH factor. Reality. Practicality. Honesty. All three are meant to apply in searching for a solution. Of the three, honesty is the most important. Why is this on his mind so very much lately?

The intuitives in ancient human times would have come to a simpler conclusion regarding the significance of these events. They would have surmised that something is deeply amiss, that all of these occurrences are signs that need to be heeded. Warnings emanating from a deeper place within the human psyche. Irrepressible warnings that speak of a great unrest and disturbance affecting this sphere known as the healing arts.

Ancient human beings would have surmised that the gods must surely be angry. They are most certainly desiring our immediate attention. They are being dishonored.

"Mother, May I?"

My nursing assistant is frustrated today. She was sitting in her cubicle facing the stack of charts with a weary frown on her face. Her red pen tapped erratically against the loathsome stack. She had spent forty-five minutes on hold with a patient's HMO obtaining an authorization for a minor office procedure. She and the other nursing assistants have been dealing with this frustration for two years, ever since our office load of HMO patients increased. They've dubbed this authorization process "Mother, May I?"

I feel sorry for the medical assistants. A typical "Mother, May I" experience goes like this: I see a patient for an office visit—usually the sole "allowed well-woman visit with the gynecologist of their choice." I then identify a problem that will require a routine minor office procedure to clarify the nature of the problem and assist in treatment. I am no longer allowed to perform the majority of these procedures unless I obtain "prior authorization." My patients on this particular HMO plan will have to make a follow-up appointment in two to three weeks to allow sufficient time for "Mother, May I." Rather than their problem being taken care of in one visit, it now takes two. Most of them are working women, and it's not easy for them to take additional time off. However, I explain, this is the way their plan works. I give them an encouraging smile, and we both are left to make the best of the situation.

My assistant then has the onerous task of obtaining the authorization. She calls the HMO, is invariably placed on hold—usually for several minutes—and at last has the privilege of speaking to an actual human being (whose qualifications for the position of power and authority held are not quite clear to us and thus are an endless topic of speculation). She relates the pertinent details and submits the specific request. She is then told that this matter will be sent for "review" and to please call back in forty-eight hours. Two days later she calls back. Hopefully, the request has been reviewed—by whom we are not certain. She can expect to be placed on hold for several minutes during this second telephone call (today, for example, she spent twenty minutes on hold) before invariably receiving approval. Mother, may I take two scissors steps forward? Yes, Doctor, yes you may. Thank you, Mother. Thank you, HMO.

An average "Mother, May I" takes three or four days to complete and creates untold irritation and anxiety among the staff. They are usually juggling several "Mother, May I's" at any given time, doing their level best to keep them all straight—who has left messages with whom, who is waiting for a call back. At times I will hear them signing off to one another before their day off. They pass off the assignment to another assistant so that nothing is missed if the awaited callback occurs when they are not working. When they're finally given the cherished authorization number, they must transcribe the multidigit number carefully, since it's the only means of verifying the transaction.

What a sorry contrast to our non-HMO patients, who can be adequately taken care of immediately, appropriately, and without any hassle.

Relocation

Regina came into the office today. She has been one of my longest-standing patients. I was surprised to learn that she had moved out of the area since her last visit. She had driven down for the weekend to visit with her family and to obtain her annual checkups with her physicians. I was curious to know why she had left and what she was presently doing for a living.

She had secured a position as a medical assistant and X-ray technician at a physician's office—the same type of job she had previously been employed at while living and working here. As to why she had left, she replied, "Because I was tired of all the hassles that I had to go through in order to try and help the patients in the managed health care system."

She went on to explain that she used to work in an office that was open seven days a week. She often worked the weekend shifts. She became frustrated because she could not help take care of the patients adequately. Her job entailed performing an X-ray procedure in the office or arranging for a more involved diagnostic procedure to be performed at the hospital. She had been happily employed in this position for several years. She recollected that in times past, if the physician felt that a test was indicated, she was able to perform it or schedule it right away. This was most often done while the patient was in the office. She recalled that the patients appreciated the good service.

In the recent past, however, the circumstances became different. If the patient came into the office for a visit and was found to have a problem that required a particular diagnostic procedure, it was not possible to perform or schedule the procedure unless "prior authorization" was obtained. It was often not possible to obtain this authorization on the weekend because the insurance companies were not open for business. There existed the occasional exception, but the vast majority were closed. The patient was then sent home to wait for authorization to be granted.

Regina's role was to pile these charts—generally three to five in number—on the desk of a nurse who on Monday would begin the authorization process. She described the process in the following manner: It would be initiated on Monday. In her experience, after the initial request was made, information given, and all questions answered, the nurse was informed that the Utilization Review Committee would meet on Thursday. That was the earliest time that a reply could be expected. In her recollection, in many instances the feedback was not available until the following Monday. Which meant that the patient was kept waiting all this time without a resolution.

All of this made Regina feel inadequate. She was not able to complete the job that she was trained to do. She felt sorry for the patients. She was often the one with the job of relaying the unhappy news to them. She can still recall the standard reply that seemed—almost without exception—to emanate from them: "I am caught between a rock and a hard place. I hate this insurance plan, but I have to take what my employer offers."

They disliked being treated like a number. She felt their frustration acutely and remembers apologizing many, many times. They were gracious to her. They realized that she was doing the best she could.

Regina jumped at a new opportunity for employment that arose in a community out of the area. There is little or no managed care there. She is employed in the same role, and it feels wonderful!

She loves her job. She feels again as if she is being useful and helpful. Most important, she feels, the patients are happy when they can be taken care of promptly and appropriately.

What is the identity of the gods who seem to be deeply disturbed by the transformation of the healing arts into a business-driven, bottom-line-worshipped, and—in many instances lately—purely profit-driven enterprise?

I think that for the medical profession as a whole we can look to Asklepios, the Greek god of medicine. It is said that he appeared to his patients as a vision in their dreams. As a consequence, they were reported to be healed.

I can imagine that he is suffering from chronic recurring nightmares.

Patients' Medical Problems and Their Expiration Dates

Shirley works as an office manager for an orthopedic surgeon. She looked tired. She was in the office for a routine annual exam. She looked almost sorry when I came into the room— I had interrupted the only period of quiet time that she had had all week. This irony was not lost on me. I apologized with a smile barely concealed. Among other usual and customary inquiries, I asked her how her job was going.

She replied that it was so much more stressful than it had been last year. She was not sure how much longer all of this could continue. As an office manager, she is responsible for timely and appropriate billing. She also keeps track of reimbursements to ensure that they have been received from the insurance companies in a timely and correct manner. Because it is a small office, she is also responsible for obtaining all of the necessary prior authorizations that pertain to patients' visits.

She related the following example as one among countless examples typical of the HMO experience. A patient was referred to their office for treatment of a problem of a moderately serious nature. An assessment was made that the proper treatment of this condition would require several office visits. Shirley then contacted the HMO and submitted a request for the approval of these visits. She described her experience of the permission process as follows.

A telephone call was placed, followed by the perilous navigation through the phone tree. Eventually, a "staff person" was reached and the pertinent information relayed. This was followed by an average time spent on hold of about fifteen to twenty minutes per transaction. She was granted her request and received approval for five office visits. The patient was then seen by the doctor and received the necessary treatments. At the end of the allotted five visits, the physician decided that the patient needed additional visits—the problem had not yet been resolved to his complete satisfaction.

At this point, the office manager was required to obtain authorization for each visit on a separate basis. The HMO would not permit authorization of more than one visit at a time. The reasons for this were not made clear to Shirley. Each subsequent visit was then authorized in the required manner—one by one, navigation of the phone tree, twenty minutes on hold, the same explanation given, over and over again. Eventually, the patient demonstrated a satisfactory recovery, and the case came to a resolution.

Several weeks after the completion of the case, additional communication was received from the HMO. This communication stated that they were not going to reimburse the physician for two of the original five authorized visits. This prompted Shirley to discuss the case with an HMO representative, who stated the reason as follows: One of the visits was not authorized. To this Shirley had an extremely passionate reply: "Of course the visit was authorized! I am the only one who performs that job. I can guarantee that it was done. I do my job very well. I followed all of the guidelines."

She received a noncommittal response to this reply. The HMO representative then proceeded to discuss the reason for the denial of the second visit. That denial was based on the fact that the patient had been seen in the office following the issued *expiration date* of the original authorization. (It is common practice for all such authorizations to be issued with an expiration date. I had not learned in medical school or in all my years of training that patients' medical problems actually possessed a *limited shelf life*.)

Due to the ardor with which Shirley presented her case, the HMO representative then reassured her that everything would be fine. They would grant an exception and reimburse for all of the visits as originally authorized. This benevolent posture lasted one month.

At the end of the passing of approximately four weeks, Shirley received another telephone call from the HMO representative. She stated that the case had been sent "for review," and denial of payment for the two visits would stand, after all.

This incited a rising level of anxiety and indignation in the hard-working Shirley. She began all over again to explain the entire situation, sequence of events, previous conversations, and so on, since this person to whom she was speaking was someone she had not spoken to previously. However, communication was extremely difficult, and our dedicated office manager only felt her frustration level rising. It was particularly bothersome because the person to whom she was speaking, who held such a position of power and influence, could not speak English very well.

Finally, overcome by feelings of hopelessness, frustration, and indignation, Shirley simply hung up the phone. She gave up. She found herself wondering: I have spent so much time on this already, and to what end?

Shirley has been working for this orthopedist for several years. The situation appears to be getting worse. It seems as though she is bending over backward, jumping through hoops, just to make it all happen. Even then it seems there is no guarantee that all of the effort will be validated.

She feels that this system is not the best for the human spirit. It seems that office staff, physicians, patients, and HMO staff have found themselves in an antagonistic relationship. This is not the way it should be. She feels strongly that there is so much that is really wrong with this system—surely the truth must come out.

Shirley thought that one of her elderly patients summarized the situation quite succinctly today. She had brought the patient back to the exam room for her visit. The patient most emphatically handed the office manager her new Medicare card along with the supplemental card—for the purpose of making a copy for the medical chart. (The patient had switched last year into an HMO and had now switched back into traditional Medicare insurance.)

The patient then told the office manager, "Don't ever let me think about doing that again! That was such a nightmare!"

An Additional Perspective

My afternoon was pleasantly interrupted by a visit from one of my favorite drug reps. He is definitely one of the best in the business. He possesses the unequaled talent of presenting his product in a manner that respects the physician's intelligence and time. By adhering consistently to this principle, he thus accomplishes his goal of moving his product to the forefront of our awareness. Consequently, because of his easy and authentic manner, I always enjoy his visits.

I perceived that he was looking a little tired, which prompted my inquiry as to how life was treating him. I also mentioned that it had been an unusually long time since his last visit. I remarked that we had truly missed his company.

He replied that his territory had recently been expanded. Therefore, he had many more physicians' offices to visit these days. This had kept him extremely busy. He commented that we were all looking very busy, as well. He mentioned that he had missed his more frequent visits. He enjoyed coming to our office, as it always gave him such a comfortable feeling.

I responded that I was glad he still perceived that feeling in spite of the office being much busier than it had been in previous years.

"This is still a friendly office," he replied.

"How are you finding the other doctors that you call on?" I inquired, unable to withhold my curiosity any longer. "Are any of them happy?"

He shook his head slowly and stated, "No, it is a real shame. I have not seen one genuinely happy doctor in a long time. Most of them appear frustrated or too busy or both."

He went on to say that, after many years in the business, he found this recent development most regrettable.

"You are not really allowed to practice medicine the way that you like anymore, are you?"

As for my specialty, which covers health care for women, their pregnancy issues, childbirth, and motherhood, I can look to Rhea, the Mother of the Gods, or the Great Mother as she is also called. I can also think of the goddess Eileithyia, who helped women during childbirth and was also known as the divine midwife. I can imagine them both—wailing, pacing, wringing their hands, and crying out in unison.

"These mortals are not being allowed to pay close enough attention! Why is this system not allowing them to do so? Someone seems woefully ignorant of one essential truth—that, while pregnancy, labor, and delivery experiences are 'natural,' they are not 'risk-free.' They never have been.

"While tragedies have always occurred in this realm that belong in the category of unpreventable, it is possible to imagine in the system that has recently evolved that tragedies will begin to occur that previously belonged to the category of preventable."

The Problem of Low Morale
Among Hospital Employees

After spending a significant amount of time in various hospitals over the course of the past fourteen years, I feel as if I have seen it all. The cross section of my hospital experience includes a large, busy university teaching hospital; a gritty, unpredictable county hospital; and small, stable community hospitals.

One little-appreciated fact is that within the hospital there exist countless numbers of employees generally referred to as allied health support staff. They include the dietitians, orderlies, housekeepers, X-ray technicians, respiratory therapists, receptionists, operating-room technicians, biomedical repair persons, and electricians. Together this group makes up a crucial work force, responsible for doing tasks that may be viewed as routine and ordinary. To the contrary, these tasks can and should be considered essential, and some carry lifesaving potential.

Personal observation, experiences of patients, and doctor shoptalk testify to a drop in the morale of these workers. This seems to be prevalent throughout this valley, as we are in the throes of change brought on by the hotly competitive managed care environment that has forced itself upon us. Increasingly, through efforts aimed at cost containment and downsizing, these employees are fearful of losing their jobs. Their departments have been restructured, and job descriptions have been redefined. This has created significant distress.

I have concerns about these persons and the messages they have been receiving regarding their importance and worth. Although the business community has entered the health care field as though it were riding galloping white horses, I wonder if it has been fully informed?

These hospital staff persons do not perform "routine" functions. They are *essential* support staff for the physicians and nurses. The manner in which they are being treated while "on the job" will undoubtedly be reflected in how well they perform their jobs.

Are they being treated like complete human beings who possess mind, body, and soul? Are they being sufficiently encouraged to commit mind, body, and soul to the performance of their duties? Alternatively, are they viewed only as bodies needed to fill scheduling needs, to perform functions? Are they being viewed as easily replaceable?

I would most certainly want my patients to be cared for in a hospital where the morale of the employees was high— in an environment in which they are cared for, encouraged, and respected as complete human beings.

If the person whose job it is to wrap and sterilize surgical instruments is not encouraged to bring to his work his entire heart and soul and does not receive authentic appreciation for doing that very important task, what happens? What happens if he is made to feel as if he is a dispensable employee, that just anyone will do? Do all of those instruments get properly and painstakingly counted, sorted, wrapped, sterilized, and labeled? (I know of instances lately where this has not happened.)

Is the person whose job it is to constantly monitor, regularly service, and keep at all times in good running order the complex high-tech equipment now so commonly used in the operating room valued and properly secure in her job so that she brings to work her entire mind, body, and soul? All are needed to supply her with the energy necessary for the constant vigilance, surveillance, and attention to detail that this job requires. On the contrary, is it the case that her job is underappreciated and understaffed and she thus finds herself overworked and left only to do the best that she can? (I know of cases involving equipment failures during surgery of such a nature that the surgery could not be completed. Imagine being in the unenviable position of explaining to a patient's family that, although the patient—their dear loved one—was asleep and on the operating-room table, the surgery could not be performed as planned due to equipment failure. What does one say, We will have to reschedule? What would the family think? What is the guarantee that the equipment will be working next time?)

Abundant examples exist. Does the dietitian, while bringing in the evening meal, take any extra time to say "hello" and visit, or is he so busy trying to keep everything straight that this encounter is reduced to a curt in-and-out relay?

Does the orderly whose job it is to transport the patient to and from the X-ray department possess any training or have any idea how to comfort the patient when, during the course of one such diagnostic procedure, the individual learns some devastating news?

Hospitals are now in the business of "servicing" patients. It appears that the entire view of the functioning of the hospital is now seen in this altered light. This is dangerous and shifting sand upon which to tread. The "product" that is being serviced comprises the chronically ill, the elderly, the emergency patient, the expectant mother, the sick child, and the elective-surgery admission. The persons employed in hospitals are not processing widgets on an assembly line. They are employed in various positions that are geared toward achieving the same goal—contributing to the health and welfare of the patient.

It is in the best interests of the patient that they perform their roles well—with enthusiasm and joy; with commitment and integrity; in essence, with mind, body, and soul.

This attitude cannot be coerced, cajoled, or extorted. For it to be expressed fully, it needs to be *nurtured*. This is what is missing in the hospital setting under managed care. Considering that the misfortunes of ill health are quite democratic, all of us need to consider that we might be patients someday. We will most fervently desire those employees to be content as they are assisting us in our recovery efforts. We will become better faster and more easily and experience an element of joy if they are putting their entire heart and soul into their job.

Yes, the intuitives in the medical community are very worried indeed. These messages are crystal clear to them, screaming in their ears, assaulting their vision.

Mother's Day

It is 3:00 a.m. I am on the labor-and-delivery floor. Wide awake. It is a relatively quiet night—if nights can be described as quiet on this unit. I am attending a patient in labor who will be delivering within the next hour or two. I am not in the sleep room. Between the nursing station with its electronic bank of monitors and the bedside I am alternating my site of vigilance. I have the sense that something undesirable is at work in this labor. Having been alerted to this possibility, I am responding by exhibiting my respect and honor to the powers that be. My vigilance is required.

I learned a long time ago to hold Mother Nature in the highest regard. As an obstetrician, I hold no illusions of control over this process of giving birth. As a two-time participant in the process, I know full well who is in charge.

It is best to realize this and pay appropriate homage and respect. I often find myself explaining to my patients and their families that I am simply a troubleshooter for Mother Nature.

If all is going well, there is little that I need to do. At the opposite and thankfully rare end of the spectrum, there are circumstances in which I cannot do enough or work fast enough. In between these two extremes, it is often necessary to watch carefully, adjust medication, observe the patient's response, reevaluate, fiddle with fine-tuning, and so on. This occurs all through the labor in an attempt to stay one step ahead of a process, to try to avert an outcome that not one of the human beings involved wants to experience. I have learned that there are no guarantees.

While I sit in the labor-and-delivery suite, I find myself engaged in conversation with one of the nurses. It is often the case in the wee hours of the night that need for conversation arises. Nights almost always offer a few snippets of opportunity for this. This is probably related somehow to the awareness that our loved ones are fast asleep. In our state of wakefulness, and perhaps initiated by our thoughts of them, it is not surprising to learn that the majority of conversations revolve around them.

As it was also the predawn hours of Mother's Day, it seemed all the more appropriate that the conversation would revolve around our children. I found myself relaying the latest update on the doings of my six- and four-year-old. The nurse found it all very interesting and relayed the differences in her children—who were grown up. She was an appropriately proud mother when speaking about her daughter's success in college and the impending move to graduate school. It pleased her that her daughter had succeeded in achieving her lifelong goal. She mentioned, as an aside, that her daughter had given her cause for concern a couple of years previously when she had discussed the possibility of changing her mind from pursuing her long-desired graduate degree to pursuing medicine, instead. This had come about from helping her premedical friends with their homework studies and finding the subject matter extremely appealing. Her mother had responded with strong persuasion against considering the idea.

"Oh, please, do not change your mind now! You have always wanted to go to that graduate school since you were little. Especially not considering the way medicine is going these days."

She was successful in her arguments and was pleased that this daughter would soon be settled in graduate school. About her son, however, she was very concerned, and her manner changed to one of grave consideration. She related the following story.

Approximately one year ago, he sustained an injury in a recreational sporting activity. He began to exhibit symptoms shortly thereafter of stomach pain and bloating. Since he was enrolled in an HMO plan, he was seen by his primary care physician—eight times in eight months. There was no improvement in his symptoms.

"I am in pain, Mom."

Mother was a nurse, and hearing these words only heightened her concern. After making inquiries among her medical contacts, she decided that a visit to a gastro-enterologist might be in order. So she contacted the office of a gastroenterologist who had come highly recommended. After she had explained the clinical symptoms and history, he agreed to see her son in consultation. However, it was necessary for her son to obtain a referral first.

Mom called the HMO to inquire as to how this should be accomplished. On her first telephone call, she was referred to a different business section, then to another section. She finally found someone who could explain the process to her.

"You can call the primary care physician's office, but the only referral allowed is to the gastroenterologist on the HMO plan." Not the preferred one who had come so highly recommended to the mother.

She explained that she had intervened in such a manner because her son was not medically knowledgeable and she was really concerned about the persistent pain. Her son is a highly successful businessman and feels that a doctor is a doctor and that he should get better. The fine details of who was on which plan and who was perceived to be better than whom were not details that he would even attempt to master. At this point, he simply wanted the pain to go away.

Mother persuaded him to request a referral to a specialist. After all, eight months seemed an awfully long time to wait with no improvement and, more worrisome, no apparent diagnosis. He requested a referral, and this was the response.

"Your mother talked to our office, so here is the referral." This was rendered in a gruff, reluctant tone of voice.

He then visited the specialist on the panel and, after receiving two treatments, still did not improve. All of this only made the concerned mother more concerned. She thinks of her thirty-two-year-old son, and she is becoming worried that something really serious might be wrong with him. This is a son who never complains about anything—especially pain. She knows full well that for him to say anything at all is significant, for him to keep complaining of feeling poorly is a cause for great alarm. He has never been ill, is very health conscious, and takes good care of himself.

He changed jobs recently and with this change had the opportunity for different health insurance. His mother implored him to select the PPO plan to increase his selection of physicians, but her son selected the same plan with the same set of doctors.

Mother's intuition was screaming in her ears: This is not good! He needs to realize that getting a different (better) doctor is what is needed. Someone who will take him seriously. Someone who is capable of finding the root of the problem. She found herself ruminating on this dilemma.

How to convince her talented, bright, successful businessman son that in medicine these days one cannot place one's faith blindly in the system? Too much is at stake. In this case, it is the health of her eldest son.

How to convey to her trusting eldest son that he should not just pick a name randomly out of a book—that it matters, very much, who is taking care of you? He has been so trusting, unwilling to upset the applecart, willing to go along with the "program," unable to sit back and ask why.

All of this in spite of the fact that after nine months of receiving medical care he has not improved, has not regained his usual state of excellent health, and has not been able to see a physician who can tell him what is wrong.

Katherine

Katherine thinks, reminisces, and thinks again.

It was all so different fifteen years ago when she graduated from nursing school. What prestige she had felt! An RN degree. Ever since she had been a little girl, she had wanted to become a nurse. She had never questioned it, really. It all had seemed so natural.

She had always known that she wanted to help people.

Nursing school had been a challenge—a wonderful, exhilarating kind of challenge. She did very well there. She can still recall her excitement at landing that first job in the hospital. It had never occurred to her then that things would change so dramatically.

"It is sad to observe what has happened over the past few years. It has been very difficult to witness the deterioration of the standards of care. What bothers me most is to see the nurses crying at the end of the shifts. The stress, the unhappiness, and their frustrations well out of them.

"Nobody seems to care. We attend meetings, but it does not appear to do any good. It seems as if the administration only cares about money.

"I watch the nurses' aides who are so excited and exude enthusiasm about their plans to enter nursing school. I do my best to try and talk them out of it. Oh, please, I say, do anything but nursing!"

I sit back in silence, digesting all of this, finding myself without words.

Her final comment: "We feel as if the world has abandoned us."

What the general public does not realize is that a medical community is a community that never sleeps. People are working around the clock. As events happen within the community, much discussion is held and considerable speculation is carried out. There is an increasing need to talk, to touch base, and occasionally to pinch each other. Increasingly, the human beings in this system are feeling the need to reach out for a reality check. Consequently, very little goes on in the medical community that is not known or that does not generate an opinion. The opinions are given most freely in the late evening and on through the long, dark night when everyone else is asleep, when the need to converse is stronger than ever. This is traditionally the time that has been allotted for reflection, observation, and expressing concern. This time has been well used lately, with no lack of subjects for discussion, and none of the commentary has been favorable.

Andrew's Lament

Andrew is employed as a biomedical electronic technician. He received his two-year associate degree and has been working ten years in this field.

When he first started, it was fabulous. The work environment was terrific. The morale was great. He felt that he was helpful to the nurses and doctors. He felt appreciated—as did other members of his department—by the administration as well as the rest of the hospital staff.

This appreciation was rendered in remarks such as "The biomedical department at your hospital is the best in the area." There was a great deal of pride in the department, pride resulting from the awareness of a job well done.

Initially, Andrew felt fortunate to have landed the job. He was one of twelve in the department. It was a highly competitive field, and he had to compete against several other candidates.

He spent the first few years of his employment in a happy state. His work was satisfying, and he felt that there were opportunities to learn and advance (in technical or managerial areas) if he were so inclined.

He liked getting out of bed in the morning and going to work. On Sunday evening, the prospect of returning to work on Monday was a pleasing one. The camaraderie at the hospital was enjoyable and pervasive. His job is one of the few offering the ability to interact with any department that has to deal with patient care—a well-known and highly regarded door-to-door repairman, if you will. A face recognized, trusted, and appreciated.

Changes began about four to five years ago. Morale in the department, as well as in the rest of the hospital, started to slip. It has fallen to rock bottom in the last one to two years. It is hard to imagine how it could become any worse.

As Andrew steps across the threshold of the hospital entrance door, he feels as if he has entered a black hole. All motivation, initiative, and cheerful thoughts are sucked away.

In this state of solemn, depressive reflection, he now performs his job.

He puts himself painfully and laboriously "through the paces."

Now when he makes his rounds, this formerly highly regarded, well-known door-to-door repairman has become the dog that is kicked. This occurs when he is the recipient of abusive statements or the venting of feelings directed his way over situations out of his control. (For example, sometimes the equipment is under warranty and he cannot repair it. This excites the fury of a lab tech who cannot see how he can do his job—all this tension over a hundred-dollar hot plate.)

Previously, he might have received some complaints from the doctors. These are not anything new. They are usually seen as evidence of the doctors' need to vent their frustrations. It is the newly evident complaints from the various staff that are the most difficult development to assimilate.

The news now is: Who is going to buy us? Who is going to be repositioned (that is, transferred to a different department, followed several months later by a cut in pay)?

The latest trend: Whose department is going to be contracted out to an independent company? The consequences of this will be that all of the existing jobs and familiar faces will be lost. Conceivably, his department could be replaced by bona fide itinerant door-to-door repairmen. These persons would have no history with the hospital, no relationship with the staff, and no previously proven in-house track record. *But a savings would be realized in labor costs.*

Over recent years, Andrew's department has been cut in half. The remaining folks are left to do the same amount of work for the entire hospital—per person this means more work. They have not only been required to know how to repair their highly technical and ever-changing equipment, they have now been asked to be experts on the contract negotiations pertaining to all of the equipment that they lease.

Other departments are also reeling under the stress and strain of reorganization. The respiratory therapists at his hospital have been cross-trained to perform EKGs (electro-cardiograms), thus eliminating the entire EKG department.

The EKG techs had acquired good working knowledge and expertise such that almost as soon as EKGs were finished, if they saw something alarming, they would notify the physicians immediately. The respiratory therapists do not have this level of expertise and are busily engaged in attending to their respiratory therapy patients when not asked to obtain EKGs. So the EKG is dutifully done and filed in the chart to await reading by the doctor.

Other employee shoptalk has created considerable concern as well. Someone has analyzed the number of beds in his hospital and has compared that number to the national average. This was correlated with all the persons employed in the various departments.

Andrew's department now has to answer as to why they have so many—read too many—technicians. This analysis was done without addressing special situations, such as the fact that his department does outside work (shared services with other, smaller hospitals, doctors' offices, etc.). This extra work adds 1,400 to 1,500 pieces of equipment that require servicing, but they are invisible to these analysts, who likewise are invisible to those employees most adversely affected by their conclusions.

The latest, most irksome change is the idea that all types of engineering work done in the hospital are to be done according to national standards. This idea is taken from the example set by the auto repair industry, where a certain amount of time is allocated for a particular type of repair such as a brake job. If it is called a brake job, then it should take no more than two hours to repair. This does not take into account the quality of the repair job or the condition of the particular brakes.

The earnest effort is under way to apply these cost-effective, efficient principles to hospitals. The concern is shifting away from quality to quantity processed.

For example, consider a malfunctioning defibrillator (a vital piece of equipment used to save someone's life when the electrical conducting system of the heart suddenly is not functioning properly). This may come into the biomedical repair room tagged with the problem "It will not discharge." Andrew's job is to verify that the problem exists. Following appropriate steps, he does this. He troubleshoots, identifies the problem, and repairs it. This can become time consuming because a multiple number of components have to be analyzed before the true culprit is identified.

He has also been taught to do an excellent job. Considering the implications and destiny of the equipment after it leaves his department, standards for excellence have been ingrained. He has been taught, therefore, that he is to inspect the entire piece of equipment when it comes in and not just fix the identified problem. After all, it is not uncommon for another defect to be found that has missed the notice of unsophisticated eyes. This might even be a critical function of the equipment that would not have been noticed until the emergency situation requiring its use arose. It goes against his training in excellence to be asked to forget these other possibilities. It causes his gut to churn.

Finally, he has been taught always to perform performance verification and recalibration as a final send-away seal that this equipment has been entirely looked over and spiffed up. It is reliable in every aspect. It can be trusted to work when needed. He sends this important equipment back with his signature on the repair log. He sends it back with a part of his integrity and soul committed.

He fears that, with national standards being put in place, turnaround time will be the key factor in determining performance standards. He fears that his continued employment will depend upon his adherence to protocol.

Some of the cosmetic aspects of his job will be eliminated. More important, instead of taking care of a potential problem right then and there, he fears that the pressure will be such that the technician will have to render a good guess that this piece demonstrating some stress will probably last a little bit longer. The repair will be "postponed" until the next time.

He fears that job reviews will be based upon production levels—that is, how many pieces of equipment worked on during the day and how much time spent on each, with the greater number of pieces and the least amount of time spent with each being the criteria set for reward. Five hours spent on one piece of equipment well done does not stand up favorably to comparison with four hours spent on four pieces of equipment with less attention to detail.

He wonders how this work would be divided among the technicians. Would they start examining the equipment as it arrives? Then, upon the realization that the identified problem would require too much time and lead to a poor evaluation, would it sit unattended to while the other, easier and quicker jobs are snatched up upon arrival?

At present, the stress on Andrew is profound. He was trained, after all, and brought up with this Midwestern axiom: If you cannot do a job well, you have no business doing it at all. He now feels as if he does not play such an important part anymore in contributing to the quality and safety of patient care. He is beginning to feel more like a factory or production-line worker.

He feels that he should leave the hospital and is considering leaving the field altogether. Looking back, he sees that it was a great choice then, but now he questions it. He wonders, Am I really being appreciated for my talents, or am I only a number on the paycheck stub?

But the greatest source of anxiety revolves around this: His name is identified with the pieces of equipment when they return to the floor. His integrity is on the line. He knows full well how and under what circumstances this equipment is to be utilized. It is these reveries that are the source of uneasiness, the beginning of a stress ulcer, chronic back pain, insomnia, and the Monday-morning dread of returning to work.

Yes, the pulse of discontent among members of the medical community is palpable to those who can perceive it. It seems to be growing stronger with each passing month.

It would appear, indeed, that the gods must be angry.

As they very well should be.

Nurses' Shop Talk

Apparently, a patient's family and friends, so appalled at the conditions encountered in one of our local hospitals while visiting, called the public health department, which made an immediate unannounced visit.

This was a first for this private institution.

A Billing Saga . . . or Where Is a Computer Whiz When You Really Need One?

One of the latest trends to evolve with the managed care revolution is how various and sundry payer organizations manage not to pay physicians. The following saga involves only one doctor's office among far too many others.

The office had been dealing with a payer organization that had subcontracted with another for payment of services rendered by physicians within the network. Due to nonperformance, this relationship ended.

It seems that claims had been filed by physicians for professional services rendered over an eighteen-month period of time. No payment had been received for a significant percentage of these claims. This particular office had generated $200,000 worth of accounts receivable, which represented claims dutifully and appropriately filed. However, when inquiries were made—politely at first, then with increasing exacerbation—the following responses were heard: "We cannot locate that claim" and "It has been inaccurately filed" (suggesting that the wrong ICD-9 code had been utilized, for example).

The business manager who oversees all of the filing of claims knew better than this. Of course they had been filed. Often, more than once. Furthermore, they were done correctly. She could testify to that. She had been involved in this billing game far too long. Too many coding conferences had been attended. Too many guidelines checked and double-checked. She was a seasoned veteran of this modern-day shell game. She knew very well the importance of accurate and timely billing. This stall tactic was becoming more than irksome. She had overhead to pay.

How many patients realize that when they receive a bill for a physician's services rendered about fifty percent goes into office overhead? In order to determine what the physician's portion is, subtract fifty percent, not from the physician's billable charges but from what the insurance entity actually reimburses the physician. Now add a twelve-to-eighteen-month delay in collecting this discounted reimbursement. Then start subtracting the hours spent in labor costs by those employees in the business office, at about twelve to fifteen dollars per hour. The remainder dwindles rapidly.

Understanding this absolutely and becoming wearied by the rigmarole, the business manager decided to become creative. This money needed collecting. Having grown fatigued by all of the nonsense, she again made copies of all the claims that added up to the $200,000 outstanding accounts receivable. These were arranged and filed and placed into stacks of boxes and more boxes.

A telephone call was made to the payer organization. A responsible person was identified. This person came to the office and was held personally responsible for delivery of the claims to the processing center. She transported the boxes and boxes. Once they arrived at their destination, a special effort was made to identify those persons who would be assigned to work on these claims. One phone call was not sufficient. Nor were two or three. Rather, the manager called every other day for thirty days to recite the following narrative.

"You have received the claims?"

"Yes."

"You are working on them?"

"Yes."

"And when might we expect payment?"

"Soon. We are still processing the data."

"Why this delay?"

It was then discovered that somehow during this transition period it was necessary to keep track of all data entry on the claims information, such as how many times the doctor orders a routine visit versus intermediate visit versus complex visit, as well as office procedures done, such as biopsies and so on. Why? To make sure that the physicians are toeing the line, staying within the actuarially generated mean. Ordering just enough of one and not too much of another.

Apparently a glitch had developed over the past several months. In a presumably cost-saving measure, the bulk of this data entry had been out-sourced to *India*. It is comforting, indeed, that the skilled work force on the subcontinent is making its impact on managed care in California. This is presumably one of the benefits of a global economy.

Except that it is not going so well. This is a great reason for the enormous delay. At least this year's excuse. Is all of this record keeping really necessary?

It appears to serve at least one purpose. With someone having been convinced that it is necessary, it now provides justification for inordinate delays in payment.

After one month's persistence, the office finally *began* receiving payment for services rendered twelve to eighteen months prior. This effort had taken up the time of the business office manager and the employees for most of the year. Finally relieved that last year was beginning to be cleared up, attention was directed to the present year's accounts receivable.

Preliminary checks with said payer organization elicited the following:

"We have no record of that claim being filed."

"You must not have coded it correctly. Please file it again."

In response to terse assertions to the contrary, indirect replies again emerged regarding transport of CD-ROMs traveling back and forth from India—not quite running as smoothly as anticipated. (This is granting the huge concession that that much was thought out in advance.)

Meanwhile, physicians' offices continue with the fifty percent overhead that will not go away and cannot be out-sourced to India. Rent, insurance, health benefits for employees, salaries, office supplies, malpractice insurance, and so on.

Many are simply wondering this: What does it take to receive payment?

Would any other self-respecting business establishment agree to run under similar conditions, especially in the heart of Silicon Valley?

Where is the innovator to solve this mess? That it be solved is imperative.

It will behoove patients signing up for insurance plans to call their physicians' offices and speak directly with the business office personnel. Ask this: What is the track record of this plan with respect to payment? How well run and responsive is the agency whose job it is to pay the physician on *my* behalf?

For if one thinks that the subtle irritation and subliminal resentment associated with identification of a plan such as the one outlined above are not somehow transmitted to patients and appreciated by them as a part of their total health care experience, one is demonstrating an extremely limited understanding of the basic imperfect nature of the human beings involved.

On Being
a Physician

"The first cry of pain through the primitive jungle was the first call for a physician. . . . Medicine is a natural art, conceived in sympathy and born of necessity; from instinctive procedures developed the specialized science that is practiced today."
— *Victor Robinson (1886–1947)*
The Story of Medicine

Identification Badge

Hospitals. These are very interesting establishments. Indeed, they are made up of a peculiar array of intersecting notions. I muse upon this often as I work. Especially when I am on call and making rounds—a physician's version of very formal and informal socializing. Formal applies to the interaction with the patients, who are being seen and evaluated. Informal applies to the chitchat, gossip, and innuendo that comprise most of the dialogue among the hospital personnel. An occasional formal discourse is held, in serious situations, but these are relatively few. At least on the floors that I am most familiar with.

As I walk past the nurses' station, I greet the familiar faces. I pass the phlebotomist who hurries on her way to the lab with her most precious cargo—someone else's blood. It occurs to me that I recognize most of these persons by sight, and vice versa. I see the laboratory technicians in the cafeteria during lunch. Some of them are also my patients. In these cases the familiarity extends beyond simple hospital courtesy.

Of course, the medical record clerks know all of us, summoned as we are, under the threat of suspension, if we do not sign off on an action that was performed days or weeks ago. An action that was done accordingly, done appropriately, but in the hurry of the moment the required signature of acknowledgment was not obtained. So we must go back and acknowledge the deed. A formal testimony of our having been present then and there and having said such and such and so on. It makes for a lot of paperwork to keep track of and is a requirement for accreditation. Consequently, these clerks know us all by sight—who comes in faithfully, who is a procrastinator, and who consistently has only four or five charts to sign off. In contrast are those who, when they call, generate a heavy sigh of resignation, for these individuals have stacks and stacks of charts that require pulling, sometimes taking up an entire shelf!

My personal favorites are the cafeteria employees, who with a vigilant and knowing glance whisper subtly or nod their head to move us to the front of the line. They whisk us through quickly. They know us all by sight and name as they sign us off in the logbook. They know we are busy and that we have work to do. Perhaps no other homage is more endearing than to hear "I've got you Doctor. You're covered." And with a wave of their hand, I am on my way to the condiment section.

All of these employees are required to wear name badges. This is a condition of their employment and has to do with many things. Hospital security plays a role. These badges ensure that all who see them can readily identify which department the employees belong to as well as their name and sometimes their status—such as RNs who have achieved different levels of professional performance, which is proudly acknowledged in boldface type beneath their name.

All wear these brightly colored badges except the physicians. This may seem odd. We, who travel everywhere throughout the building and arrive both during the day and in the middle of the night. We, who know every entrance and exit and the location of every well-stocked refrigerator in the place, with a familiarity second only to knowledge of our own homes. It is, after all, for many intents and purposes a very close second.

For this is our "house." A place in which we have free rein. A place where we can come and go as no other employee in the building can. No room in this place is absolutely, truly off-limits—except, perhaps, those rooms designated for the exclusive use of members of the opposite sex.

We act, therefore, as if we own the place. And it shows. And . . . we do not wear name badges.

It is not necessary, at least in the community hospital of which I am speaking. All the employees here know us by name, by sight, by profile, by tone, by temper, and by character. They know us better, perhaps, than those at home.

They wait for us, you see. We are responsible for giving them directions—orders, if you will. We direct the nursing staff as to all appropriate medications and treatments. We inform the dietary department as to what to feed our resident patients. We tell the laboratory what type of lab test to order and when we want the results. We tell the orderlies where they will take the patient and at what time. We inform diagnostic imaging as to what type of X rays, ultrasounds, MRIs, and so on we believe are necessary.

We do all of this for our patients. And we do it whenever it needs doing—day or night. We are the "directors" of the hospital. All of these employees are awaiting our orders. They know who we are; they know what we do. All of them are employed by and receive their paychecks from someone else, but nothing happens in the patient care department without the physicians.

We are fully aware of this awesome responsibility and carry it with us—in place of a small and woefully inadequate plastic badge.

Our authority and right to wander and order and direct are validated by these persons.

"Yes, Doctor," the nurse says as she repeats the order.

"Yes, Doctor," the phlebotomist replies. "I can add that test if you like."

"Yes, Doctor. I can pull the on-call team in from home for your emergency surgery. I can have them here in half an hour," the nursing supervisor tells us as we call to explain the need to operate at 2:00 a.m.

"Yes, Doctor," the ultrasound tech says. "That exam can be done at 8:00 a.m. We will make sure that it happens. . . . And call you right away with the results? Yes. Certainly."

"Send two units of blood to OR three and stat!" And it happens. Just like that. No further questions asked.

No, little plastic name badges can never dream of validating this type of authority. We do not need a name badge to announce it. We wear something else. It is in our aura as we "act like a doctor." And all of these employees know what that means.

How would we describe these employees without their physician "directors"?

All dressed up with no authority upon which to act.

Who Wants to Know, Anyway?

As I sit and reflect upon the closing weeks of last year, a small but significant incident comes to mind regarding a telephone call received from Emily's insurance company. It was requesting information about her cesarean section that I had performed a few days previously. They wanted to know why it was done, who the assistant was, and a few other minor details. My nurse assistant and I were very busy taking care of the urgent problems that always occur around the holidays. We found this query to be quite irksome, as we had to take time out of an already hectic day to reply. Ten days have passed since this transpired. After considerable reflection, I have come up with a better idea.

Why not discuss this type of situation directly with the CEO of the insurance company? I am assuming, after all, that he or she is directly or indirectly responsible for drafting the guidelines and is apparently very interested in all the details. So why use an intermediary?

I would like to speak to the CEO myself, at the time when the action is occurring. That way, we can be sure to transmit accurate details and eliminate any possibility of the vague inaccuracies that sometimes occur when relying on recall memory alone. I can imagine the following conversation.

"Good morning, Mr. CEO, this is Dr. Doctor calling, from San Jose, California. How are you doing?"

"Huh . . . it's the middle of the night! Why are you calling? I was asleep!"

"I wanted to give you an update on the condition of one of the enrollees on your insurance plan, Mrs. Patient. She's been on your plan for approximately two years. I'm sure that you know her well. . . . Hmmm, not quite ringing a bell? That's OK. I'm sure that it will come to you. I realize that you are not quite awake. However, I wanted to inform you that she needs a cesarean section—*now*. These are the reasons to support the decision, and this is a synopsis of my management of the entire twenty-nine hours of her labor. . . . Do you have any questions? No? I take it that I have your approval to proceed? Yes? Thank you very much. This is the right decision. I should not need to bother you anymore tonight. I hope that you can get back to sleep. . . . Me? Thank you for asking. I will not be sleeping for a few hours yet. I have work to do. Surely you know that Ob/Gyns work nights? Oh, just recently promoted . . . Didn't cover this at the corporate retreat? . . . Well, maybe next time. I have to get moving along. Good night."

I can then imagine going back to the family and the patient and with a great sigh of relief saying, "Well, I have obtained the CEO's permission. We can proceed."

Now, the more I dwell upon this fantasy, the more I experience a strong desire to take it a bit further. I really want someone to develop the transporter of Star Trek fame. Because really, in order for the CEO to get a full appreciation of the situation, I think that he or she should obtain the information firsthand.

I can imagine a sort of on-call roster made up of CEOs from all the insurance companies. This way, they could truly gain deep and lasting understanding regarding all of the procedures that induce such intense curiosity.

I would like to place one telephone call and discuss the case with the CEO. With great anticipation, I would then walk to the transporter room. I would expect a couple of minutes' delay to allow the CEO the time necessary to change out of his or her pajamas. After all, first impressions are so important. After the arrival of His (or Her) Eminence, I would personally present an hour-by-hour breakdown of the events that have occurred, not leaving out the slightest detail. After all, they want to understand, don't they?

We would then meet the patient, husband, and family. I want the CEO to fully appreciate the fear, pain, extreme anxiety, and overwhelming fatigue that the patient is experiencing. I want the CEO to meet the extremely concerned and usually stoic husband. We also must not forget to stop and chat, however briefly, with the floor-pacing, hand-wringing contingent of extended family, friends, and neighbors. After thus being "fully informed," I am certain that the CEO would agree with my decision. And . . . since the CEO is already here, why not ask him or her to assist with surgery?

Some level of basic and adequate training could be offered. This could be incorporated into an MBA program, one would think. Or the truly committed could sign up for a year of rotating internship. I can imagine several programs that would be willing to set aside a few spaces for them.

Additionally, this would be a cost-saving measure, because the CEO would not charge the assistant's fee. (There seems to be plenty of room in the present compensation packages to allow for this addition.) Just part of the job description, as they say.

If implemented, this scenario would certainly go a long way toward decreasing physician/office frustration with paperwork and eliminating needless interruptions. And wait . . . what an insight! . . . *This would be a great team-building exercise!*

"I swear by Apollo the physician, and Aesculapius, and Health, and All-heal, and all the gods and goddesses, that, according to my ability and judgment, I will keep this Oath and this stipulation. . . . I will impart a knowledge of the Art to my own sons, and those of my teachers, and to disciples bound by a stipulation and oath according to the law of medicine, but to none others. I will follow that system of regimen which, according to my ability and judgment, I consider for the benefit of my patients, and abstain from whatever is deleterious and mischievous. . . ."
— *Hippocrates (460?–377? B.C.)*
The Oath (tr. by Francis Adams)

Utilization Review Strike

I staged a private utilization review strike today... and it felt wonderful!

What is utilization review? It is the process by which hospitals, insurance companies, and peer review committees keep track of and thus document utilization of services. It is a very large umbrella that covers areas such as frequency and nature of laboratory testing, frequency and type of diagnostic studies (X ray, ultrasound, MRI, CAT scan, and so on), frequency and nature of specialist consulting, and, of course, length of hospital stay. It also encompasses the frequency and nature of surgical procedures performed and whether or not they are inpatient or outpatient. Documentation is performed regularly on parameters such as complication rate, length of stay, and so on. I could go on and on regarding utilization review, because it covers such a large territory. Over the course of the past five years, it has mushroomed into a large, billowing, dusky, and murky cloud that has penetrated in an insidious manner into the very heart of the practice of clinical medicine.

All doctors are being monitored in a seemingly infinite variety of categories. It is all being kept track of on a huge and elaborate computer system. We are reminded of this often in letters and other forms of communication from hospitals, insurance companies in general, and HMOs in particular.

The HMOs have latched onto the concept of utilization review tenaciously and are most responsible for its promotion. Committees have been established and guidelines published as to what is "appropriate utilization" of medical services per diagnosis. These guidelines are described in specific terms such as suggested medication, treatment pathways, and appropriate situations for specialist consultation. Utilization of diagnostic studies is addressed. Ultimately, definition is given as to what constitutes appropriate length of stay in the hospital as correlated with the admitting diagnosis.

The driving force behind utilization review is cost containment. Initially, physicians were informed that inappropriate utilization had been occurring. Thus, we were strongly encouraged to comply with the new guidelines and do our fair share to assist with achieving the goal of bringing down health care costs. A direct result of this new thinking was the concept of shortened maternity stays.

"Someone" performed an analysis of the length of stay on the maternity ward and decided that two days after a vaginal delivery and three days after a cesarean section constituted "inappropriate utilization of services." "The analysis" apparently revealed that an entire day could be dropped from each category without adverse effects on mother or baby. "The analysis" definitely revealed that substantial savings would result.

I can still remember the first time I learned of the new policy at its inception a couple of years ago. I shook my head in disbelief. "They" cannot be serious! I had been in practice approximately six years. I had taken care of countless new mothers, and the policy in place during that time seemed perfectly adequate. Almost all mothers and newborns were actually recovered and ready to go home within the stated parameters. The physicians also had the "luxury" of prolonging the hospital stay an additional day when it was medically appropriate. I recall having exercised this option on several occasions on behalf of those who needed it. They appreciated this and were very grateful.

So surprising was the initial pronouncement on the shortened maternity stays that it seemed quite unreal. Surely this was nothing other than a bad practical joke! However, "they" were not joking. The HMOs initiated the policy, with all the rest quickly following. How was it enforced? By increasing the presence and authority of individuals known as utilization review (UR) coordinators. Some were employed by the hospital, and others were employed by the HMOs directly. Their job was to review all the inpatient charts daily and determine if an additional hospital stay was indeed "appropriate." They were acting, of course, according to "guidelines."

I was quite annoyed when the telephone calls began. The UR coordinators would make their way around the hospital *after* the physician had done so, and the calls would arrive around mid-morning. I was invariably in the office and dutifully summoned from a patient consultation to receive the message. I was then required to explain to the UR coordinator my reasons for continuing hospital stay when I was "outside of guidelines." In the beginning there was some leniency. If I presented my case well, the coordinator would generally act as a liaison to the HMO, and my requests were generally honored. This did not last long.

The situation was transformed and the nature of the dialogue changed. I began to hear the following statement: "I am sorry, Dr. Doctor, the HMO will not cover any additional stay. The patient must go home." (Ready or not.)

My recourse at that time was to obtain the telephone number and name of the contact person at the HMO to personally plead my case. (The scheduled patients in the office, some of whom had waited several weeks for their appointment, were suddenly required to wait a little longer, as this telephone call took priority.) Again, initially there was some success. However, after a short period of time this proved to be fruitless. The replies became sure and definite. The answer was no, period. No recourse existed for discussion.

Discouraged and downcast, I trudged reluctantly across the hot asphalt parking lot to relay this unpleasant news. (You see, I was still the physician in charge, so it was my responsibility to write and sign the discharge order—*ordering* them to go home, literally.) My stomach was in knots by the time I reached the floor.

Thus did a sad, unwelcome, unrewarding element become a fixture of morning rounds. Nowhere was this manifested more completely than on the postpartum ward. Disbelief and disappointment registered on the faces of mother, father, and family when presented with the early discharge news. It was an emotionally charged interaction. I had to explain to them, these trusting innocents, especially the most completely trusting innocent—that seven-pound sleeping angel in its mother's arms—that these were the rules mandated by the insurance companies. They were backed up by the hospital and enforced absolutely, no exceptions allowed. It was not the "right" thing to do. The patient and family knew this. The physicians, nurses, and allied health staff knew. We were powerless, behaving in effect like marionettes, carrying out the act as if we were being pulled and pushed by forces outside our control.

I complied with strict adherence to these guidelines for a period of time; then I couldn't stand it anymore. I began to stage my personal Utilization Review Strikes. The disharmony was too much to ignore. The sense of injustice was so great that I just could not comply. Who were these people, anyway? Invisible in the wings but very much in charge, they could not see that a time that should be accompanied by feelings of joy, celebration, encouragement, and compassion instead became tainted with the feeling that something malevolent was at work. I was no longer able to participate in this farce.

I went back to my old ways. Thinking for myself, reaching my own decisions, vowing to send these innocents home only if they were really ready. How could I do otherwise? I entered the room with an open mind to answer the question, Is she ready to go home? Most of the patients were, and the discharge was appropriately planned. Some were not. In these cases, I produced the necessary documentation and did not send them home. The nurses applauded my efforts, and the patients were very, very grateful.

I am "on strike" again today. The first patient I went "on strike" for had just had her first baby. Elizabeth had delivered her baby by vaginal birth. She had no particular medical difficulties or problems. She did, however, require an episiotomy—which is considered routine. She therefore fit all of the requirements for the twenty-four-hour discharge.

That is, until I interviewed her. Walking into her room, I could sense the pain, the fatigue, the overriding confusion, and the doubt.

"How are you doing?" I inquired gently, knowing that I was trespassing on her feelings.

I received a grimace and a hesitant "OK, I guess" in reply. She elaborated. "My bottom is sore, I have trouble walking, and I can't sit very well."

Forcing myself to carry on with the charade, I ventured, "Do you think that you could get along all right at home today?"

Again, hesitation, then the reply, "I'm not sure."

I can interpret body language. Elizabeth was *not* ready to go home. I performed my routine checkup. I knew that she should stay in the hospital. She would be the beneficiary of additional nursing care, additional support, concern, and compassion. Not to mention additional time for healing. In essence, this is the definition of "good medical care." When I relayed my decision to her and her husband, I was the recipient of an instantaneous smile of relief and gratitude along with the words "Thank you, Doctor, I just do not feel ready to go home. Thank you very much!"

The second patient that I am "on strike" for was at the end of her allotted forty-eight-hour stay following a cesarean section. Again, a review of Harriet's chart revealed that she also satisfied the requirements for discharge that day. So I entered the room utilizing my primary mode of receiving information—intuition and feeling. I sensed immediately the tension, anxiety, and uncertainty. Outwardly, she "looked fine." Again, I inquired, "How are you feeling?"

"Not great. I'm congested and I have a bad cough."

"Do you feel like going home today?"

"Only if I really have to."

"So you would rather stay?"

"Yes, I am really tired, and I do not feel well."

After listening to Harriet, my decision was easy. She was not ready for discharge. Appropriate chart notes were written. Harriet will stay an additional day.

I have a strong hunch that Elizabeth and Harriet would have been sent home if another physician had been making rounds today. I suspect that they were aware of this.

Once I gave myself the freedom to stage a Utilization Review Strike when appropriate, hospital rounds became tolerable again. I cannot participate in any protocol that is not beneficial to the patient. *Why it was ever assumed by the powers that be that I should do so is beyond me.* Surprisingly, I have not received any hassle regarding my "strike" patients. I strongly suspect that recent federal legislation mandating longer maternity stays is helping, since in one year's time current guidelines will be history. All of this does beg the question, *In what other circumstances might Utilization Review Strikes be considered?*

Postscript to Utilization Review Strike

Interesting follow-up today regarding Elizabeth and Harriet.

When I returned today to revisit Elizabeth, I was the recipient of a grateful smile and a thank you upon entering the room. This was followed by "I feel so much better today. Thank you for the additional time. I am now ready to go home." I responded to this with the customary heartfelt congratulations before issuing appropriate discharge instructions.

Harriet's situation was quite different. I was called by the nurses last evening to see her. During the course of the afternoon, she had developed a worsening cough and a fever. When I examined her that evening, it was obvious that she was not well. Something was wrong. After listening to her description of her problem and completing the exam, I suspected that she had bronchitis and/or asthma.

She then told me the story of having had an extremely difficult time receiving appropriate treatment for a similar problem a few months ago. She is in an HMO. She described an unsettling tale of needing four or five visits to her primary care physician's office before someone finally listened to her and established the correct diagnosis and initiated treatment. She described a prolonged and tiresome recovery from that illness, which she attributed to receiving "the runaround."

She was afraid of reliving this unfortunate experience. I reassured Harriet that this would not be the case. As it turns out, since she was in the hospital, I could bypass the primary care physician and obtain consultation with a specialist immediately. It is noteworthy that, had she been discharged earlier in the day, I would no longer have been able to help her. She would have had to deal solely with her primary care physician. Such are the rules and regulations of her HMO.

Harriet was acutely aware of this. After explaining to her that I had arranged for a pulmonary specialist to see her that night, she and her mother expressed great relief. The specialist arrived, ordered appropriate diagnostic tests, and established the diagnosis of pneumonia. Treatment was begun immediately. How thankful I am that she was in the hospital and was taken care of so well! Harriet and her husband thanked me this morning for taking such good care of her.

As for myself, I am just glad that I listened to her yesterday and believed her.

Capitation . . . and Ethics

A few days ago I spoke with a physician who believes that participation in capitation reimbursement arrangements is unethical. We were huddled in conversation at the nursing station, having arrived at almost the same time to see a mutual patient. We were both at the end of a long on-call shift and were feeling the luxury of a few minutes' time to discuss— what else?—the present state of medicine. I had considerable curiosity regarding capitation arrangements, and he was very willing to share his viewpoint. He has chosen not to participate in any HMO plans that reimburse physicians in this way. He's lucky to have this luxury. For most physicians, the choice is limited: Either participate in the plan by capitation or choose not to participate.

I'm one of the lucky ones also, as I am presently being reimbursed by other means. However, I keep hearing rumors that capitation is coming down the road; in fact, it may be just around the corner. I would not want any part in it. This is how it works.

The physician is reimbursed per patient on a per-month basis. The fee is generally low, perhaps ten dollars per member per month. The physician agrees to take care of the patient, no matter what the nature of the patient's problems may be, for that fee. Whether patients are healthy or have a chronic illness, whether they never come to the doctor or have to come once a week, the payment arrangement does not change. After agreeing to this reimbursement scheme, the physician then opens his or her practice and starts "signing up" or "taking on" new patients. Physicians' practice habits are then closely monitored by the HMOs. They keep track of frequency of laboratory testing, use of diagnostic studies, and referrals to specialists.

In order to promote the proper incentives to assist in "lowering the cost of health care," there's an additional wrinkle. The physician is not paid the entire ten dollars per patient per month up front. Rather, a portion—say, two dollars—is held back until the end of the year, then distributed to those who did a "good job." That is, those who ordered the least amount of laboratory testing, diagnostic studies, and referrals to specialists. What would be the ideal patient population under this scheme from the point of view of the primary care physician? He or she would want to have a large number of patients, to be sure. Preferably, they should also be in good health and not have any need to see the doctor. How can such a system work in the best interests of those patients who have serious medical problems that might require diagnostic testing and/or specialist referral?

I can see why my physician colleague has chosen not to be a participant. As for myself, I can't imagine practicing medicine in a position so full of conflict of interest. Nor would I participate as a patient.

I know that when I visit my doctor (who does not participate in any HMO plans) she is free to order any diagnostic test as appropriate and without delay. She is also free to exercise her medical judgment to perform any necessary procedures, unencumbered by any insurance company.

I cannot imagine what would happen in my dentist's office if he were reimbursed in this way. I see him twice a year for cleaning, on his recommendation. As it stands, he is reimbursed for each visit. I'm glad he is. It's important to me. I can only wonder, What if he received payment under a capitation scheme? That would mean that he would be reimbursed whether or not I ever came to the office. Would those cleaning visits drop to once a year? Would he still be motivated or have any time to personally check my teeth at each visit, as he does now? Would his reception desk be so busy that I would be put on hold when I wanted to make my appointments? Would all of the increased paperwork cause intolerable stress among his office staff? Would this result in increased staff turnover? Instead of the familiar faces I have come to know so well, on each visit would I now find someone new and inexperienced? If he had to increase his patient load to make up for decreased reimbursement, would I face delays in the waiting room? Would he still have time to check my blood pressure on every visit? Would he have the "luxury" of being able to spend a few moments chatting about my family as he does now? Let us hope that no one has any ideas to modify dental insurance. Let's leave the status quo alone.

Back to the question of ethics and capitation. It is interesting to hear the occasional physician speak out against capitation. I was mulling this over as my physician colleague and I finished our conversation. I had finished my charting and had placed the chart in the order rack. I left him in quiet conversation with the nurse, explaining his orders for the day. I headed over to the office to open the piled-up mail from the previous week.

I have seen this topic addressed from time to time in newsletters from various national physician organizations. So far the jury is still out as to what the results will be. I suspect that the physicians involved in this type of decision making are thinking about it long, hard, and very seriously.

As I sat at my desk facing the stack of mail, a brightly covered package caught my eye. Upon opening it, I was struck by the remarkable coincidence that on this day, after this conversation, the package contained the American Medical Association's 150th Anniversary Edition *Code of Medical Ethics*.

It makes for interesting reading and is very timely; and I wonder, *Has any other physician read it?*

"The well-equipped clinician must possess the qualities of the artist, the man of science, and the humanist, but he must exercise them only in so far as they subserve the getting well of the individual patient. He must feel directly responsible to his patient, not for him—to someone else."

— *Sir Alfred Webb-Johnson (1880–1958)*
Medical Press 216:312, 1946

Permission Slips

A few years ago, I could send my patients to the cardiologist when I suspected a heart condition, to the endocrinologist when I discovered a thyroid goiter, and to the gastro-enterologist when I suspected a serious digestive disorder. Since I'm the only doctor most of my patients see each year, they appreciated the fact that if there was something non-gynecological that was concerning them I could assist in taking care of the problem. This has all changed with the advent of the primary care physician assigned to the role of "gatekeeper." This means that all specialty referrals must be authorized through the primary care physician's office.

If I see a patient for her annual "well-woman visit" and I happen to find a thyroid nodule, I can't do anything particularly useful for her except explain that she's going to need additional testing and specialist treatment. Her next step is to make an appointment with her primary care physician so that he or she can verify the problem and then authorize the visit to the endocrinologist. I often hear the lament, "Why do I have to take time out of my busy schedule just to obtain permission from my primary care physician to see the specialist?" This question is answered with the dubious but accurate statement, "This is how your plan works. There is no getting around it."

I'm not sure how many of my patients actually go on to make an appointment with their primary care physician. They're very busy. Perhaps they don't feel the problem is urgent; perhaps they think the situation will improve with time. I also have reservations about what might happen when they're in the primary care physician's office. Will the patient actually obtain the referral that I feel is important? Or will the primary care physician feel otherwise? I know the primary care physicians are under pressure to minimize their referrals to specialists.

In order to sleep better at night, I have devised the permission slip as a strategy. The permission slips have this general format:

> Dear Dr. Doctor,
>
> Please send my patient (I'm asking for your permission) to the endocrinologist for evaluation of her thyroid nodule.
>
> Sincerely yours,
> Dr. Doctor

I then make a copy for my records and give the original to the patient. All the while, I impress upon her the importance of making an appointment with her primary care physician. In this way, I know that I am doing everything I can to ensure that she receives good medical care.

Ironically, most primary care physicians don't like the current setup either. A physician colleague confided in me how much she dislikes her role as gatekeeper. We were discussing this last week over lunch in the physicians' dining room. We were surrounded by others sharing the same lamentations. The time necessary to obtain all of the authorizations and approvals for the procedures, tests, and so on is overwhelming. This is *not* the reason why they attended medical school or endured the rigors of residency. Many of my primary care colleagues have to employ one or two people whose sole job it is to spend the day communicating with insurance companies to obtain these authorizations.

Danielle is presently under my care. She is forty-two years old and expecting her second baby. On her first several visits, my time was occupied with addressing all of her medical needs. She has had a chronic problem with low back pain. We could do very little to assist her, as she needed to obtain care through her primary care physician's office. I had also found a large umbilical hernia and realized that consultation with a general surgeon was in order. We were not able to authorize this, as it was not pregnancy-related. So a permission slip was faxed to the primary care physician's office.

Dear Dr. Doctor,

I have discovered a large and symptomatic umbilical hernia on Mrs. Patient. Please send her to the general surgeon for consultation. By the way, here is who I recommend . . . .

Sincerely,
Dr. Doctor

Danielle was sent for follow-up to the PCP's office to make sure that authorization for the visit was received. After several faxes between our office, the PCP's office, and the HMO administrator, the approval was obtained. The process is never guaranteed to run smoothly, and it's very exhausting. I now find myself performing surveillance of all of these additional steps, keeping track of the hurdles erected between Danielle and the specialist. I have to stand back and personally monitor each laborious leap—double-checking to make sure every step is being followed. I have to remind people when something is forgotten. I ask at follow-up visits, "Did you receive your authorization? Did you make your appointment? Was it faxed to the proper place? Was the authorization number given to all of the parties concerned?" Tiresome work. *Work that can't be set aside because I am held accountable if Danielle does not receive appropriate care.*

Why is this better than the old days, when I could say: "You have an umbilical hernia. Please make an appointment with the surgeon. Here is the card with the phone number and address. They will be expecting your call."?

Happy New Formulary to You

It was a treat to open my mail over the past week or two and receive the new and revised formularies from various and sundry insurance plans—HMOs and non-HMOs alike. A formulary is defined (by one such insurance company) as a list of U.S. FDA-approved prescription drugs determined to be safe and effective, that is regularly reviewed and updated to reflect current medical standards of drug therapy. The pamphlet further states that, when one or more equivalent drugs or brands exist, the formulary need not include all such drugs. The goal is to include prescription drugs that may have the potential to keep costs down and to keep health care coverage more affordable. The pamphlet mentions what an excellent and empowering concept this formulary embodies. That is, the physician will benefit from the educational literature provided from time to time, and the formulary will encourage the patient to become better educated regarding her medications. The hope is that the patient will begin to take on a more active role and participate more enthusiastically in the health care process. All of this sounds reasonable to me and to many if examined on a superficial level. However, when the particulars of the situation are examined, it becomes troublesome.

I have received five nonidentical formularies in the mail recently—all from different insurance companies. They list different preferred drugs on their formularies. They are not even of similar size. Two of them are pocket-size booklets—one of these is eighty-two pages in length, the other ninety. The three remaining formularies are printed on handy 9-by-12-inch quick reference sheets. One of these is actually laminated. This, I assume, is for my benefit. Someone has obviously considered the very real possibility of coffee being spilled on the precious pages in my morning somnolence, hence relieving me of any concern that the formulary would be rendered unreadable. I gather that my job is to read, keep on hand, and/or commit to memory these formularies. It is particularly important to keep this in mind when I am about to prescribe a medication for one of my patients. I wonder, Where do I place all of these formularies? If I happened to wear a white lab coat (which I have not done since completing residency), there would not be enough pockets or even any large enough to achieve this goal. Besides, it would feel rather bulky, and it would be difficult to walk around. I can also imagine that bending over to retrieve the odd dropped pen would most likely result in some of them falling out. I would have to spend a considerable amount of time throughout the day picking them up.

This now means that, when I interview a patient, I must first ask the question, "Mrs. Patient, please tell me what your insurance plan is so that I can be sure to consult the correct formulary prior to prescribing any medication." If I fail to do so, the insurance company or the pharmacy will call back with the not-so-gentle reminder, "Dr. Doctor, the medication that you prescribed is not on the formulary. Please choose a substitute."

From a practical point of view, I am lacking sufficient pocket space to accommodate storage of the formularies. My desk, bookshelves, and workstation are filled to the brim already. I also am *not* a hard disk drive, and this information cannot be downloaded into my data banks. Besides, I feel as though my "data banks" are already busy and overloaded with more important subjects. So I feel sorry for the trees that gave up a happy existence in the woods to help generate these "educational materials." Aside from receiving a rather cursory glance, they are not paid much more attention. I would rather deal with the "courtesy" call.

Call me old-fashioned; however, I prefer to go about this differently. I like to actually talk to my patients, find out how they are feeling, and become knowledgeable of their particular sensitivities regarding medications before I decide on appropriate treatment. I also choose to obtain guidance regarding choices of medications by one or a combination of the following: clinical experience, discussion with my colleagues, and attendance at educational meetings.

I like to obtain my information directly from the respected leaders in the field. I do not particularly care to receive secondhand information and recommendations—especially considering that cost considerations are most likely becoming the primary motivation. A recent example comes to mind.

Melinda is a careful, considerate forty-seven-year-old. She came to the office earlier this week. We had a lengthy discussion regarding a number of issues. One that was troubling her greatly was insomnia. She is being affected by menopausal symptoms. The 2:00 a.m. night sweats were bothersome, and the associated insomnia debilitating. Among the options discussed was a short-term prescription for sleeping tablets to allow for adequate rest prior to other therapies being initiated. She does not like to take medications because she has always felt that she is very sensitive to their side effects. With this in mind and after considering all of the options, I chose the medication best suited to her. I discussed this with her, and she was grateful. All went well until the following day, when I received the telephone call from the pharmacy.

"I'm sorry, Doctor, but this medication that you prescribed is not on the patient's formulary; please choose another." (Oops, I forgot to check that formulary book.) Why didn't I think of that yesterday? I suppose that I was just paying too much attention to Melinda and became "wrapped up" in the discussion. My goal was to actually select the "right" medication. This was the focus of my thoughts. Nothing else entered my mind.

I mulled the news over and called her. I explained that in this particular situation I felt that the medication selected was the only one that would suffice. The alternatives, I felt, would cause unacceptable side effects. I did not recommend a substitute.

What recourse did she have? Only to pay for this out-of-pocket in the short term. We would have to deal with the insurance company later, by requesting an exemption to the formulary. This process is a more involved and arduous version of "Mother, May I?"

This incident disturbed and irritated this gentle artistic soul. Who is in charge here? she wondered. What was the benefit of having pharmacy coverage under her HMO plan? It also brought back a painful recollection for both of us regarding an earlier experience.

Melinda had been diagnosed with and treated for breast cancer approximately two years before. She had been doing well and had recovered from the treatment. Then, six months before the incident described here, she happened to find a new lump in the same breast that had been treated for the breast cancer. This was anxiety provoking, and even more so when she learned that, since she was in an HMO plan, she had to bring this situation first to the attention of her primary care physician. He ordered a mammogram, which demonstrated normal findings. She requested and assumed that she needed a referral to her breast surgeon for further evaluation. The primary care physician, after reviewing the mammography findings with her, advised a waiting period of a few weeks in order to see if the mass resolved spontaneously.

My first awareness of this series of events occurred when I received a copy of the mammogram report. I reviewed the section regarding Melinda's history and read that a new lump had been found. I was immediately concerned and called her. I assumed that she must have already seen her breast surgeon, as it had been a couple of weeks since the mammogram had been performed. I can still recall my feelings of dismay, disbelief, and extreme disappointment when she relayed to me that she had been asked to wait. Wait for *what?*

If this lump represented a recurrence of breast cancer, waiting was extremely unwise. I knew this—as did she. I racked my brain and wondered, What could the primary care physician possibly have been thinking? Why didn't he render the referral?

I know that he is a good clinician, and I consider him to be a good doctor. Was he overworked? Did he actually see this patient himself, or did an assistant take care of this problem? Was he concerned about receiving a "poor report card" from the HMO for allowing too many specialty referrals? Had he, in fact, already exceeded his "quota" for this month, and was this the reason why Melinda was told to wait?

Many, many questions. No answers. Overwhelming disbelief and disillusionment. All the while, I realized that Melinda was worried and frightened. There was little that I could do. I reflected upon the fact that, had she been on a non-HMO plan, she would already have been to see the general surgeon. She would have been able to go there directly—no referral needed, no gatekeeper nonsense, no unnecessary delays.

Being honest with her was all that I could offer. I spent one-half hour on the telephone with her after office hours on a Friday evening. I was so sorry that she had this type of plan. I was embarrassed at having to play even a peripheral role in this type of management. We decided that the first thing to do on Monday morning would be to call her primary care physician's office in order to correct the situation.

Melinda and her husband had a terrible weekend. When denial is stripped away, the cold, hard facts are unpleasant to face. The art projects remained in limbo, for nothing could be attempted in her distressed state of mind.

Monday morning arrived at last. With it came the resigned determination to call her PCP. Melinda spoke to the authorization clerk and resolutely stated that she was not getting off the telephone until she received permission to see her breast surgeon. She asked the assistant how she would feel if their positions were reversed. She mentioned our conversation. She received the authorization. She then came to see me, and we discussed this sad, poignant victory.

With persistent nagging aggravation in the background, Melinda made an appointment with her breast surgeon.

A wait of a few more days was followed by the removal of the breast mass. Fortunately, it was benign.

I exhaled slowly in relief when I learned this. I realized that I had been holding my breath for nearly two weeks—or so it seemed.

Between the distress Melinda suffered with her breast biopsy and this formulary "annoyance," it was now that I first began to wonder... *What type of health care delivery system was I participating in?*

Anger . . . Frustration . . . Denial:
Consequences of the Lost Voice

I am surrounded by unhappy physicians. I am not referring only to those physicians in my immediate sphere of acquaintance, such as the members of my specialty or the hospital or even the county medical society. The boundary of this unhappiness appears unlimited in my estimation. However, if asked for a specific boundary for the purpose of discussion, it would seem safe to include the physicians who practice medicine in the San Francisco Bay Area. This must include a few thousand physicians, accounting for an astonishing amount of unhappiness. How can this be?

I have heard my fellow physicians complaining of feeling powerless in the face of the recent changes in medicine. I have read articles in medical publications that speak to the frustration and anger that physicians are experiencing. That this anger extends beyond my immediate associates was demonstrated in a series of columns that appeared in the local newspaper a few months ago. At that time, seemingly untold numbers of readers, including physicians, felt the need to vent their anger and frustration. It was not always like this.

I can remember what it was like when I first started private practice eight and a half years ago. I recall that the medical staff was excellent. There existed a sense of camaraderie and benevolence that was sweet music to the soul of a physician straight out of a county residency program. The atmosphere was upbeat, the availability of high-quality consultants exceeded expectations, and the focus was clearly on delivering the highest quality of medical care possible.

What a crying shame that much of this has been lost! The same physicians remain in their roles, carrying out the duties that their respective specialties have assigned to them, only doing it with evident toil, frustration, and increasing fatigue. That they remain committed to delivering quality medical care is the single constant factor that has been sustained over time. They are increasingly hampered in their efforts to achieve this goal. This is the greatest source of their unhappiness. Why do they choose to participate in a system of medicine that is the source of such unhappiness? Why do they feel powerless? Who has given them this mistaken impression? Why do they remain silent? Why the denial? This entire evolution of the practice of medicine depends absolutely on the physicians' voluntary participation in all of the various rules and regulations. Since it is the source of so much profound exasperation and frustration, why do they continue to participate? The answer lies in acquiring an understanding of the process by which physicians receive their education and training. For it is oftentimes the case that during this lengthy and arduous process the individual loses his or her sense of power, self-esteem, and own voice. This happened to me.

It happened so gradually that I am not able to pinpoint the moment in time at which it occurred. I can recall specific contributing examples. I was first made aware of it approximately two years ago. I was involved in community work, and a very dear friend bluntly stated that I had "lost my voice." I felt the greatest surprise. What could he mean by this? I was perfectly capable of speaking and expressing my point of view. I was capable of communicating well with family, friends, and patients. I was capable of carrying on a good conversation. I puzzled over this comment for many weeks until I discovered what it really meant. The loss of one's voice means the loss of being able to express one's inner feelings and thoughts. In addition, it follows that one loses the ability to recognize them as having validity or importance. For myself personally, it meant that I had stopped believing that what I thought or felt might actually be interesting to anyone else. Loss of one's voice can be seen to go hand in hand with the loss of one's power. I began to reflect upon my life to determine when this had occurred. For, once it was pointed out to me, I could see that this observation was correct. How and when had this happened to me? It was important to discover the reason.

I reviewed my childhood and adolescence, and as I reflected on the person that I was at eighteen—exuberant, lively, feisty, and ready to have a run at life—I realized that my voice was intact at that point. I remember my college experience as the happiest of times. I had many friends, and we enjoyed ourselves and our adventures immensely. I was able to excel academically and gained admittance into an excellent medical school. I remember the privilege of associating with such a talented group of diverse and interesting classmates. The first two years of medical school offered associations and adventures of a different kind, though still enjoyable. I then recalled and mused over the last two years of medical school and my residency experience. These years should be grouped together, because they represent a continuum along the path of learning clinical medicine. It was at this point in my reverie that I realized with a sense of foreboding that I had come to the answer. It was during these years that I had lost my voice. I realized that it was the price I had to pay in order to receive this most wonderful and unique of all educations—I must add, however, that this price was too steep. I will recall only two instances to exemplify my point.

The first example occurred during my third-year clerkship during general surgery. This happened to be my first rotation, and I was so excited about finally learning what it was going to be like to become—at last—a real doctor! General surgery is an exciting rotation, the residents were always very busy "doing something," and the Attending Physicians were very important personas. I enjoyed my time on the rotation immensely, except for one episode. It occurred during an operation. It was generally assumed that we could expect a pop quiz on the particular anatomy at any given time. We were expected to answer correctly and were very much motivated to leave a good impression on the Attending Physician. This accounted for many late-night reviews of the particular anatomy of the planned case for the next day. All of the medical students wanted to make a good impression, and we were eager to please. I suspect that our demeanor was viewed much as one views the mannerism of puppies. We were naive as well. I remember being in my surgical attire and being "scrubbed in" on a particular case when I was asked a question. I ventured an answer, but in my state of nervousness and from my desire to get it just right the wrong answer was given in a nervous stammer. I was laughed at. It was a quiet little snicker from the Attending Physician. The scrub nurse joined in with a comment of her own. I was humiliated. I could feel the tears stream down my face and was at a loss as to what to do next. No further commentary was given. I was left in silence to ponder my ignorance.

It was one of my first lessons: Do not be too eager to speak up. When you are trying to say what you really think and feel, do not leave yourself too vulnerable—you might be in for a nasty shock. I was left to ask my dear and kind resident for advice regarding this incident. "Act like a duck," he said. "Learn to let the water run off of your back. Toughen up." There would be more of that type of incident to come in the years ahead.

The second episode occurred in residency. Again, it occurred in my first rotation. I was in a clinic that treated pregnant women with high-risk medical problems. I had been a "real" doctor for just one month. I remember having a great curiosity about these problems and began asking questions. I was motivated to learn as much as possible. After all, this is what I would be doing for the rest of my life. I recall being made to feel completely inadequate at my lack of knowledge. This was communicated to me in such a humiliating and biting manner that I was brought to tears on more than one occasion that *first day*. I left the clinic more than once to seek solace in the graffiti-covered walls of the county hospital rest room. Once I regained my composure, I was able to return. I barely survived that grueling day. The fact that I would have to return to the clinic and face repeated episodes of this type for the remainder of the month's rotation was extremely depressing.

I survived this experience by learning not to ask any questions, not even the most important ones. I remained as quiet as possible, like a mouse, so as not to bring any undue attention to myself. Any subsequent negative commentary brought back the words of advice from my medical school experience: Act like a duck, do not let these people *get* to you; toughen up. Easier said than done for this sensitive soul.

I mention these stories not to cast any negative thoughts toward these Attending Physicians but rather to illustrate what actually happens to residents and medical students during training. I feel that both Attendings felt as if I needed to toughen up. This was their manner in teaching me that lesson. The lesson was learned at a great price.

To complete this picture, I need to mention the conditions under which interns and residents actually work. It is fairly commonplace to expect interns to work a minimum of twenty-four hours, if not longer, at a single time. In addition, this shift is to be worked with no actual expectation of sleep or food at any regular or predictable interval. It is also to be worked without complaint, if one is to be considered a *good* intern. It is not just one twenty-four hour shift that is expected. It is a sequence of many, over and over again, during the course of a minimum of three years. That truly compassionate physicians can emerge from this environment is a testament to perseverance against all odds. I am pleased to say that I know many such survivors. However, even these survivors may not realize that, while they were able to emerge with their compassion intact, they may not have retained their voice. A price was paid.

It has occurred to me lately that once individuals are subjected to this type of dehumanizing treatment and "abuse," they are susceptible to being taken advantage of subsequently. In a manner analogous to victims of child abuse who then grow up to enter dysfunctional relationships, I see that my colleagues have done the same thing. I am speaking of their relationship with the HMOs in particular, and with the insurance industry in general. Having lost their sense of power and control over many routine and ordinary acts of the day—added to these individuals' having also lost the right to express legitimate questions and concerns—has made these physicians ripe for the picking. How else to explain their participation in a health care system that causes them so much grief, that causes them to question why they went into medicine in the first place, and that allows them to continue to participate when so many members of the outside community are raising serious questions? It has occurred to me lately that practicing medicine under managed care rules and regulations is bringing back many unpleasant associations from residency. Voiceless . . . powerless . . . dehumanizing . . . intolerable.

When will all of this stop? When the physicians realize what has happened to them and truly understand why it is they continue to participate. It is their *voluntary participation* that makes the entire system work—as well as their *continued silence.* When will they realize that, like Dorothy in *The Wizard of Oz,* they are already wearing the ruby slippers?

"It is certain, that some men are indeed called to be doctors: and so are some women. They are, as we say, born doctors: they were shapen in Medicine. So apt are they to their work, and it to them, that they almost persuade me to hold opinion with Pythagoras, and to believe that in some previous existence they were in general practice. Or their ability may be the result of inheritance: but we know next to nothing about inheritance, neither is it imaginable by what physical processes the babe unborn is predisposed for one profession. Still, there are men and women, but not a great number, created for the service of Medicine: who were called to be doctors when they were not yet called to be babies."

— *Stephen Paget (1855–1926)*
Confessio Medici, Ch. I

Why Become a Physician in the First Place?

Why did I really choose to go into medicine? Why is the present version of the practice of clinical medicine causing me to experience so much anguish? If I had it to do all over again, knowing what I now know, would my decision remain the same?

These are soul-searching questions. I have been asking these very same questions of myself with increasing frequency of late. I have been involved in conversations with my colleagues in which this very same discussion has arisen. We are all not quite sure of the answers, primarily because the thought that we would be brought to the point of even formulating these questions would have been considered unthinkable five years ago. This state of mind is not confined to my locale. I caught a glimpse of evidence that this type of consideration was creeping into national physician consciousness while reading a professional journal a few months ago.

I was reviewing an article regarding an area of interest within my specialty when my attention was directed to a member survey at the completion of the article. Many of the questions were relevant to the article and carried the purpose of soliciting the readers' opinions. My eye was caught by one of the last questions. It stated, "If you had this to do all over again, would you still choose to become a physician?" I recall feeling taken aback by such a bold question. I had not ever seen it raised before in this context. It was a sure sign of the times, I remember thinking. I had the greatest curiosity to know what the respondents had to say. The question caused me to pause and prompted additional thought and intensive personal reflection. After many months of introspection, I have come to the answer for myself. Yes, I reluctantly replied, I would do it again. I came into this world to become a physician. It was a calling. I wonder, How many other physicians feel as I do?

I can still remember the moment at which I became cognizant of this calling. I was twelve years old. It was in the summer. Growing up in the middle of farming country offered much time for solitude and to commune with nature, one's inner voice, one's siblings, and the occasional visitor. It was during one of these visits that the question was asked of me. I cannot remember who asked it. "What would you like to be when you grow up?"

The answer suddenly popped into my head—unbidden but instantly certain. "I think that I will become a doctor," I replied with a steady and unflinching gaze. This was certainly a surprising reply from the visitor's point of view. I remember that she tried to hide her incredulous feelings. I can now understand the rationale behind her reaction. There was no apparent reason why this child standing before her in grubby jeans and with disheveled hair, having just spent the bulk of her time outdoors divided between the task of weeding the garden and contemplating the best approach to take to this almost hopeless task, would choose to become a physician. There had never been any family members in the profession. Funds were not available to sustain the many years of education that this endeavor would require. How could I possibly have decided on this?

The year was 1970. While there was much going on in the rest of the country and even the world, it had not reached this small midwestern farming community of 1,200 persons. Although much strife and controversy had been occurring, we were only peripherally aware of it. It was occurring "elsewhere." It was a prosperous community. I recall it as a relatively happy time—full of hope and optimism. The only serious conversation revolved around the price of corn and soybeans.

I believe that our guest made a reasonable recovery and inquired whether I was certain of this. I replied that I was. It seemed as though I was supposed to do this. Additional explanation seemed unnecessary. I could perceive the puzzled but polite glances between the guest and my mother. My inward response was, Why are they surprised? It seemed perfectly logical to me. It was what I would become. As adults

I suspect they felt overcome with an urgent need to remind me of a few of the details that this grand idea embodied.

"You will have to gain admittance to a good college."

"I know."

"You will have to study very diligently and obtain very good grades."

"I know."

"Somehow you will have to obtain scholarships or loans along the way."

"OK!"

It is likely that a few additional practical points were brought up subsequently, as this conversation continued over the entire tenure of my high school days. It did not end until I actually left for college. I listened to these questions politely and gave them as much consideration as a teenager could; however, for the most part I remained unconcerned. I knew it would work out. There was no doubt in my mind. It did.

I performed well in college. I exceeded everyone's expectations. I obtained the necessary loans and scholarships. I was able to obtain admission to one of the top ten medical schools in the country. I encountered another example of the discrepancy that manifested itself with regard to my calling and the actual process by which it was practically obtained in my contemplation of the standard medical school application form and, in particular, my response to the query "Why do you want to become a doctor?" *Because I am meant to do this* did not seem adequate. I felt the need to elaborate. I achieved my preteen goal of becoming a physician with an expenditure of considerable effort, but it was not particularly arduous. It was within my capabilities to achieve this goal. It was a manifestation of my calling. I could not escape this calling— nor did it ever occur to me to do so until recently.

The ideal manifested in the calling did receive a jolt during the clerkship years of medical school. Why that particular style of indoctrinating medical students into the profession exists was beyond the comprehension of my soul. However, my soul is a pliable one, and from an overall standpoint the benefits exceeded the drawbacks. The education was superb, and the faculty was second to none. There will always remain a special place in my heart for the talented and gifted group of individuals who made up my class. It was truly a privilege to be counted among that number. The residency years beckoned.

What occurred there was a most significant shock to the soul. I surmise that I have stories and recollections that can be shared only with graduates of similar large county hospital residency programs. The reality extends beyond the believable, the environment was most taxing, and the entire experience was almost beyond the limits of physical endurance. We made it through, however. We survived. The fact that many left their voices behind—and, along with those, their sense of power—was distressing to this soul. It took eight years of reentering the real world, living normal and routine life experiences, and forming associations and friendships of a nonphysician makeup to allow this soul to fully recover. A part of me will never be the same.

However, in measuring the result against the vision that the soul carries—the calling—a reconciliation can be made. It cannot be disputed that the clinical education was superb. It was there that the first lessons of real medicine began. The fledgling steps taken along the path to learning the mysterious art of medicine occurred there. It was a most precious gift. I am grateful for the resident who initiated this process for me. It is a mystery not easily explained or taught. It is not found in textbooks. It has to be learned in the field or in the hospital—on real people, in real situations where the penalty of making a mistake is the highest, in an environment where no mistakes are allowed. The soul accepts these most useful and priceless advantages and in the end has forgiven the manner in which they were taught.

We (my soul and myself) have now arrived at the third and final obstruction to the fulfillment of the vision of the calling. Managed care. We have been living, breathing, and experiencing this creation the past few years. It has taken that long to fully comprehend the nature of this beast. It is not to be tolerated. If one assumes that the soul is eternal and timeless, it then follows that it carries with it the wisdom of the ages. Seen in this light, there can be little surprise that the soul finds the present situation so disagreeable. I believe that my soul is of the opinion that the present situation can be judged to lie along the continuum between incredulous and reprehensible. With each passing day, it feels as though it is moving with hastening speed away from the former and with greater certainty and urgency toward the latter.

Utilization Review . . . Live!

It had been a relatively uneventful "on-call" day—no emergencies, no difficult or sensitive problems, no lengthy delays. All in all, the situation was looking quite favorable by late afternoon. I was excited by the prospect of actually being able to make it home in time to eat dinner with my family. That is, until I received the four o'clock telephone call.

While I was glancing through a patient's chart, my assistant informed me that a nurse from the hospital was on hold and wanted to speak with me. I was unaware of any pressing business regarding any of the hospitalized patients. Therefore, I assumed that it must be a question regarding a routine medication change. Delaying my entry into a patient's room, I then gambled on the assumption that this would be a very short conversation. I agreed to pick up the receiver. I am not a good gambler.

The nurse informed me to my greatest surprise that one of my partner's patients needed to be discharged from the hospital.

"Now?" I replied. "Are you sure?" I continued—recovering quickly.

"The utilization review coordinator has just been by and has finished reviewing the chart. She has instructed us to notify you of this decision."

I could sense the first tender shoots of indignation sprouting. However, I repressed these feelings and continued. "Please do me a favor and pull the chart. Did Linda's physician actually make rounds today and write a note?" I was ninety-nine percent sure that he had, but I wanted to have all of my facts straight.

The nurse did as I requested and replied, "Yes, there was a note. He had been in earlier."

I continued, "Is there any mention in that note of sending her home today?"

"No" was the reply.

"Now please tell me . . . did Linda request an early discharge?"

"No, she has not." A sigh of relief escaped, and a sense of triumph began to replace the feeling of indignation.

"Well, it is very clear to me that the only appropriate course of action is to respect my partner's clinical judgment in the case. I am informing you most certainly that Linda is not to be sent home tonight." I relayed this to the nurse and was feeling confident that the matter was settled. I returned the phone with the greatest degree of satisfaction to its resting place.

I then redirected my attention to the waiting patient's chart. After bringing myself up-to-date with her history, I prepared to enter the room. It was then that I heard the receptionist's voice on the intercom. "The utilization review coordinator is holding. She would like to speak with you."

The discipline required to maintain politeness under adverse circumstances is a lesson ingrained from the earliest moments of the clinical educational process. I was grateful that I had obtained a mastery of this subject. It would serve me well in this situation.

"This is Dr. Mahony. How may I help you?"

She reminded me at this point that Linda's three postoperative days were at an end. It was advisable that she be discharged to home this evening. She further elaborated that she had reviewed the chart and could not find sufficient documentation to justify an additional overnight stay.

With the greatest effort, I maintained an even tone in my voice during the reply. "I am reluctant to override the medical judgment of my partner, who is the *physician of record* in this case. This is my assessment. I have already discussed this with the nurse. Linda should not be discharged."

Her reply: "Can't you call your partner at home to discuss it with him?"

"No," came the most painstaking reply. "It is his day off. I have too much respect for his time away from the office. I will not be interrupting him at home."

She felt the need to elaborate that it was unlikely that the insurance company would cover the additional day. Therefore, Linda might have to face the possibility of paying the hospital bill herself. She further elaborated that this would be approximately nine hundred dollars.

My reply was that I could not be concerned with what the insurance company might do in the future. The issue at hand, I replied, was the medical appropriateness for discharge. My partner had already made it clear that he was not intending to send her home. It was his medical judgment that dictated his assessment. I would not render a decision to the contrary. This was most particularly so because *I do not even know this patient.*

Seemingly unfazed by my remarks, she concluded her remarks with the reminder that in her opinion, after reviewing the chart, she could see no justification for a continued hospital stay.

Feeling overcome with a combination of reluctance, irritation, and a sense of coercion, I replied, "After I finish seeing the patients in the office, I will personally visit Linda and *render my own judgment.* I will make no guarantees at this time." The conversation, thankfully, concluded.

I finished seeing my patients in the office and found myself apologizing to those who were last on the schedule. As a consequence of that telephone call, I was, at that time, unfortunately running forty minutes behind. It would have been hard to explain the reason why to those disgruntled few. I needed to speak to the utilization review coordinator? Hardly an emergency.

I composed myself while walking across the hospital parking lot. How would I introduce myself? I had not met this patient before. How would I explain the reason for my visit so late in the day? It was after dinner time. Perhaps Linda would think that I was from the hospital volunteer crew stopping by to solicit her possible interest in tomorrow's paper. This would be an interesting encounter.

I reviewed the chart prior to entering her room. It only confirmed my earlier assumptions and resolutions. I took a deep breath and entered the room.

"Hello, we have not yet had the pleasure of meeting. My name is Dr. Mahony. I work in the same office as your physician." Linda and her husband exchanged polite and inquiring glances. She then removed her dinner tray from its close proximity to her bed.

"I'm sorry, I hope that I have not interrupted your dinner."

"No," she replied. "I had just finished."

Now the hard part. . . . "I am here . . . uh . . . to see you. The . . . umh . . . utilization review coordinator suggested that I stop by for a visit. Do you know her?"

"No."

"Did you meet her?"

"No."

"I see . . . so she did not actually talk to you?"

"No."

"Well, there appears to be some discussion regarding whether or not you should be sent home tonight. You are not aware of this?"

"No."

"I see. Well, do you mind if I ask you a few questions?"

"No."

"What do you remember about your physician's visit this morning? Specifically, I am wondering when he thought you might be able to go home."

"He mentioned that it might be tomorrow or the next day at the latest."

"I see. Now, please tell me honestly, how are you feeling? Do you think that you are ready to go home this evening?" And so on. I completed my interview and received all the information that was necessary.

After reviewing the chart and assimilating all the information, I clearly saw that it was not in her best interest to be discharged home tonight. I then dutifully recorded appropriate chart notes and returned to Linda and her husband.

"Please be reassured that you will be staying through the night. We [your physician and myself] have your best interests at heart. It is our most fervent desire that you recover in a timely and uneventful manner. Have a good evening, and I am sorry for having disturbed you."

As I left the hospital, I could not help but wonder—what would she think?

"If you follow these the noble objects of your profession in a proper spirit of love and kindness to your race, the pure light of benevolence will shed around the path of your toils and labours a brightness and beauty, that will faithfully cheer you onwards, and keep your steps from being weary in well doing—while, if you practice the art that you profess with a cold-hearted view to its results merely as a matter of lucre and trade, your course will be as dark and miserable, as that low and groveling love that dictates it."

— Sir James Young Simpson (1811–1870)
Physicians and Physic, Ch. 1

Stepford Docs

I was speaking with a professional colleague a few weeks ago, and I was impressed with her astute observations. She is involved in the type of work that requires much travel during the week. In her travels, she has the opportunity to interact with many physicians in several local hospitals.

"The physicians seem as though they have just given up. I remember that a couple of years ago they appeared very angry and energized. They now appear blasé and almost lifeless. It is as if the fight has gone out of them."

I had perceived the same phenomenon, and I was very concerned. If physicians allow themselves to feel any emotion at all, it is only an encapsulated show of anger and frustration, and then for only a short period of time. Their appearance for the most part seems to have components of forced resignation and studied indifference. This is what I would term a "Stepford Doc." It seems as though these physicians apply the professional veneer upon arrival at the office, wear it all day, and shed it upon leaving. They carry out their duties with the skill and expertise honed by years of experience. It is possible, however, to perceive cracks and fissures in the veneer. It seems to be getting perilously thin in some instances.

Where are their feelings? What happened to joy? What about passion? Are they not entitled to feel a love of life? How about just feeling a love of practicing their profession?

Is this Stepford Doc veneer merely functioning as a necessary coping mechanism adopted in response to the massive changes that have affected our "professional lives"?

Has it become too painful to actually examine with a critical eye the day-to-day events that require our participation? Are we now reduced to playing a part in this passion play and reading our assigned script—like it or not?

I am acutely aware of the stress that this has created among the physicians I know. I share this awareness with their spouses, children, friends, and associates. I am also reminded of it every year when my annual premium is due for my personal disability insurance policy. When I initially applied for this policy eleven years ago, it was considered a low-risk policy. In other words, physicians at that time were expected to work quite uneventfully up until their retirement years. It was anticipated that the disability policy would have to be used only for rare and unusual cases of disability, such as accidents or serious illness. In recent years, record numbers of physicians have applied for and have been receiving benefits under the category of stress-related illnesses. So many have done so that the premiums for my type of policy have skyrocketed. The difficulty of receiving approval for a policy has similarly increased. Every spring I am warned of the dire consequences of allowing my policy to lapse by a brightly colored notice printed with bold capital letters.

Why all this stress? Why the flight from experiencing the day-to-day routine?

Have physicians subconsciously abdicated their leadership role in medicine?

And, in so doing, can we not bear to look at, think about, feel, or fully acknowledge the consequences that such an abdication has wrought?

Optimism . . . a Rare Sighting

While speaking with a physician colleague today, I realized there was a character and component of his conversation that I had not discerned in conversations with physician colleagues in far too many months lately—optimism.

I learned that his upbeat state was based on the fact that his practice was primarily made up of persons carrying PPO or indemnity insurance. There was a small HMO component.

I remarked upon his uplifting demeanor—it appeared so striking to me—and he replied, "I am not as pessimistic regarding the future of medicine as you are."

"That is because you have not been involved extensively with HMO-type practice."

"That is true," he agreed.

I replied, "There are many physicians who believe that the only way to survive is to continue participation in HMO-type health insurance plans. I think that continued participation in HMO-type medical practice will accomplish nothing other than to drive those participating MDs to an early grave."

He responded, "I predict that the HMOs would soon start to go bankrupt."

I replied, "It remains to be seen what will happen."

I do not know many physicians who would agree with that pronouncement—as much as it would be their secret desire to see it come to pass.

If so, what type of health care delivery system would replace HMOs?

How to Regard a Physician? (Somewhere Between Deity and Drain Fixer)

It seems to me that there has been a significant amount of confusion among physicians lately regarding their self-image. Who are they? How are they to be regarded?

In one sense, this appears to signify that the physician community is playing catchup with the general public, who have been asking these questions for several years. An additional element contributing to this identity crisis of sorts has been the manner in which the insurance industry has blurred (was this deliberate?) the status and value of a physician.

This blurring of the image has its roots in the title "provider." It has been several years now that patients have been receiving their "provider directory." Among the pages, they will find the names of their *physicians* listed. Why not call it what it actually is—a physician directory?

Let's examine the term "provider." It is a bland, unassuming title lacking distinction, as if anyone can do it. The term "provide" also brings certain associations. Provide what? Provide the service of delivering medical care. The acceptance of this philosophy is, of course, what the insurance industry has now accomplished. In the process, the mystery has been deleted, and the professional status and reputation that the practice of medicine previously enjoyed have been placed in serious jeopardy.

In all of my years of practice, I have never heard a patient say, "Thank you, Preferred Provider!"

To the contrary, I hear "Thank you so very much, Doctor" or "We are so very grateful, Doctor, for all that you have done."

Physicians have had great difficulty with this development. "Service industry" is not a term that is utilized during medical training. Rather, physicians spend all of their time, energy, and academic pursuits learning about the mysteries of the human body and mind. Intensive education is directed at understanding the myriad complexities of the human organism. Once such an understanding is obtained, relentless effort is aimed at learning how to initiate repairs and corrections when called upon to do so. Many noble efforts have been made by physicians since time immemorial in the pursuit of desirable ends. To attempt a cure. To improve the ailing human body. To alleviate suffering. To be present and witness the joyful beginning of life and to witness the passing of life with dignity, compassion, and professional expertise.

This is my recollection of the *intent* of all my education and training.

Certainly, it is also clear to me that not just anyone can do it. Not just anyone can gain admittance into medical school. Not just anyone can obtain the essential and precise grasp of science, biology, and recent technology—all prerequisites for obtaining the medical degree.

Not just anyone can endure the rigors of premedical education, sustain additional testing in medical school, and survive the harsh, unpleasant reality of the residency experience. Not just anyone can perform surgery well, in the appropriate circumstances and without mistakes. Not just anyone can make intuitive medical diagnoses by fully integrating the information given by the patient, by the laboratory, by the recent history, and by the clinical gestalt that exists in the examination room.

Not just anyone can listen to mothers talking about their newborn babies and hear in one mother's tone of voice, nature of dialogue, and inflection the one key descriptive phrase that, when correlated with the experienced eye of "clinical diagnosis," selects that one child out of all the children as having the serious life-threatening illness.

Not just anyone can provide excellent prenatal care. This is accomplished by taking the time to really become acquainted with the expectant parents. Taking the time to listen in an open-ended manner to the answer to the seemingly innocent question, "So, how are things going today?" Not just anyone has the ability to discern and identify the eight percent of pregnant women who are destined to develop complications of preterm labor. Especially considering that the signs in the earliest stages are so subtle that it takes a practitioner in the art of medicine to identify them.

Many physicians I know do not feel that just anyone will do. We know better. We have obtained this awareness through our own experiences as we have come to realize our own inherent strengths and weaknesses. There is an unreserved admiration for colleagues who can do something "better than we can." Collective physician intelligence can divide members of the physician community into excellent, very good, good, and everyone else. The nonphysician community will rarely hear a word spoken about "everyone else." This would be in violation of an unwritten rule in the physicians' code of silence. However, they will hear plenty spoken about excellent, very good, and good—so pay attention.

Physicians are the last persons on earth who would even dream about selecting a name randomly off an arbitrary list of physicians in order to select a personal physician. We also would not accept any restrictions in being able to select the best physician for ourselves or our family, as presently is the case under many insurance plans. No, we know too much and we know better. We take ourselves to the excellent physicians. No one else will do. We will gladly wait in their waiting rooms without complaint. We will wait several weeks for an appointment if necessary. We will be very respectful of their time. We put ourselves into their hands completely to make us feel better, treat our illness, fix the present malady of the body, and operate if necessary. We would not put ourselves into the hands of anyone who is less than excellent.

Many, many physicians desire to have the ability to treat patients in the same way. We would not send them to see someone who in our opinion is less than excellent—in other words, to anyone we would not go to ourselves. This is the entire basis for the referral system of high-quality medical practice. This has been in existence, one can only speculate, since medicine has been an honored profession. Referrals were carefully thought out and handed out with great consideration following significant deliberation.

It should not be surprising that recent developments have caused great consternation among physicians—particularly those with high standards. These physicians are the ones who complain most bitterly about the term "provider." It rankles them. They dislike it intensely. They do not like the connotations that the term implies.

While it has often been stated that the physicians work on a fee-for-service basis, this is not equivalent to saying that medicine should be considered a service industry.

That the boundary between these concepts has been blurred has not been overlooked by physicians. One can also surmise that its promotion has been advantageous to the insurance industry. It seems to have allowed the industry to gradually consolidate power and influence over physicians and the general public.

Perhaps some of the recent perceptions have occurred as a consequence of a backlash against the regard that physicians were held in during the earlier part of the twentieth century. Physicians at that time were held in the same regard as a deity. They were treated as such during their education and training. This attitude was additionally encouraged by the status given to them in the hospitals and by the public at large. Like any illusion, it began to fade to reveal the human beings behind it. Human beings possessing feelings and frailties and carrying imperfections—like other human beings.

A fall from grace seemed inevitable, but was it necessary to plummet?

Doctor shoptalk reveals a belief that in some instances physicians are being reimbursed on a per-hour wage at a rate less than that of our dear friends the plumbers. A physician recently stated in a local paper that his hourly wage is now approaching thirty-five dollars; he mentions that many of his colleagues are reporting no better. A good plumber in this area charges sixty dollars per hour.

While the particulars of reimbursement will continue to be debated, the general feeling is that our relative worth in society has been diminished. A physician is average. The job is ordinary. It is not anything special. This is far from the truth.

There is a happy medium between bland, unassuming provider and deity. It would be entirely appropriate to view physicians as follows: extremely capable, learned individuals who possess above-average intelligence, strength of character, integrity, and compassion. They have passed all the necessary and grueling prerequisites to satisfy the requirements to be granted the rite of passage from usual and ordinary citizens to exceptional, talented, committed, and extremely well educated professionals. Individuals who most certainly need to feel as though they have value. That all the hard work, effort, self-sacrifice, and ongoing personal sacrifice are worth it.

Not just anyone will do. Ask any physician. He or she will tell you the truth.

"These are the duties of a physician: First . . . to heal his mind and to give help to himself before giving it to anyone else."

— Anonymous
Epitaph of an Athenian Doctor, A.D. 2
(Quoted in the Journal of the American
Medical Association 189:989, 1964)

Co-dependency and Isolationism

"How are you doing?"

"Awful."

"How is your day going?"

"Horrible. It is long and busy and there is far too much to do."

"How are you feeling?"

"Tired. I have been up most of the night. I was taking care of an emergency patient. I settled all of that and then made rounds. I was running late by the time all of this was attended to and was running too far behind at the office. The waiting room was packed! The patients were really upset. I am exhausted."

These are expressions that I have heard over and over again in various modifications since I became a physician. I hear them, of course, being uttered by other physicians. When I happen to eat in the doctors' dining room—which one of my esteemed colleagues refers to, with tongue planted firmly in cheek and with the greatest affection, as the doctors' whining hall—I hear a constant stream of this type of dialogue. It goes without saying that the volume and passion supporting this dialogue have increased remarkably lately. Sometimes it is hard to digest lunch. This is typical behavior for co-dependents.

All of this complaining is valid and appropriate. What is the content of the whispered comments while doctors sit huddled at the nurses' station? What about those fervent opinions rendered as they sit in the dining room? Many topics are discussed. Among them on any one day would be the quality of the nursing staff, the care that their hospitalized patients are receiving, the quality of the laboratory services, and the hassles in the office with respect to the increasing paperwork involved with the authorizations. Let's also not forget to mention the jam-packed, mission-impossible schedules and the days that seem never to end and then end only in exhaustion. Their evident and increasing fatigue and the gnawing, growing sense that their patients' discontent is most certainly on the rise are also perceived. While all of this is certainly appropriate and potentially could be put to desirable ends, it goes no further in most instances. In other words, it does little good at all except to add to the enlightenment and astonishment of the fly on the wall.

Very little thought is devoted to actually taking action on these most appropriate concerns. Action, if taken, is fleeting and ineffective and encourages no additional expenditure of energy in that direction. Besides, the physicians are too busy already.

"What good would it do?"

"Things will never change, anyway."

"What's the use?"

So the conversations continue. They have a palliative effect on the physicians—at least we can give them this much credit.

The root of this co-dependency is the internship and residency experience. That type of experience is beyond true comprehension by the nonphysician and eludes succinct explanation. It is a life-changing experience in many respects, and co-dependency evolved as a way of coping with it all, a way of obtaining mutual support at a time when such support was absolutely critical. It is now so ingrained in the physicians' psyche that I often wonder if they realize they are participating in this passive supporting role. Having learned oftentimes most painfully that trying to change the system was futile and that speaking out left one open to reprisal, it is easy to see how co-dependency would evolve.

Along with the co-dependency came isolationism. I think the combination of these two characteristics is a contributing factor in the present unsatisfactory state of the physician-patient relationship. The majority of physicians I know socialize exclusively with other physicians. This is because it is comfortable for them to do so, since their colleagues, by default, are the only ones who can truly understand and appreciate the incredible stresses and strains involved in being a practicing physician. The only ones who can console when consolation is needed, distract when distraction is called for, and listen when listening is required.

The rite of passage from regular, ordinary citizen to physician is such an arduous, tumultuous path that it can be appreciated only by another physician. Physicians, in many respects, can be judged only by a jury of their peers—fellow physicians. No one else possesses the slightest clue.

Given the comfort of being in the company of fellow physicians, it is easy to see why exclusive socialization evolves. It is a very natural consequence. At these social events, it is possible to obtain a glimpse of the person behind the mask and beneath the white lab coat. The air is relaxed and carefree. Physicians finally feel that they can safely let down their guard and be themselves. On rare occasions, someone will act on a whim and adopt a lighthearted mood—telling a joke or performing an outrageous stunt or otherwise acting "out of character." He or she has been overcome by the supportive camaraderie and remembers the bridge to a happy, carefree youth. A bridge burned a long time ago as a seemingly necessary step prior to inheriting the cloak of professional obligation. On the odd occasion, this bridge is suddenly resurrected and the person flies across, caught up in the moment. Out of time and space, on the spur of the moment, the gesture or joke is over, and all respond with pure, uncontrived laughter and mirth. But, almost as quickly, the moment is gone, the laughter dies, and the bridge is recognized as the mirage it is. All are silent as it shatters and the pieces fall to the ground. The heavy weight of professional responsibility is taken on once more.

I have been thinking lately that it would behoove physicians to reestablish social relationships with members of the community at large. It would be beneficial at a community service function, for example, to listen to the stories, laments, and problems that the "patient" members of the community are experiencing. If the physicians actually had to meet these "patients" on a regular social basis, I find it unlikely that this present version of managed care would continue. If these two parties, now predominantly moving in separate circles, would meet and talk on a regular basis, it seems to me that things would change. In the interest of improving the physician-patient relationship, I would propose a series of weekend retreats. The participants would include all of the physicians listed on the provider panels and all of the enrollees on the particular plans. Representatives of the insurance industry would not be invited to attend this exclusive "members only" event. However, in the interest of improving provider relations, it would certainly seem reasonable to ask them to pick up the tab.

I can envision that several mediators would be utilized, as interest in this event would likely exceed all expectations. Small groups would be formed made up proportionally of physicians and patients. Both sides would be free to speak, to discuss, to inquire, to understand, and to listen. Stories need to be told and experiences shared. There is much that these two parties need to tell each other. The time seems to be ripe for such an event. I can imagine that, once the discussion began, the mediator might well step back and let the dialogue continue with an animated life of its own. It would be expected to continue long into the night, with both sides finding the need to converse and achieve at last the full comprehension of the truth and experience the relief that comes with full and complete understanding.

At the end of the weekend, the two groups would meet with their respective peers for debriefing. It would at this point be possible just to begin to imagine that solutions are within reach and that rectification can begin. Most important, it would be realized that it is fully within the power of these two distinct parties to do something about the present situation.

What new direction would be selected?

What new changes would be demanded?

In what state of affairs do we enter the twenty-first century?

Commercialization and Confusion

I found myself admiring the great variety of handbags, luggage, pocketbooks, and wallets. I appreciated the fine textures and wonderful aroma of new leather. My olfactory system was virtually on overload as the sweet smell of leather competed considerably with the stimulating aroma of freshly brewed coffee emanating from the adjacent espresso bar. I was left in a state of indecision. Which was the more pressing matter: selecting a billfold, or purchasing a double mocha, whipped cream, with a sprinkling of chocolate and two sugars?

My reveries were interrupted by the monotone of the overhead paging system, and I was brought back to my senses. I was momentarily confused as to the particulars of time and space. Where was I? Was this a boutique? Was it a department store? Was it the lobby of a hotel? No, no, and no. I was in the hospital cafeteria.

We have been treated in the past few months to all types of entrepreneurial delights. A few weeks ago, while enjoying lunch, all had the opportunity to browse among an elaborate display of books. Something for every occasion was present.

Today it was luggage. What will be next? It is summer. Perhaps an opportunity to select a new swimsuit would be appreciated by the staff. All of this shopping pleasure is enhanced by the nearby espresso bar.

It sure makes for a confusing picture. Uncertainty about the nature of the institution arises. Just where am I, and what is the purpose of this place?

I remember when the only commerce in the hospital was the gift shop. It was run quite amiably by members of the volunteer staff. The purpose of this enterprise was clear, and the contents of the shop spoke to serving that purpose. It was stocked with items that would bring solace and comfort to a patient in the hospital. It was available to family and friends to utilize when something "extra special" seemed to be in order.

So what is the purpose of the luggage and books and who knows what next? It is an interesting development. It has been puzzling to me. As I ponder and observe, I can see that I am not the only one to raise an eyebrow or two. Not quite sure what to do with all of this commerce, we are confused. What is the purpose of the institution?

Commerce or patient care?

Is it a hospital or a department store? Maybe that is the point. Maybe we are supposed to be confused. If we are not quite sure about the nature and purpose of the institution, then we will not be able to easily interpret our experience. If the frame of reference is blurred and indistinct around the edges, we may not be sure how to judge what we see and encounter. What is the precise context within which to place certain events and circumstances?

Is it a hotel or a hospital? What is the reference point? How do we measure performance?

Is it room service that is wanted, or nursing care?

Are there orderlies here, or bellhops?

Should one tip the dietitian (caterer) who brings in the lunch tray?

Is it more important to sell premium luggage in the cafeteria, or to have adequate nursing staff on the floors above?

I admit that I have a fondness for the espresso bar and it probably enhances my work efficiency. As for the rest, I prefer the commerce represented by the hospital gift shop. It remains a quiet little reminder of the intent and purpose for which the hospital was originally built.

Access Issues

Patient access to physicians under managed care is under intense scrutiny. The presently accepted wisdom is that restricted access is necessary to control costs. And while the health insurance industry claims that this practice has caused no harm to patients, those of us involved in the day-to-day grind know better.

From a general surgeon:

"I am not sure what is happening between the patients and their primary care physicians. I find them asking me to treat urinary tract infections and routine yeast infections. They say it is too difficult to obtain an appointment with their primary care physician."

From a physician who treats patients for cancer:

"We have finally gotten to the point where we are concerned about the delay in diagnosis for cancer, and thus initiation of treatment. The patients are suspecting that their cancer should have been diagnosed much sooner than it actually was. They have started voicing their concern about this. We are now advising them to send a letter expressing their feelings and complaints to their employers, who, after all, insist on paying for this 'cost-effective' health insurance. This is, after all, a product that the employer or someone is actually buying. The serious flaws need to be pointed out."

From a physician who sees patients with lung cancer:

"I am so disturbed by the apparent delays in diagnosis of lung cancer that I find that I am being very honest with my patients. I tell them that this should have been diagnosed six months ago. This is something that I never would have considered doing five years ago."

From a patient who spent six months going to the primary care physician for a cough and "funny bumps" on her neck before she finally received a referral to a specialist who quickly diagnosed her with lymphoma:

"I knew all along that there was something wrong with me."

From a patient regarding her neighbor:

"She had been treated in an HMO for some time regarding chronic back pain. Feeling uneasy and perhaps suspecting something worse, she changed insurance and selected an internist who was also an oncologist. In a short period of time, she was diagnosed with bone cancer."

I am *not* describing the disenfranchised population. These persons have health insurance; many are well educated and sophisticated. They are very aware of what is happening, and they possess keen powers of observation. It is difficult to constantly listen to this dialogue. This problem is apparently not confined to our area. One of our trade journals ran an article recently speaking to the point that HMOs seem to be cooling to the idea of using the primary care physician as a gatekeeper. The reasons given were as follows: The process of prior authorization has proven costly, sometimes interferes with good care, and has angered patients. The article explains that the original intentions for this concept were good. It points to the model of the British National Health system, in which every citizen is entitled to care by a general practitioner. When comparisons were made to our system, the feeling was that too many patients were seeing specialists for treatment that could be better (and less expensively) rendered by the primary care physician. When managed care began sweeping across the country with the intent of cutting health care costs, the general internist or family practitioner was nominated to be the physician with primary responsibility for the patient's medical needs. (*Tag. You're it!*) This gatekeeper role did not immediately engender enthusiasm on the part of the primary care physician. The article states that the primary care physician did not view it as a "good news" position. The doctors I know responded along a continuum between reluctance and loathing.

They cooperated with the changes because they basically had no other choice. Besides, in the beginning, the physicians were coming from a position in their professional lives that was largely marked by contentment. From the optimism that arises out of ignorance, all went along with the change, however reluctantly, truly believing that it would not turn out to be that bad.

Having gained the perspective of time, we can see that it has been much worse than anyone would have predicted. An analogy can be drawn to the process of setting up a fictitious business. The role of primary care physician as gatekeeper was given to these family practitioners and internists along with a new job description, and they had to proceed—like it or not. The trouble was that they had no training in this new "fictitious role." While they were supposed to continue to provide medical care, they were also held responsible for holding down medical costs. The incentives, rules, and authorization processes were not understood beforehand. They were caught broadside by the powerful responsibility of cost reduction. Perhaps they have lost their bearings while being subjected to this unstoppable force. These are human beings, after all, not gods. Was it too much too fast? Were the consequences thoroughly considered in advance?

The article mentioned earlier asked an excellent question. If the health plans abandon the concept of primary care physicians as gatekeepers, where will this leave the physicians? Probably with many asking why they were talked into playing this part in the first place.

When I recall how we practiced in those days known as "BMC" (before managed care), I recall a completely different medical community. Left to our own devices, we shared a certain kind of commonsensical intelligence. The overriding principle was first and foremost to take excellent care of our patients. The family practitioners and internists seemed quite able to do a marvelous job of providing this level of service for their patients. They were able to adopt a unique practice style that was based on a synthesis of their basic personality, their inherent strengths and weaknesses, their particular training, and their particular interests. The style of practice in their office was customized—taking all of these variables into account. Some family practitioners provided obstetrical services; others might have a particular interest in other areas of medicine that they were free to pursue. Some internists had a particular expertise in kidney ailments; others had expertise in pulmonology. In spite of these differences, all had in common that they had developed a pattern of practice with a level of comfort, pace, and efficiency that worked well for them and for their patients.

The question of who had the primary responsibility for patient care seemed to depend upon a great many variables. For women, the gynecologist seemed to have this role. For other persons, the internist or family practitioner did this job. In other circumstances, the specialist had the primary responsibility. If a patient suffered from cancer, the oncologist often assumed the primary role. If the patient had a severe autoimmune disorder, the rheumatologist would assume the role of being primarily responsible for the patient. If a patient suffered from allergies, then the allergist would be the primary physician. And so on.

We had a great deal of freedom then, patients and physicians. The patients had unlimited access to any specialists, who were readily available and quite content to quickly see and take care of any patients referred. There existed many avenues to the specialist's office. The internist or family practitioner could refer when indicated. The indications were based on their particular expertise and experience—not prescribed by arbitrary protocols. The gynecologist had the luxury of referring patients to the specialist. More important, the patients themselves seemed to possess the uncanny ability to select the appropriate specialist for themselves when they became ill. This interplay among patient, generalist, and specialist seemed to work in a fine balance. It was an easy flow—one could count on it to work smoothly. It was predictable and reliable, this unstructured model of delivering high-quality medical care. I recall that in our community the patients were by and large content and the physicians were amiable and worked well together in a system that allowed wisdom, common sense, and experience to guide physician selection. Patients were passed off almost reverently from physician to physician with the patient's welfare the overriding concern.

As we fast-forward to the present, we find ourselves in a drastically altered environment. The same persons involved are operating under someone's idea of improved, albeit cost-effective, medicine. One of the characteristics of this new system is the increased patient load at the primary care physician's office. It is as if these physicians have been rendered so busy attending to the covered lives huddled in their waiting rooms that they have become unable to see the invisible line that starts outside their door. A line that no physician would ever have wanted started and that no patient wants to stand in. The single most disturbing aspect of this newly created medical model is the suspicion growing in our patients' minds about all of us who agreed to participate in this model. Whom do we serve? Just where does our loyalty lie?

Have the reputations of the primary care physicians been tarnished by participation in managed care? If so, then theirs have not been the only ones. It seems as though all of us should be wondering: Why did we let ourselves be talked into this in the first place?

Reference for the article mentioned:

Holoweiko, Mark. "Bypassing primary-care physicians: HMOs cool to the gate keeper concept." *Medical Economics* (May 1997):42–52.

"Life is short, and the Art long; the occasion fleeting; experience fallacious, and judgment difficult. The physician must not only be prepared to do what is right himself, but also to make the patient, the attendants, and externals co-operate."
— *Hippocrates (460?–377? B.C.)*
Aphorisms, I.I (tr. by Francis Adams)

The Physician as a Figurehead

In the not-so-distant future, it is easy to imagine that, at the current rate of transformation, modification, and justification, the physician will to all intents and purposes be relegated to the status of figurehead. The primary argument made in order to promote acceptance of this end result will be based on economics.

Health care costs were too high. It was necessary to control the pace of these escalating costs. When the focus was aimed at health care costs, physician costs seemed to top the list—not only with regard to their expensive wages, but also with regard to their expensive practice habits. Discussion and identification of these problems were followed by a ready solution: Cut both of these costs.

Reimbursement rates were cut first. This created quite a stir initially, but the physicians adjusted. They had no choice. Often it is a one-sided decree: "This is what your services are worth. Take it or leave it."

This was repeated with increasing frequency and enforced so studiously that eventually the physicians acquiesced, adjusted their practice habits, and accepted the reality of the situation. This still creates rancor in some circles, as significant numbers feel as if their services are being obtained "below costs." This is a hard concept to explain, as people think about health care only when they are ill—which is a low-frequency event, since the majority of persons are healthy.

This results in too few people actually thinking about the health care system changes and too few people making decisions for those unfortunate folks who will be affected by these changes when they become ill. When it may be too late to rectify them.

Leaving the wage issue behind, the more important objective is to control physicians' behavior. The rationale for controlling their behavior has been their "expensive practice habits."

Therefore, formularies were created to restrict their prescribing privileges. Rather than being allowed to pick and choose among all available medications, physicians must choose among limited selections listed on formularies. This is all being done under the auspices of cost control. If the errant or free-spirited physician attempts to prescribe a medication he or she feels is most suitable for the patient, the invisible barrier will rise to thwart the attempt. And in this process the physician will be dissuaded from any future endeavor at unfettered and freethinking decision making.

For the most part, doctors have long been excluded from any serious decision making regarding hospital administration. Thankfully, exceptions do exist and appear as a welcome oasis on the desert horizon. Unfortunately, it has been all too common for physicians to hear the following: "The business of running hospitals is not in your domain. We have hired appropriately trained and educated individuals to do this."

In these situations there is an effort to retain an advisory board, but whether any advice rendered is actually followed seems questionable. Legitimate concerns are voiced periodically regarding patient care issues, medical equipment failures, nursing staff, and so on—all of which are witnessed and dealt with day in and day out. In response, we often hear "Thank you for your enlightening input. We are working on this problem area and will get back to you."

This is often followed by the lament "The harshness of the economic climate mandates that adjustments be made."

The physicians' silently groaned reply is *Just how far will the standards drop before someone says, "Enough is enough"?* It is a silent groan because they have learned by now that if it becomes audible it will fall on either deaf ears (administration) or untrained ears (the general public).

Protocols by which to practice medicine are gaining increasing favor. These are popular because patients can be categorized to fit recognized symptom patterns and thus be easily diagnosed. Ready-made treatment protocols have been formulated so that a physician need not think about almost anything anymore. In fact, why would a physician even be necessary under these circumstances? Any trained health care professional can ask technical questions, record replies, and enter data while facing the computer screen. Diagnosis and treatment protocols can be retrieved. Following a brief discussion with the patient, the health care professional sends him or her off with the ready-made treatment in hand.

In this scenario, the art of medicine remains an elusive entity and most likely makes the protocol types nervous.

"How can you be sure that the patient is having this problem? You have not asked all of the required diagnostic questions. Where is your documentation to verify that you have followed the protocol? Why haven't you tried treatment A? How do you know that it will not work?"

The intuitive individuals enter medical school and arrive with one foot in a room that they can quickly enter. They (being the minority) are often at odds with the sensate thinkers, who are very aware that the room exists but have difficulty identifying the doorway.

Intuitive physicians see the art of medicine in its beauty and majesty and fully appreciate its mystery—if given enough time and allowed the freedom of thought to practice medicine in this manner. Medicine practiced in this manner is medicine at its most fulfilling and most exciting and is truly awe-inspiring. This point of view is shared by patient and physician to an equal degree.

When intuitives are obligated to practice by protocol, all of the joy and passion is drained away. They themselves pay a steep personal price for being obligated to practice in this manner. It is not sustainable in the long run. The ultimate price that the intuitives pay is the price of their own soul—so detrimental is the loss of the art of medicine to them. So it is unlikely that they will stay. They will leave this system of medicine, or they will leave medicine altogether. *The art will leave with them.*

Who will remain? Those individuals who, by and large, are content with protocols, do not mind that their pharmacological choices are restricted, and are not bothered by the fact that every test they order is being monitored by the insurance industry—justified under the heading of "economic credentialing." These individuals are also unruffled by the knowledge that the environment of the hospitals in which they leave their patients is, largely, out of their sphere of influence. Finally, these physicians will perform all of these duties for whatever price the insurance industry feels they are worth.

All of this is accomplished for the sake of cost containment.

Who wants to play the part of the patient, and who wants to play the part of the figurehead?

Synchronicity

It was a wonderful day for synchronicity. I have learned of two female physicians who have dropped all participation in managed care. I learned about the first while requesting a referral for one of my patients. This specialist had recently gone out on her own to provide medical services on a straight fee-for-service basis. Completely tired of dealing with the hassles of managed care in her previous employment, she had come to the conclusion that life was too short to put up with that nonsense. She expressed the desire to take good care of patients, to give them good service, and to eliminate the hassles associated with trying to take care of patients within the constraints of managed care.

As I spoke to her today, I could sense the excitement intermingled with anticipation and hesitancy. These feelings are consistent with someone who is following her heart and wanting to do what is right for the patients and herself— taking off on a wing and a prayer, hoping that the patients agree.

One hour later I opened one of our medical journals to read a feature article on a female physician in another state who recently dropped her participation in all managed care contracts and has switched to straight fee-for-service. The article states that her particular medical marketplace is composed of eighty percent managed care. Her decision was considered a radical one.

The doctor's stated reason for taking such a drastic step includes her belief that she could no longer practice good medicine under managed care's increasing constraints and shrinking reimbursements. She mentions having had unfavorable experiences with the formularies by which she was required to abide.

In addition, the article highlighted many of the frustrations that the physician dealt with in regard to obtaining reimbursement from all of the HMOs and other managed care entities.

At the present time she bills her patients directly, and they, in turn, bill the insurance company for reimbursement.

So far, the article states, the doctor has managed to attract enough patients willing to receive services in this manner. Others in the article were quoted as saying that it would be difficult for a physician to survive without participating in managed care.

I particularly liked the doctor's comment about her office since dropping participation in managed care. She describes it as being a nicer place. "I didn't realize how much it was bothering me to fight for payment all the time and feel unjustly rewarded. You feel somebody is taking advantage of you. Now, when patients come in, I know it's because they think I do something special, not because it's only a $10 copay."

At the end of the article she says, "All I want is to do good medicine and get the patient-doctor relationship back."

Reference for the article mentioned:

Bell, Carrie Sears. "Dump managed care? This gynecologist did." *Medical Economics* (May 1997):11–18.

Efficiency

One of the payer organizations that our office deals with experienced a recent change in its computer system. This was accompanied by internal reorganization. Our office is required to obtain all authorizations for our patients from this entity.

The reasons for the new computer system and reorganization were mentioned from time to time in memoranda received from the organization. Depending upon my inclination, the attention paid to these documents varied considerably. In the midst of the adjustment period, I felt overcome with a powerful urge to retrieve these memos. What was the reason for this change? Perhaps it had to do with increasing efficiency.

Since these changes have come about, our office staff have reported the expansion of "on hold" time to a period that ranges between one and two hours. This is the time needed to attempt to obtain authorization for one procedure on one patient. After facing the difficulties in actually getting through to the office in question, the staff are treated to the following as a reward for their efforts:

"I will place you on hold now."

The difficulty encountered in obtaining this privileged bit of communication is such that the office staff are extremely reluctant to break the connection.

All of the "on hold" waiting is taking place during working hours, that is, when the staff are already preoccupied—talking to patients on the phone, bringing patients into the examining rooms, checking on urgent lab results, and assisting in follow-up.

Consequently, they now find themselves camped out in front of the "on hold" line—passing off this privilege with great care from assistant to assistant as the "watch" changes. I can see them trying to juggle all of this, along with their other duties, with one ear pressed to the speaker phone (wasn't it invented for just this purpose?).

As the assistants attend to their attentive watch, listening to the less-than-soothing Muzak interrupted by occasional recorded commentary, their patience begins to wane. How much longer would this delay continue? Their minds must begin to wander a bit. I could imagine them wondering how many pencils could be entwined end to end in the telephone cord between the mouthpiece and the main unit. This is accompanied by nervous drumming, twirling of stray hair strands, and chewing of already shortened fingernails.

In the midst of these reveries, a human voice startles them and they react as if it has come out of nowhere. The Utilization Review Representative speaks!

They are advised that they are allowed three requests only. What about the remaining half dozen sitting before them? The reply . . . "You must call back."

Two years ago this type of idiocy that now passes as the norm would have provoked an outburst of righteous indignation. The only response now is a muted, irritated sigh, followed by more nail chewing, finger tapping, and involuntary eye twitching. They have learned that it is futile to buck this system. Subdued and resigned, they pick up the receiver and dial again.

I understand that we will all soon have the opportunity to vent our concerns and frustrations regarding this computer system to a representative of this organization. I have only one question: What precisely are the merits of this health care delivery system?

In all fairness, this situation improved gradually over the following weeks. By fall, the kinks in the system had been worked out, and the authorization process returned to the usual state of subdued irritation. This entry remains to highlight the painful transitions that physicians' offices have been put through under the edict of managed care. This is approximately the third such tumultuous transition that we have been subjected to—all mandated under the guise of improving the system. The effects on the office staff are cumulative, and no one believes that this is the last one.

A colleague of mine recently summed this up in a meeting discussing physician stress: "I understand the stress imposed on the working physician, and I appreciate the coping techniques that have been suggested. But my problem is this . . . I am convinced that while I am sleeping the [insert favorite expletive] are up all night thinking of new ways in which to make my life miserable the following day."

"Just as time can bring rain, roses, flowers, and shape all things from their beginnings to their end, and no one can stop it, so can it also make diseases break out at will. The physician must never forget that time can do this, or he will be unable to discover what is possible and what is impossible, and to understand what he can nevertheless undertake to inspire people with respect for the medical art that God has created, and to prevent the disease from getting worse, for this cannot be the intention of God. Time is a brisk wind, for each hour it brings something new. . . . but who can understand and measure its sharp breath, its mystery and its design? Therefore the physician must not think himself too important; for over him there is a master—time—which plays with him as the cat with the mouse."

— *Paracelsus (1493?–1541)*
Hohenheim's German Commentary on the
Aphorisms of Hippocrates, Ch. I, Sect. 3
(tr. by Norbert Guterman in Selected Writings)

Time

The summer months adopt a frenzied pace in an obstetric practice. The peak delivery time generally occurs during the summer, and the gynecological aspect of the practice tends to increase as well. This, perhaps, coincides with the end of the school year. Many women see the summer as the time to finally attend to matters of personal health. A problem that may have been bothering them for several months has been put off due to the demands of juggling school and work schedules. Summer provides a respite from the hectic routine and gives them time to take care of themselves.

Occasionally, circumstances arise—as in the present case—when a mini new pregnancy boomlet coincides with the delivery boomlet. The statistical blip of an unusually high number of newly pregnant women coincides with the number of women having babies. Under these circumstances, the office can literally buzz with activity from dawn to dusk, with the hospital humming with activity from dusk to dawn.

Such has been the case this month, with the pace in the office proceeding at a breakneck, barely tolerable speed. Just when I do not know how it is all going to hang together, two quiet days will materialize—a gift to allow catchup on "routine and ordinary matters."

The pace has been heightened this year compared to previous years, as there are more patients requiring visits, testing, and follow-up. Before the increased percentage of patients enrolled in HMOs, with the corresponding increased office load, I recall a time when I had the luxury of calling back all of my own patients to discuss concerns, answer questions, and explain lab work. I was able to do this in a leisurely manner—either on the telephone or during a follow-up office visit. The patients liked this; it is the way it is supposed to work.

I can no longer work this way. I have had to shift over to a "priority basis" callback and triage system. The urgent problems are attended to immediately, and the time allowed for routine callback has lengthened.

As the day begins, the messages are prioritized as emergency, urgent, and routine. The appointment requests are similarly analyzed and divided into today, tomorrow, and next week. Same-day appointments are few and far between; such is the case with this allocation of the limited resource known as time.

It is the inability to have time for patient callbacks that is the most bothersome. I now come in on my day off to make some of these calls. Thus, the day off, an essential breather that used to serve the role of reenergizing the soul, becomes just one more scheduled day—with work right in the middle of it. I actually enjoy talking to patients and do like to discuss matters on the telephone. I am aware that they are waiting to hear about the results of a biopsy, a laboratory report, or an X ray. I could have one of the assistants do this for me, but I like to do it myself. It feels very satisfying, particularly when the conversation ends with "Thank you for taking the time to explain this so well. I really appreciate it. I know that you are busy."

Uneasiness has settled in lately while performing this medical juggling act. Am I doing an adequate job? How are my patients doing? What do they think? They serve as my ultimate litmus test. If I am not doing my job correctly, they will certainly let me know.

One particular callback delegated to the routine stack was on my mind. The lab result was normal. However, before calling Marilyn back, I wanted to consult a specialist to double-check my conclusions. I also needed time to read about possible side effects of medications. I was waiting for those quiet days when this opportunity invariably arises. The quiet days did not materialize. The specialist did not own any time this hectic week to call me. My time was being devoured by emergencies.

While reviewing my stack one day, reshuffling the callbacks, I made Marilyn's problem the top priority, as it had been some time since she had been in. I started working on it. In the back of my mind, I wondered how she was doing and whether this delay was of concern to her.

Marilyn came to my office at 4:45 that afternoon to tell me exactly how she felt. Disappointed. Angry. Frustrated. Upset.

Between her tears, she told me that she had been kept waiting too long. Why hadn't I called? It was so very important to her that she learn the results. She pressed me urgently. Why had it taken this long? She had gathered up enough courage to arrive and sit in the office to tell me exactly how she was feeling. Irritated. Distressed.

These honest expressions of sentiment hit home to this empathetic physician. She is absolutely right. Of course, I explained the entire situation to her—the emergencies; the inherent unpredictability of an obstetrician's practice, particularly in the summer months; my own efforts; my distractions; and so on. They were hollow-sounding excuses in the presence of so much grief—even though they were true.

She understood. She is familiar enough with the workings of a physician's office. However, she expected better. She expected more from me.

Excruciating disappointment . . . again.

We continued our discussion for forty-five minutes after-hours, talking and listening. I was able to make amends and repair the breach in the physician-patient relationship. It is exhausting work, this repair and reconciliation. Thankfully, I was successful.

The visit ended and I was able to secure an appointment for her with a specialist the following day.

I then returned to my desk and looked at the stack of shuffled charts piled adjacent to the telephone—an ever-present reminder of unfinished business. *How are all of these waiting patients doing?*

The time was 6:30 p.m. I made a few more calls, left a few messages, and arrived home at 7:30. I then faced the household of happy children and husband, who were eager to tell me about their wonderful, delightful, ordinary routine day. I tried to shake off the cloak of solemnity that accompanied me from the office and settled irrevocably around my shoulders in the dining room. I was unable to exorcise this feeling. Consequently, I sent all of the cheerful folks off to the library. It was necessary to stay behind. Quiet reflective time was needed. Rumination on time was in order.

Additional time would have prevented this incident. Time that I did not own. Time that I could not reproduce by binary fission. Time that needed to be borrowed or stolen from another patient. Time that recent and very complicated emergency patients had taken away from Marilyn. Time is the resource being allocated, and the efficiency experts have whittled it down to a per-patient allotment that makes every office schedule akin to walking a high-wire act.

The consequence of insufficient time was sitting in my office chair this afternoon, sobbing, trying to dry her eyes, trying to maintain composure so as to speak coherently to me. She was determined to make her feelings known to me.

In this task she succeeded beyond her wildest expectations. Little did she realize . . . her agony was secondary only to my own.

Around and Around We Go

Having heard so much regarding the authorization process from my staff, I decided to personally try it out for myself. Was it really as bad as they say? My curiosity had been heightened over the past few months and could be contained no longer. An opportunity presented itself four weeks ago.

During a routine well-woman visit, Dorothy requested some medication for a yeast infection involving her skin. It was a simple request, and I quickly obliged by writing the appropriate prescription. She was grateful and left the office en route to the pharmacy.

She telephoned the following day to say that when she arrived at the pharmacy she was told that the medication was not on the formulary of her HMO. She had asked if there was another medication that was equivalent. Was there a generic substitution?

The pharmacist answered no. There was no available substitute, and if she wanted the medication she would have to pay fifty-two dollars.

Dorothy was surprised. However, knowing that she needed the medication, she paid for it and called our office.

"Could you help out?"

This type of situation had happened to her previously in her primary care physician's office. Apparently, she was able to obtain retroactive coverage for the medications after a request for an exemption to the formulary was filed.

It seemed perfectly reasonable to me that if substitutes were not available the medication should be covered.

I volunteered my services on her behalf. I located the telephone number of the appropriate administrative office and called.

I spoke to a staff person and was referred to an office designated to handle such requests specific to our county. (*Was there a county-to-county variation? This thought crossed my mind.*)

I then placed the second call. I spoke to a person and relayed the entire story, including all of the details, in the precise manner that only physicians can when they start becoming bogged down in administrative matters that appear to have questionable merit. (A little alarm starts to beep, restlessness appears as if out of nowhere, and a little voice whispers, *Why am I spending time on this?*)

I was rewarded for my efforts by being referred to a second office and was pleased to listen to all of my options via voice mail.

The voice mail stated that I had reached the office of the UR committee for hospital admissions and discharge benefits. Please leave a message. *Apart from the benefit of actually being allowed to leave the hospital, what other benefits might they be referring to?*

Realizing that this was the wrong extension, I called back.

I spoke to a different person, explained the entire situation, and was told, "I have no idea who can help you. I will refer you to the provider inquiry department."

She transferred my call, and I was left to be entertained by a recording as I was placed on hold.

I was reminded periodically that all of the "specialists" were busy and to please stay on the line. *Interesting play on words. I thought that I was the specialist.*

I then was able to speak directly to the specialist, who, after listening to my story, stated that she could not help. I would have to speak with the insurance company directly. She informed me of the 800 number.

I called this number and again listened to a voice mail message. Enter subscriber ID number. I was not interested in pursuing every convoluted and potentially unlimited branch of the phone tree. Instead, I requested to speak directly to a human being.

While on hold, I was able to listen periodically to the benefits of exercise with respect to prevention of heart disease. *It seemed appropriate to suggest that they include a blurb on the benefits of stress reduction techniques as well. It would be most advantageous to those persons kept waiting on hold.*

My patience was rewarded at last when I spoke to a human being, explained everything again, and was referred to the pharmacy department.

Victory was in sight, and my anticipation was rising as closure to this story seemed imminent. Unfortunately, I listened to yet another voice mail recording, pressed the appropriate numbers, and was placed on hold again. From time to time I was reminded: "All of our customer service representatives are busy. Please stay on the line." *Momentary confusion again. Had I dialed the local department store?*

No, I was a physician on a medical mission trying to play my role as patient advocate.

Properly reoriented, I then succumbed to the pleasure of uplifting symphonic music while continuing to remain on hold. More reminders followed about how busy they were, that my call was important. Keep holding, ... More music, ...

After fifteen minutes had elapsed, my efforts were rewarded as I received instructions to place all pertinent information on a recording with the promise that it would be taken care of promptly. I took a little tally. Total time: twenty minutes, including fifteen minutes on hold.

Total number of human beings spoken to: five.

One week later I had not received any reply. So I called again.

This time I was able to speak to a service representative. She inquired. "Are you a provider trying to verify coverage?"

"No, I am a physician trying to determine why a medication was not included under formulary benefits. I am trying to request an exemption to the formulary."

"Oh, I see. I will refer you to the utilization review department."

More music, repeated messages about the virtues of patience, remarks about appreciation of your services, benefits of exercise, and so on. All followed by a reminder to please wait for the next available specialist. (That word again.)

"All of the specialists are assisting other callers. Your call will be answered by the next available specialist." *This specialist, in the meantime, was kept on hold with several urgent callbacks of her own beckoning.*

After five minutes on hold, I decided to place the telephone on speaker mode so that I could attend to pressing matters while waiting. My neck was beginning to feel cramped, and my right arm was beginning to tingle as numbness began to set in.

I could not do this, however, because I could not locate the volume control knob that would render the speaker function audible. It would do little good to activate the speaker function if I would be unable to acknowledge the specialist when she came on the line. I certainly did not want to miss that longed-for moment. After fruitlessly trying the two or three most promising knobs and most likely candidates, I was left with the forlorn conclusion that my telephone did not possess one, or if it did it was not working.

Out of concern for the prevention of brachial plexus nerve palsy of my right arm, I diligently began to alternate between right arm and left arm. This was less than satisfying because I am right-eared. To hold the phone with my left arm to my right ear was not a posture that could be sustained comfortably for any reasonable length of time.

I then wondered about the perceived benefits of isometric exercise, with strengthening of the deltoid muscle group specifically coming to mind. Perhaps the insurance company could incorporate this into their automatic messaging relay program that one listens to while on hold. I could certainly imagine an improvement in the attitude of all those poor souls resigned to suffer a fate similar to mine if they could be apprised of such a potential benefit.

Fifteen minutes passed—occupied in this manner. The stack of phone calls and messages on my desk appeared to be gaining greater importance and urgency. Such as calling a patient regarding an abnormal mammogram report, and calling someone else regarding an abnormal pap smear.

Then my choice became this: remaining on hold to play my role as advocate or attending to urgent business on hand. In the end, after waiting twenty minutes, I relinquished the receiver. The other charts could wait no longer.

As I picked up the telephone eight days later, I realized that almost three weeks had elapsed since I had been called by Dorothy. I remembered that I had promised that I would get back to her soon. She probably thought that I had forgotten. With this awareness, I dialed the number again, musing on the old saying "The third time is a charm." I boldly resumed my quest. I listened again to this voice mail.

"If this is an emergency, call your PCP immediately." (*Ah . . . I guess those providers are good for something, after all.*)

"If this is an employer, press one.

"If this is a hospital, press two. All other business matters enter subscriber ID number followed by their birthday."

Three additional minutes about helpful health benefits, exercise, diet, and so on. *Nothing, however, regarding deltoid muscle enhancement.*

Then a receptionist answered. I was connected directly to the pharmacy department. I enjoyed the privilege at last of engaging in dialogue with a utilization review person. I relayed all of the pertinent details, *again*.

I then repeated my request for consideration of an exemption. I was relieved that at last I appeared to be getting somewhere. After clicking on her keyboard and asking a few additional questions, she offered this explanation: "It was refused because there is an over-the-counter alternative to the prescription medication."

Astonishing! This was the last thing that I expected to hear. I was unaware that such a product existed. Based on the conversation that my patient had had with the pharmacist, he was likewise unaware that this product existed.

Recovering, I asked for the name of this product. She then pressed a few buttons on her keyboard and told me the name of a popular medication used to treat vaginal yeast infections.

Flabbergasted, I replied, "You cannot be serious. I am ready to believe almost anything except this. You cannot really mean that you are recommending that a medication designed and formulated for intravaginal use be utilized in the treatment of skin fungal infections?"

Her explanation: "They have the same active ingredient, so they are considered equivalent."

Incredulousness mounted with this disclosure. I replied by informing her that although they had the same active ingredient they were not formulated the same; therefore, they could not be equivalent. Sensing my increasing exacerbation, she referred me to a supervisor.

I spoke to the supervisor and relayed my concerns, issues, and original request.

She, in turn, clicked on her keyboard, checked her computer screen, and verified the first person's declaration. There was an over-the-counter equivalent. Therefore, the prescription medication was no longer on the formulary. I was longing for clarification. What was the name of the over-the-counter equivalent to the prescription medication?

She then gave me the name of the vaginal yeast medication. I immediately objected and reiterated all of the salient concerns. She quickly recovered, clicked a few more buttons, and victoriously stated: "No, it isn't the vaginal yeast cream that we are talking about. There is actually a product that is identical to the external skin fungal medication. It is available over the counter. That is why the prescription was denied."

Confusion. "Then why did the pharmacist tell the patient that no options existed to the medication, if what you are telling me is true?"

"I do not know the answer to that question. All I know is that effective January first of this year the product is available and it is no longer covered on the formulary."

After this thirteen-minute volley, I was more uncertain than ever. I ended the conversation and called Dorothy.

I explained all of the particulars. She, too, was perplexed as to why she would have been told that no options existed if, in fact, the insurance representative was correct.

I asked for and received the number of the pharmacy and dialed the number. I was able to speak to a pharmacy assistant and relayed the entire story—requesting an explanation.

I was placed on hold. She then informed me that no such over-the-counter product existed. I insisted that she double-check, based on my most recent information. She placed me on hold, discussed this with the pharmacist, and personally searched the shelves. She came back on the line to inform me that she had found the over-the-counter equivalent of the external skin yeast medication.

The obvious question escaped my lips. "Why wasn't Dorothy informed of this when she specifically asked for this three weeks ago?"

Technicalities surfaced at this point. Because the alternative medication is an over-the-counter product, it is not considered in the same category as a generic substitution for a prescription medication. Technically, the pharmacist was correct. There are no generic substitutions for this product— that is, no other *prescription substitutions*. The fact that an over-the-counter substitute was available seemed to surprise all parties concerned.

Having finally obtained clear and succinct understanding, I called Dorothy and explained everything. The technical aspect of the transaction was not particularly pleasing to her. She would have preferred to put her fifty-two dollars to better use. I suggested that she bring this up with the pharmacist at her next visit. She then relayed the following ongoing prescription saga that began with her new HMO last year.

First of all, she was no longer able to see her allergist due to HMO restrictions. He had taken very good care of her for many years. So her allergy shots stopped. Her problem with chronic sinus infections and congestion worsened. She was required to stop taking a prescription medication that helped greatly with control of her symptoms, as she was told that a combination of two other over-the-counter products produced the same effect. Somewhere along the way, she also had to stop seeing her internist with whom she had enjoyed a long-standing relationship. He was not on the HMO panel.

Dorothy fiddled with the over-the-counter alternatives, essentially self-medicating as she felt was needed, but the results were unsatisfactory. It simply did not work as well as the prescription medication. She now finds herself with a chronic upper respiratory tract infection or inflammation, treating herself as needed with over-the-counter options. She finds that her functioning capability is reduced due to this chronic illness. Unless she finds herself "half-dead," she does not bother to call the primary care physician. What is the use? It is just a waste of time.

She knows what she should be getting, but she is not able to obtain the right treatment. She received good treatment in the past. She knows better. What really worries her about doing this "home job" of mixing the over-the-counter medications is the nagging concern about a possible reaction with the medication that she takes for her heart condition. This concerns her considerably, as she is under the care of a cardiologist.

She made an attempt to obtain coverage for the prescription medication by calling the insurance company and requesting an exemption. This was of no use. They did not yield. She then asked the primary care physician to call. Apparently he did so—to no avail. The request for exemption was denied. She then relayed the following story.

She arrived one day at the pharmacy to obtain her monthly refill of heart medication. She was informed that she had to accept the generic medication. She had been taking her other medication for ten years. She was uneasy about changing. However, she was talked into making this switch.

She then suffered through one of the worst weekends of her life. She was bothered by the most disturbing heart palpitations and elevated blood pressure. She was so concerned that she called her heart specialist first thing Monday morning. He was furious.

He called the pharmacy and was very explicit in his thoughts and desires. He left strict instructions that under no circumstances was Dorothy ever to be given generic medication. Once Dorothy resumed her nongeneric medication, her symptoms resolved.

Six months later, she dispatched her husband to the pharmacy to pick up her medication. He was advised to accept the generic substitution. Knowing better, he refused and went home to explain this to Dorothy. She became very angry. With great indignation, she went to the pharmacy and was very explicit in expressing her feelings and opinions on this issue.

"It should be clearly seen on your computer screen that I am not to take generics."

After checking carefully, the pharmacist apologized and said, "You are right. I guess my hand had inadvertently covered part of the screen. I was unable to read that cautionary note at the bottom."

All of this brings to mind: Who's on first? . . . What's on second? . . . and "I don't know what's on the formulary" is on third.

In the interest of enhancing provider relations and improving customer satisfaction, it would seem appropriate that a "call for action" hotline be established. As for the volunteer staff members who would make up such a panel, I can think of none more qualified for this position than all of the upper-level executives of the HMOs, insurance companies, and go-between administrators. It would seem an ideal opportunity for them to satisfy their community service and public relations requirements.

Once the superb qualifications possessed by the staffers became widespread knowledge, I predict that demand for such a service would be great—indeed, possibly even overwhelming.

So overwhelming, in fact, that it may require that the hotline be staffed twenty-four hours a day. *Imagine that!*

"It may seem a strange principle to enunciate as the very first requirement in a Hospital that it should do the sick no harm."
— Florence Nightingale (1820–1910)
Notes on Hospitals, Preface

Operating Below Costs: Hospitals

Various reports are circulating in the medium of doctor shoptalk regarding several hospitals in this area. These reports are unfavorable and address concerns regarding quality of nursing staff, availability of ancillary support services, quality of medical equipment, and so on.

There is a belief among many that these problems can be attributed to the decreased revenue that hospitals are receiving. That is, decreased reimbursement from third-party payers due to decreased per-day reimbursements, decreased length of hospital stays, and decreased reimbursement for billable charges, supplies, laboratory tests, and so on.

In response to the decrease in revenue, hospitals have had to cut back on all essentials—those ingredients mentioned above. The problem with this trend is that at some point the hospital begins to operate "below costs," that is, performing services for less than the cost of those services. Essentially, operating in the red.

I want to extend that definition of operating "below costs" to include the very real line below which these hospitals may drop and find themselves operating under conditions below the safety margin—that is, when the quantity and quality of all the essential ingredients drop to the point at which patients might actually be endangered by their hospital stay.

It seems as if the hospital administration keeps using the argument to the staff that decreasing revenues justify the cuts in ancillary support services. It is not possible to afford this "excess."

This continued pursuit of a bottom-line, bare-bones, operating-below-costs strategy seems to have no end.

Someone needs to draw a line on the ledger in indelible red ink. This should be marked with a warning in the margin: *Below this line endangers patient safety, and we cannot operate below it.* That would define precisely the point where operating "below costs" would be.

So far, in all of the years I have spent listening to administration, insurance industry executives, and business community leaders, this concept has not appeared as often as one with common sense would think it should. I wonder if it has even been spelled out in all of the training that these persons undergo.

It is important to do so, because it seems that some hospitals at this moment may very well be operating below this red line. Woe to the patients who are unwittingly admitted to them in order to receive medical care.

Operating Below Costs: Physicians

Many, many, many laments—and then more—abound among physicians concerning declining reimbursements from the insurance companies regarding their fees for services. At first, this may elicit no sympathy from the general public, who perhaps believe that physicians probably make enough or possibly too much. This sentiment was brought on by the excesses in the past regarding physician reimbursements and the escalation of fees that occurred in the 1970s and 1980s. With this escalation of fees apparently taken too far, the insurance industry stepped in to control costs by starting to negotiate lower fees for services—with the physicians' cooperation. These original discounted fees were negotiated and were acceptable to the physicians.

Had the insurance industry maintained the practice of bilateral negotiations, much of the present prevailing sentiment of discontent would be nonexistent.

I don't suppose the public realizes that at present the fees are determined unilaterally. The insurance company, HMO, and federal government simply state: This is our reimbursement schedule. The only negotiating issue revolves around this—take it or leave it.

It's unfortunate that the physicians didn't call this bluff a few years ago when it set in in earnest. Perhaps a chance at bilateral negotiations could have been resurrected and the present seething mass of discontent prevented.

When I started practice in 1988, I thought that the reimbursements were reasonable. While they could have gone down a little, they should not have fallen to the present state. I share this sentiment with every colleague I know.

The source of the present discontent revolves around the physicians' feeling that they are operating "below costs." In other words, they feel deep down inside that they are being required to perform services below their own personal costs.

What are the costs of practicing medicine? Many. First and foremost, one must factor in the many years of study and training (a minimum of eleven years including college). During this time—the golden years of early adulthood that span the ages 22 to 30—the physician-in-training is sequestered from the world and in many instances loses touch with it. There is a price that is paid for the single-minded devotion to the study of medicine that needs to be factored in "post-training."

That brings us to the realities and responsibilities of everyday practice.

When a physician opens a practice and accepts patients, he or she is required to be available for a patient's needs twenty-four hours a day, seven days a week. The difficulty is that it's not one patient but typically between a few hundred and two thousand. All of these patients are carried around in the physician's black bag of responsibility *twenty-four hours a day, seven days a week, fifty-two weeks a year*. Sometimes the weight of the bag becomes such that it is necessary to set it down and rest a bit. It's not possible, however, to leave it behind.

The physician carries this responsibility to bed (you might call in the middle of the night), on his or her day off (you might have an emergency), and on vacation (he or she cannot even plan a vacation without first arranging for another physician to cover patients during the planned absence).

So important is this concept of being available to you (the patients) that it's not possible to obtain hospital privileges without completing the section: Who will be responsible for the care of your patients when you are unavailable?

The constant weight of this ever-present responsibility has a cost.

What does it feel like to be "on call"? I have heard many of my colleagues report increasing anxiety, insomnia, and uneasiness on the night *preceding call*. Sometimes I awake at 3:00 a.m. preoccupied with what emergency problems or surgery or difficult clinical problems *might* have to be dealt with the next day.

These nights are followed by nights when I am actually on call and can't sleep because any minute the phone *might* ring. Needless to say, it doesn't help the spirit to realize that in the midst of this on call–induced insomnia one has to work a full schedule the next day.

There is a cost of being awakened from a dead sleep (on those call nights when sleep easily comes) and having to drive to the hospital quickly through the still of the night when everyone else is asleep. Upon arrival, one is required personally and professionally to perform emergency surgery just right, with no mistakes allowed, at 4:00 a.m. in the same manner and attitude and composure as if it were 9:00 a.m.

Recently while on call I experienced the type of night in which I received a telephone call every thirty minutes throughout the entire night. After the first few calls and with fatigue setting in, I found myself jarred awake with increasingly spasmodic movements of my limbs—as if my nervous system were being subjected to repetitive injury. As I drifted in the twilight between awake and asleep, I reached a quasi state somewhere between consciousness and REM sleep.

In this state, the periodic ring of the bedside phone would jolt my body like an electrical shock. This continued all night long. In the beginning, the mind can rationalize this abuse of the body as being consistent with professional obligations and contributing to the welfare of the patient.

As the night wears on and the disturbance continues, it becomes increasingly difficult to ignore the feelings of agony, pain, and alarming fatigue that the body is relaying to the brain. In essence, there is a cost involved in that in the rendering of one's professional responsibilities one is made to feel like a pithed frog in the morning. Especially considering that this pithed frog is expected to put in a full day at the office.

There are also the desirability and necessity of completing ongoing education requirements, such as attending professional meetings and finding reading time for professional enhancement.

Finally, there is the time away from family. Often unexpected. The evenings when one is delayed at the hospital and dinner happens in your absence. Many times, bedtime happens in your absence too. There was the time when I suddenly left the neighborhood barbecue (having been paged for an emergency). Then there are the missed school activities, plays, and events due to emergencies.

There are costs involved.

The prevailing sentiment of physician discontent has to do with the fact that these important considerations have not been factored into the reimbursement equation. As such, the equation is lopsided and the physicians are left feeling that their services are being extracted "below costs." It is important that these persons feel as if the level of ongoing personal self-sacrifice is being adequately reimbursed.

The public interest will not be served if the very best decide it's just not worth it anymore.

The real problem in this operating "below costs" scheme lies in the fact that, faced with decreased reimbursement *per service*, physicians have responded by speeding up, seeing more patients per day, taking care of more problems, processing more paperwork, and performing more surgery. These are human beings—not robots. The pace is prohibitive.

There is a growing awareness that the candle is also burning at the other end. One has the deep sense that the speed of that burning will hasten if one continues at the present pace. While there are many noble pursuits in life that would warrant continued participation in spite of attaining this realization, participating in managed care medicine is not to be counted among them.

Ashes and Soot

I have been attending the most marvelous conference called "Empowering the Healer." I am writing on the evening of the last day.

It has been magnificent! The lineup of speakers was wonderful, and the keynote sessions were fabulous.

Several speakers addressed concerns regarding the impact of managed care on physician wellness. One speaker described it as an unpredictable and hugely frightening dynamic force, with the assault on autonomy leading to outrage and with disequilibrium leading to anxiety and anger. Declining finances are leading to stress, depression, marital tension, and divorce. Finally, the issue of the assault on ethics was discussed, particularly with respect to patient privacy issues, which the physicians appear to be powerless to do anything about.

Another speaker addressed concerns about the state of medicine in society—concerns about declines in status, erosion of the public trust, and the issue of the integrity of the medical profession being ill-defined.

Yet another speaker addressed the increasing numbers of physicians reporting for treatment due to "impairment." An increase that he attributed to managed care.

In the midst of all these grim reflections, great excitement existed. It revolved around the seminars presented on the importance of taking care of oneself, maintaining balance in life, and practicing stress-reduction techniques—all intended to ward off burnout.

The most exciting messages for me were from the seminars recognizing the importance of the spiritual dimension of healing: the role of the spirit in healing, the emphasis on the mind-body connection, the power of the mind to heal, and the latest in energy medicine.

It was the last that filled me with zest and energy. I am buoyant at the prospect of practicing medicine by incorporating all of these important elements. Being with all of these wonderful people was like a homecoming of sorts—an intuitive spiritual physician delighted to be counted among the ranks of others.

The joy and pleasure of having found such precious company on the face of the earth will remain with me always.

As I anticipate the last day with excitement, I find that sleep eludes me. I am now so reenergized by just being here that I cannot sleep. But that is not the only reason.

I very much want to practice medicine incorporating all of the things that I have learned. I know it is important to have a nontoxic work environment, that the energy and attitude of all involved are important. I know that I should have some free time each day. I should take up tai chi or yoga to decrease stress.

I have been validated in my belief that spending more time (not less) with patients contributes in a statistically significant manner to enhancing their wellness—as well as my own. I have learned that the nonverbal communication between physician and patient is more important than ever thought before. I have learned that mood affects the immune system.

I want to practice medicine in a nurturing, healing, mutually acceptable environment. Thus, the paradox glares before me: All that I have learned at this conference I cannot do on Monday. Medicine under these conditions and medicine under managed care are mutually exclusive concerns.

I am in many respects like Cinderella at the ball. For all the euphoria of my present state, at the stroke of midnight tomorrow it will disappear.

On Monday, I will be brought back to ashes and soot.

"No one should approach the temple of science with the soul of a money changer."

— *Sir Thomas Browne (1605–1682)*

We Are All in This Together

Much news lately regarding the for-profit sector of the health care industry. Not much of it has been favorable.

There has been an explosive growth in this sector over the past few years. My curiosity was piqued by the recent news. I placed a call to a stockbroker. I had a simple request: "How many for-profit health care companies exist, and how many are publicly traded on the various stock exchanges?"

She expressed surprise at such a naive question. "Well, there are zillions. I could not possibly begin to tell you how many there really are."

I persisted because I really wanted to know. "Is it possible to obtain a list—a computer printout, perhaps? Just how many are there?"

Making some comment about the enormity of such an undertaking, she reiterated, "There are so many. It would be hard to know where to begin."

The conversation ended. My curiosity was only enhanced.

The local newspaper was helpful this morning when an article appeared about one such for-profit company. This company is the world's largest health care company. It was described as a $20 billion giant with approximately 350 hospitals, 550 home health care offices, and scores of medical businesses in 38 states. Other businesses included surgery centers, mammography centers, and laboratory services.

Of course, one must not forget the for-profit HMOs.

The company in question is not the only one. It is merely mentioned as the largest—perhaps not for long. There is speculation that a takeover bid might be in the works—with another for-profit company eyeing to purchase this one. Thus would be created a huge for-profit health care corporation with nearly 500 hospitals and $30 billion in revenue.

Viewed from the perspective of a physician who has witnessed the change from nonprofit, through managed care, to the present for-profit, this is not heartwarming news. I think of the vast number of patients who have been affected by these changes. This immense number who now receive a staggering amount of their health care services via for-profit entities.

So who does the for-profit entity serve first? Lip service and gloriously written mission statements are overflowing with "concerns about high-quality health care . . . and goals of providing the finest medical care possible."

Are these mission statements written to make the portfolio appease the stockholders? To appease that uneasiness that will not go away, in spite of slick advertising campaigns, smart brochures, and the somewhat out-of-date argument that "these changes were necessary because of escalating health care costs and inefficiencies with the cumbersome, unsophisticated nonprofit system?" Is all of this done to ease the consciences of those persons who are receiving a return on their investment—an investment realized when a person who is ill, vulnerable, sick, or even dying utilizes the health care system?

This is the simple, underlying truth that will not go away. The public relations efforts have been intensified lately, perhaps in response to negative press. Are these efforts being launched to make everyone forget, feel better about it, or not really think about it?

A personal opinion here. The patients received better care under that old, outdated, inefficient, nonprofit health care delivery system. It was a cleaner system. It was very clear who came first then. Everyone involved, from the housekeeper to the board of trustees, operated consistently with this single, straightforward goal in sight: The patient came first, period.

Did things need to change? An economic argument could fill pages. I will grant that with all systems things eventually need to change. However, with all of the for-profit entities taking such a commanding presence in this arena, one has to consider this: A comparison needs to be made between the amount of money now being paid to satisfy the profit motive versus the reported amounts lost due to waste and inefficiency under the old system.

In other words, is the sum total exchanged in the business any different from the sum total exchanged previously? Or has there just been a massive redistribution of wealth? Way back when, all of the money went back into improving the experience of patient care. How much has now been diverted to satisfy the profit margin?

All of the shareholders should realize that they should not believe the slick brochures and advertisements. They should instead listen to the stories of their family, friends, neighbors, and any physician friends that they have. Quality of health care has dropped over the past few years. Issues of quality exist today that were unheard of when I began practicing, only nine years ago.

While there are many reasons for this, it seems time for everyone to separately evaluate all the changes that have occurred and seriously ask which of these changes are detrimental to patient care. What additional changes still could be made? What modifiers should be placed?

After all, who are the patients? They could be anyone. They could be you.

For all the faults of the nonprofit system, one single virtue remained. The patients came first. In the present situation, it seems that no one is sure about this anymore.

For the shareholders, it may come down to this: What is more important, increased growth of your stock portfolio, or decent, reliable health care when you, your family, your friends, and your neighbors become ill?

We are really all in this together, linked in more ways than we can possibly imagine.

An Investment Opportunity

I was waylaid on the return trip to the office by a powerful bit of intelligence. It seems that Wall Street investors have found even more fertile ground than previously imagined.

It is not enough to have created for-profit hospital chains, surgery centers, home health care agencies, and laboratories. It appears that the truly ingenious among them are proceeding much as General Sherman did through the South. *This land must be conquered, and I am going to march right through to the sea.* Will this march go unheeded?

Perhaps, spurred on by easy and early conquests and rewarded handsomely for their efforts, they now proceed unabashedly toward the heart of medicine. They proceed with calm, cool confidence as if asking "Why not? Who can stop us now?"

They do this in spite of increasingly unfavorable press reports regarding various for-profit ventures. They proceed despite ethical concerns. They proceed despite growing anger incubating in the population at large. Are they none other than extremely well dressed carpetbaggers come to town? And why does everyone cooperate?

The latest for-profit investment opportunity allows shareholders to purchase shares in a national company that has as its business goal the purchase of doctors' practices.

At present, many solo or group practices are corporations. Depending on the structure of the corporation, it is usually the case that the physician partners own shares in this corporation. These are privately held shares and are in place solely as a matter of satisfying requirements regarding setting up a corporation. These corporations do not sell shares to anyone else. There are no dividends or yields with respect to these stocks. If someone leaves the corporation, the shares are "bought out" and someone else "buys in." This previously was the extent to which transfer of these shares was transacted. They had a relatively unexciting life. They rarely appreciated significantly, paid no dividends, and were not ever worth a great deal.

The physician owners of these shares saw them only as official documentation of their stake in the company—a necessary step to take in order to be "committed."

Apparently, to those folks used to buying and selling lots of shares and speculating on futures and looking at indexes, foreign markets, currency fluctuations, and bond markets and listening with bated breath to what the Federal Reserve Board was going to announce next with respect to interest rates, this was unbelievable! Those high-flying types who have helped the Dow Jones Average soar to record-high levels just could not believe the gem of an opportunity that befell them. They must have felt like Columbus seeing the New World. All of those riches to be harvested and taken back for the good of the mother country!

Physician businesspersons are relatively naive. Too many of them are swayed by the sophisticated, persuasive types— those persons who are so well versed in marketing strategies that they would attempt to convince the Mother Teresas of the world that they should buy shares in heaven.

These suave folks have convinced certain physician groups, those small, unassuming physician-owned corporations, that it is in their best interests to arrange a trade, if you will. Those boring old shares can be transformed, with a little Wall Street magic, into the real type of shares. The kind that people can buy and sell. Preferably, the more, the better.

So it is set up like this: A national corporation with shares sold on the public stock exchange pays these physicians a significant amount of money for their business. In return, the physicians now agree to work for the corporation. They sign a contract that usually requires that they remain on for a few years. This guarantees that the physicians will keep their practices busy. Thus, the investors will realize a return on their "investment."

This return is realized as the physician takes care of the sick and needy (but, most likely, only those with health insurance or another type of guaranteed payer, that is, government). Each time the vulnerable, the ailing, and the ill present themselves to their physician, the investors realize a return on their investment. The more sick people being taken care of, the greater the return. The more physician groups that can be brought under this umbrella corporation—as quickly as possible—the greater the growth accomplished and the greater the "revenue" generated at each quarterly earnings announcement. The projected growth of these new companies will be followed with excitement and heated anticipation, and higher yet will the stock price rise.

It should be mentioned that the physicians are now being paid a salary by the "executives" of these companies—who may or may not be physicians. The billing office is now centralized. And the bills for services may be done nowhere near where the doctor is actually providing the service. This cuts costs and is efficient, this central billing office. But who is doing the billing? What codes are they using? Who is accountable if the billing is done incorrectly? Of course, the motivation of the billing office is not any different from any other billing office: to collect money. The more, the better.

What of a physician's practice habits? Who or what influences the course of treatment? Whose interests have priority—patient, physician, or shareholder?

Of course, this for-profit organization is increasingly billing for-profit HMOs and insurance companies. So the money travels from one shareholder group to the other. I imagine that, if one is savvy and maintains a balanced portfolio, it will even out all right in the end.

Yes, these shareholders and Wall Street wizards have found fertile ground, indeed. All will be wonderful, until they or their families actually present themselves to receive medical care from such entities.

Then it will finally hit them, as must have happened to General Sherman and his surviving troops as they torched the South and laid it to ruin on their way down. Having accomplished their goal, it would have occurred to them that they then needed to turn around and *walk back*.

They would then find themselves choking upon the stench, and their eyes would be stung by ashes as they stumbled across the charred ruins of some of the finest estates that ever existed.

I had occasion to speak with an MD out of the immediate geographical area regarding a mutual patient.

I was impressed with how quickly she was able to come to the telephone. Even more noticeable was her easy, relaxed manner, as well as the ease and friendliness exhibited by her office staff.

It reminded me of the good old days.

Physician Burnout

From an internist:

"The stress is overwhelming! I am working as hard as I did as an intern. The volume of patients and the acuity are unbelievable. The energy outlay required is not sustainable."

He has heard through the grapevine that 25 percent of internists are leaving another local HMO. He hopes to hold on for four more years before getting out. He worries every day that he might not last that long. He may come in to work and suddenly say, "That's it. I'm done."

He shook his head over a recent article that suggested not training physicians due to the predicted doctor glut. *They* do not have to worry. What *they* have failed to take into account is the attrition rate. There will end up being a shortage instead.

"I Am Going to Be a Doctor When I Grow Up, Just Like Mommy!"

My four-year-old uttered these words a few days ago in a proud and determined voice. I cringed inwardly. Outwardly, I smiled with far more enthusiasm than I felt.

It seems ironic that, as I consider this, I realize that when I spoke those words it probably elicited a great deal of happiness and excited anticipation from my mother. Even more to the point, all of the hard-core feminists who were an influence on the women of my generation would have been very pleased to hear those words.

"It is working at last! Just as we predicted it would!" I could imagine them shouting.

Having made it to the rank of a highly educated professional woman, I would act as a role model for my daughter, thus encouraging by action and accomplishment the idea that she could achieve the same or even greater milestones. This is the line of reasoning that pervaded popular thought during my early adulthood. It made a great deal of sense then. It is slightly shocking to see how early on in life this form of modeling actually takes root.

My four-year-old daughter is keenly aware that I am a physician. She understands that this is important. She knows that I go to the hospital to deliver babies. She has been asking for some time now to come with me and help. I tell her that she will have to wait until she is a little bit older. Recently she has decided that she no longer wants to be confined to merely helping; she wants to take on the whole job. "I am going to be a doctor, Mommy, just like you!"

Not so fast, little one.

I know too much. My mother was naive. In all good conscience, I cannot pretend to be so.

Before I give my blessing to such a noble pursuit, I would like to see some changes. There are approximately fifteen years in the interim—perhaps things will improve.

I would dearly love to see some changes, for instance, in the educational process for medical students, interns, and residents. Large doses of compassion and consideration for the human beings involved in this noblest of pursuits need to be incorporated. How about just a glimmer of consideration to the thought that there may be more to human beings than merely a complicated array of protoplasm?

Even greater changes need to be made in the practice of medicine before I would give my consent to this endeavor. Now that I have been forewarned, I will be keeping my finger on the pulse of medicine during the next decade and a half.

If I do not see substantial changes, I will launch an intensive, all-out effort. I will bring all of my considerable powers of persuasion to the forefront. All in an effort to change the mind of my strong-willed child. It would not be easy. I do not underestimate the enormity of the task, but I would not back down from it.

Maternal instincts of protection and preservation would be activated. I would not want her to make a decision that she would regret later. No effort would be spared in this endeavor. Too much is at stake.

It would be a grievous insult to her lively intelligence for her to practice medicine under the present circumstances.

It would be a shock to her lively, inquisitive, and engaging personality to be subjected to the present methods of training and educating physicians.

It would be deleterious to her soul to allow this pursuit if present circumstances do not change.

If in spite of my valiant efforts I do not succeed, I would graciously relent and leave her with the following words of age-old wisdom: "Remember, it will not be the end of the world. You can always change your mind."

Reclaiming Sacred Ground

We have now journeyed through most of the year, and by now you understand the source of my distress and anguish. We turn now to hope and to possible solutions for reinventing our health care delivery system. At this point it is abundantly clear that change needs to happen.

My solution is presented on two separate but converging levels. The first focus is the repair of the physician-patient relationship. For reconciliation to occur—and reconcile we must— it is necessary to reimagine this most important of relationships. We need to define, discuss, and restate it, as it is obvious that the present model is woefully inadequate.

Prepare yourself for a completely different way to practice medicine, presented on the pages that follow. It is a style of practice based on my own observations and experiences that also draws from the collective wisdom presently emerging in society as a whole. It is quite a departure from typical thinking, and it is my hope that you will agree that it is an intriguing one.

The second part of the solution involves the advocacy of two concrete alternatives that can assist in the repair of two facets of the health care system. I will discuss the Medical Savings Account in the context of its restorative effect on the physician-patient relationship, and I will discuss the Planetree philosophy as it applies to improving the hospital experience. I believe that all of us will benefit from implementation of these changes, and it is for the purported benefit of all that this book is written.

Now prepare yourself for a fresh look at the physician-patient interaction. While it may initially appear to be new and different, it could arguably be said that what I am describing is in fact timeless. . . .

"The cure of many diseases is unknown to the physicians of Hellas, because they are ignorant of the whole, which ought to be studied also; for the part can never be well unless the whole is well. . . . This . . . is the great error of our day in the treatment of the human body, that the physicians separate the soul from the body."

— Plato (427?–347 B.C.)
Charmides, 156.E (tr. Benjamin Jowett)

Soul to Soul

If physicians came to regard all patients as possessing body and soul, an extra dimension would be added to the physician-patient relationship. The focus would shift during the interaction from the mind to the soul, with the physician's soul being attentive to the messages relayed by the patient's soul. I believe that the soul is the source of energy and power for the mind and body and wants acknowledgment. One can imagine the following consequences of such a change in perception.

The color of the skin of the body would be insignificant, except for those areas confined to the diagnosis and recognition of skin disorders. Likewise, the language generated by the mind and spoken by the body, as well as particular customs characteristic of and defining of cultures, would be recognized as interesting manifestations of the human experience. While they would be appreciated for their aesthetic value, they would pale in comparison to the presence of the soul. Thus would the interaction between the physician's soul and the patient's soul become the dominant part of the interview.

When necessary, the physician would feel the need to reach out and touch the soul. The physician would want to connect with it and offer consolation regarding its fears for the body—fears of illness, fears regarding upcoming surgery, fears regarding treatment.

One can imagine this extra dimension as being useful in making hospital rounds, as well. One can walk about the hospital and hear the groans of pain, anguish, and isolation emanating from the medical and surgical floors. One can hear the agonizing scream of fear and pain, followed by the cry of joy, emanating from each of the souls on the labor-and-delivery unit. One can hear the quiet sighs and glimpse the most tentative movement of limbs from the newly born souls in the neonatal intensive care unit. One can be made aware of the intermittently conscious souls in the intensive care unit.

And one can glimpse terror in the eyes of the souls in the emergency room.

It is a powerful and sobering dimension—this soul dimension—and it is crying out to be acknowledged.

The Mystery of It All

The practice of medicine does not appear to be a series of random, sterile events. My experience would suggest the opposite occurs—it is a series of sequenced, specific events tailored to the needs of each patient and physician. Sometimes, it is so specific that it appears to reach well beyond mere coincidence—it takes on an air of something predetermined. It is as if all the souls who decided to practice the healing arts and uphold the sacred mysteries held within have taken an oath committing themselves, in a fashion, to this belief. Likewise, it is as if all the other souls—the patient souls— seek us out when they need our ministrations and expect us to fully honor this commitment. Many of these souls bring important messages about themselves that can greatly enhance their experience with the physician and with all others who practice the healing arts. All that is necessary is for the practitioner to be receptive.

These messages are particularly apparent in the practice of obstetrics. Perhaps it is the altered physiology and the powerful sense of mystery that wraps around the woman that make her more able to transmit these messages. Thus amplified, they render the physician more able to receive them.

I can think of more than one newly pregnant woman who has remarked with a nervous manner and vague uneasiness on the perceived offensive nature of the genetic screening questionnaire, a fairly nondescript form that asks a series of questions regarding one's health, family history, and risk factors. It is standard procedure to ask these questions, and the form has been in use for many years. I dutifully listened to all of the reasons they did not like the form, why they found it offensive, and so on. In vain I tried to allay the apprehension inexplicably present at every early visit. It demanded attention. I was at a loss as to how to deal with this and was left after each visit wrapped in the concentric rings of the patient's anxiety.

All was made painfully clear when they received the results of their genetic screening analysis four months into their pregnancy, demonstrating that the baby in their womb was affected with Down's syndrome or another type of chromosomal problem. I would be called upon to assist them at this most distressing time, help them cope, and counsel and console them at the time of their greatest need.

Remember, we knew this was going to happen. You promised to help us through it.

A few years ago, I was taking care of Gail during her first pregnancy. From the very first visit, there was an extra dimension present in the room. *Pay attention!* I could appreciate this warning as clearly as if she had been shouting at the top of her lungs. I reviewed the history, and nothing particularly alarming was apparent. So wait and see. The same aura remained at every visit. At the seventh monthly visit, the intensity of the aura increased considerably. I needed to take some action. I questioned her in detail regarding preterm labor symptoms. She denied having any of them. However, to pacify the aura, I decided to perform a pelvic exam, just to be sure. To my shocked surprise, I found evidence of cervical thinning (effacement) and softening—the earliest signs of preterm labor. Gail was sent to the hospital. The evidence of the culpable contractions appeared on the uterine monitor. When these were pointed out, she said, "Oh, that is what contractions feel like."

Treatment was started. I spoke with her husband later in the evening. This was such a disruptive event in their lives. He remarked more than once, "It is the strangest feeling. As if you picked this up, almost before it really happened. How did you know?"

Remember, I am the one with preterm labor. You promised you would find it early and prevent preterm delivery of this child inside—who means more to me than anything else in this world.

It has happened more than once, during a routine prenatal counseling session regarding a test called an Expanded AFP, that I have felt overcome with the need to go into an elaborate explanation. I have found myself carried away with an unusually detailed and complete discussion regarding all of the precise ramifications of the test, as well as the procedures done when the test results come back abnormal. At the end of such a visit, I would wonder why I had done that—it is something that I do not usually do. The Expanded AFP is a test designed to pick up abnormalities in the development of the spine and neural system, as well as many of the chromosome anomalies. The women are given a booklet describing this test, and the majority of them are sophisticated and have obtained an easy grasp of its significance and ramifications. It is unusual to have to explain it directly to them, as it is something they already understand. I would then spend the rest of the day chastising myself on the recollection of this dialogue, as I was concerned that I might have caused the patient to worry unnecessarily. That is, until the tests returned with an abnormal result. Great care and consolation were then required to be given to these women who had been shaken off their very foundations.

Remember, we were the ones who were going to have this problem. You were to be our obstetrician.

I will never forget the few women whom I have cared for who bring their warning messages into the room with them at their first prenatal visit. The accompanying anxiety and fear compose a dense mantle and a shadowy presence that beg to be recognized. I was unaware of the significance of this disturbing element when I first entered practice—there was no frame of reference for it, except "physician uneasiness." I learned very quickly, though, that these women require careful follow-up and, sometimes, even more frequent visits. They bring with them the terror of the soul for what is yet to come. For it is these women who develop the serious illnesses—those "dark mysterious illnesses" of pregnancy that defy logic and understanding—that may end their life. One needs to watch carefully and maintain vigilance, for these illnesses need to be picked up in their earliest stages in order to avert the otherwise disastrous outcome. Having learned to interpret these messages, one never forgets them. When such a woman walks into the room, I am brought immediately to full and complete attention. I know the nature of my task. The rest of the pregnancy stretches before me like a long and treacherous detective game. When will the nature of the beast be revealed? I pray that I will be able to catch it in time.

Remember, you promised that you would take care of us. You promised that you would save our lives.

Then there are the patients who bring messages for *my* benefit, and the tables are turned. They have come to assist me.

During a series of presurgical consultations several years ago, I noticed that Estelle was reading a book with an interesting title—something about different personality types. Out of curiosity, I asked her how she liked it. Estelle replied that she liked it very much and that she thought I was an intuitive physician. How could I perform surgery, being such an obviously (in her estimation) intuitive individual?

I was taken completely by surprise. I had no idea what she was talking about. However, the weighty significance of her comment lay between us. She would not let go of the subject until she was sure that I had grasped my end of it. I found myself explaining that a doctor takes several years to learn surgery. It is something that is practiced over and over again until it is learned well. She was reassured by this, and needless to say her surgery went well. I did not forget her comments and ruminated on their puzzling nature for several months thereafter.

Two years later, I would take my first Myers-Briggs evaluation. I was overcome with the sense of profound relief that accompanies someone who is searching for something that they did not even know they needed: the ability to understand self. I tested out unequivocally in the category of an "intuitive feeler."

Estelle's comment finally made sense. Sensate persons, a Myers-Briggs category that can be said to be "opposite" that of intuitive persons, tend to assimilate precise details readily, and thus Estelle presumed this type of person would have the advantage in learning the technical and highly detailed art of performing surgery. The intuitive person might have the advantage in reaching the diagnosis, having the innate frame of reference and decision making that make learning the art of diagnosis easier. In reality both sensate and intuitive approaches are needed to make good physicians. The key is for each physician to understand clearly what his or her inherent inclinations are and to realize that the real work involves cultivating and expanding that type of thinking or skill that does not come as easily. This is just one of many reasons why medical education and training are lengthy, but it also explains why the practicing physician only improves over time—this type of learning is lifelong.

About the time when the changes brought on by managed care came to fruition, my intuition was bursting at the seams with ominous foreboding about all that would come to pass. I found myself in the midst of angst rooted in self-doubt and despair. In this state, at a routine annual checkup, a patient brought me a present.

"I thought that you might like this."

I thanked her for this unexpected surprise and opened the present. It was a book titled *The Celestine Prophecies*. I had heard nothing of this book. Like most physicians, I was unaware of the immense spirituality movement in this country. I was unaware of the popularity of this book.

"It is a best-seller. Enjoy."

A few weeks later, intrigued by the title, I jumped in. It was a cold, refreshing plunge. The book would serve as a wake-up call to my inner being—to my soul. *This is what you are missing—the spiritual dimension.* This book would be followed by many others, all devoured as hastily and urgently as a famished, malnourished child devours a plate of food set before her that is full of nourishment and sustenance beyond the wildest imagination.

Also in the midst of my managed-care-induced angst, Patty came into my practice. She was forty-one and expecting her first baby. She exuded such joy and wonder and unbridled happiness during her first and most longed for pregnancy. With her actions, she reminded me repeatedly to appreciate something that had all but been stomped out in the too busy, exclusively service-oriented medical care system that had evolved: a sense of joy that had been all but drowned out by the clamor, the rules, the distractions, the restrictions, and the daily grind. She reminded me of the value of time taken to appreciate the unfolding delight and awe of a woman's first pregnancy—a pregnancy that affects women so profoundly that it is the one they will always remember with the greatest clarity and the fondest of memories.

I have been the recipient of other surprises, as well. An elderly patient has made it a habit to always bring me a special present every year at the time of her annual exam. Last year, while I was in the throes of deep, dark despair and was seriously considering quitting the business altogether, she brought me a book about the art of Italy—a delightful picture book—full of images that I could lose myself in. This was followed a few months later by a patient who gave me several passes to our local art museum.

"I thought that you might like these."

Both of these women came to remind me that what I value most about medicine—the art—was slipping away.

Finally, all through the last year, many patients came in with these messages:

"You are unlike any other physician I have ever met. You are very different."

"It has taken me twenty years to find a doctor like you. I thank God that I have found you. Promise that you will not retire on me."

"I know now why I selected your name out of my provider directory. You are just the perfect physician for me. You do not know how grateful I am for having met you. Thank you so very much."

The following dialogue occurred last week:

I entered the room and introduced myself to someone for the very first time. She startled, with a sense of recognition all over her face.

"You look so familiar. Surely, we must have met before! Don't I know you from somewhere?"

After a comprehensive review of geographical, social, volunteer-related, and school- and children-related activities, we were certain that we had not met previously. The interview and examination were completed, and she concluded, with an extremely puzzled look on her face, "Gosh. I feel like I know you."

No, it is not random. It is not sterile. It is full, rich, and embodied. I only have to remember this and it gives me the strength to keep going. To practice medicine in such a manner is to give testimony to the mystery of life itself.

"Wherever the art of medicine is loved, there also is love of humanity."

— Hippocrates (460?–377? B.C.)
Precepts, VI

The Art of Medicine

It is Saturday morning. I am working in the hospital—making it all happen. I have been paged to the Emergency Room. I am making my way there via my favorite staircase. It is nice and quiet. It is little used, and it is rare to ever meet a soul on the way down. I like it that way—especially on the way to the ER. For I never know what to expect. It helps to clear my head with solitude and meditation as I prepare to meet the unknown. It functions much like a labyrinth, this staircase, with its repetitive step, step, step, landing, turn, step, step, step, landing, turn, all the way down. I enter at the periphery—the top floor—and by degrees methodically make my way toward the center. By the time I have reached the bottom, my mind is still and quiet as I emerge from the stairwell into the bright lights and hustle-and-bustle chaos of the ER.

I say good morning to the charge nurse as she looks up in weary confusion, momentarily off-stride as she takes a moment to recognize me.

I ask about the person I need to see. I learn that she arrived in the middle of the night. She has been here several hours already.

"Where is her chart?" It is not in a file. The charge nurse doesn't know and brushes this aside with the same gesture with which she tucks back an escaping lock of hair.

"It was here a minute ago. I'll look for it. She is in room four."

Several years ago, seeing a patient without first reviewing chart data (sensate details) would have been unsettling. This is because most physicians are taught to interpret information and reach decisions primarily by using data—lab reports, diagnostic imaging results, and so on. There is a sense of security about matter-of-factly typed, indifferent reports. It is OK to learn this way, but the beauty of medicine lies in the intangibles. Therein lies the secret to the art of medicine.

With crisp authority, my heels click on the tile floor as I near Anne's room. I am certain that she can hear me coming.

She knows that this tread is new. I am not the nurse, not the orderly, not the ER doctor who has already evaluated her and then called me.

Knowing this, I stop and knock gently on the door, announcing myself by voice before I step around the curtain that has prevented her from viewing my approach.

"How are you doing?" I smile with reassurance as I greet her. Then I am open to full and complete perception, as the intuitive processing channels are now wide open.

"Not too well. But I am better now." She replies with nervousness and uneasiness—appropriate for someone who has come to the ER in pain and has been waiting for several hours for the right person to figure it out.

That someone is me, I explain, and I ask her simply, very simply, to tell me why she came. What brought her here at 2:00 a.m.? How is she now? Compared to then, how does she feel? How is the pain . . . now?

All the while that she is speaking, I do not take my eyes off her face or let my attention stray. I am oblivious to the noise and clanks and cries of the hallway. I am a tracking beam searching unerringly for the elusive clue—that one or two bits of information—sometimes given offhandedly, almost accidentally, by the patient, *the* clue that will tell me what I need to know and how I need to act.

For all the exterior calmness, honed by years of experience, I know that this is serious stuff—potentially, deadly serious. I cannot err. The stakes are too high. This accounts for the intensity of the gaze. I cannot make a mistake. As a physician, this is one of the earliest lessons.

I listen, assimilate, ask, and gaze. She has had recent irregular menses, vague symptoms of pregnancy, and then the sudden, sharp abdominal pain that precipitated the nighttime rush to the ER.

Three things could be wrong. She could have an ectopic pregnancy (a pregnancy in the wrong place—outside of the uterus and a life-threatening situation). She could have an early pregnancy with a ruptured ovarian cyst. Or she could have had a complete miscarriage.

There is an easy way out of my diagnostic dilemma. That would be to perform surgery—to have the security of looking and evaluating with my own eyes. The surgery would be a diagnostic laparoscopy—a look-and-see type of operation. Some physicians would have done this. The question would have been settled quickly and easily. These physicians rely heavily on sensate details, and surgery is the ultimate in sensate, that is, look-and-feel, details.

I am not one of this type of doctor. Surgery, even so-called routine surgery, is not without risk. So it should be done only if I think that she really has an ectopic pregnancy (thus mandating surgical treatment), *not* to prove to me that she does not. I should be able to discern without surgery whether or not she has an ectopic pregnancy.

I will hang my hat on the art of medicine. This is nothing other than finely honed and practiced intuitive thinking and feeling. Sensate details are helpful, such as a CBC (complete blood count), vital signs, and ultrasound results, but to the practitioner of the art they confirm the diagnosis, they do not render it.

I listen for quite some time. I perceive it all and I leave the room. I relax substantially. She has told me her entire story. In between the lines, in between what she has actually said, lies this truth: She does not have an ectopic pregnancy. She looks and feels "too good." She has no demonstrable sense of foreboding. She is manifesting no evidence of impending doom.

No, this is a body that is on the mend. Yes, something dramatic did happen at 2:00 a.m.—something very scary, to be sure. But that something is subsiding, receding. The body is repairing this mishap as we speak. I discerned all of this while she spoke. It was in the tone and inflection of her voice, and I was allowed a privileged glimpse through the window of her eyes into her soul.

She will be all right. I am relieved. I exhale and loosen the knot in my shoulder as I make my way to the nurses' station. Someone has located the chart.

Sensate data galore await my perusal. She has a normal hematocrit—no sign of internal bleeding. Her vital signs are stable. Both reassure and confirm my assessment.

I am then surprised by the ultrasound report: *a large amount of free fluid in the pelvis!* Now come intense concentration and rethinking of the entire scenario—*again!* For this is either one of two things—fluid from a leaking cyst or internal bleeding.

I pause to integrate this surprising sensate data into the existing intuitive framework. Where does this piece of the puzzle belong? I weigh the balance. Ruptured cyst fluid versus internal bleeding. Was I wrong about the possibility of an ectopic pregnancy? If so, she would need surgery as soon as possible.

I walk slowly back to her room. I speak softly with her as I discuss these results and bring her up to date. All the while, I am listening to and focused on something else. Something beyond her.

No. She looks "too good." I will not operate. This has to be fluid from a cyst. I will admit her, instead, for a short-stay period of observation. I will check up on her at intervals during the day. I will ask her how she is doing. I will wait very patiently and will be paying exquisite attention to her answers. She will tell me all I need to know.

Anne was gratefully sent home the following morning. The discharge diagnosis: complete miscarriage with a presumed ruptured ovarian cyst. Clinical condition: markedly improved.

The Soul as Night Watchwoman

I believe that I have a soul residing within this body of mine. This is hardly an earth-shattering statement. Being an avid reader, I have seen the evidence of a renewed interest in spirituality in this country. I have seen this by simply glancing at a newsstand, browsing in a bookstore, and listening to friends and acquaintances. I have not always been so sure of this. Belief in the concept that we are all souls living in these bodies of ours has come only recently to me. As I reflect upon my rigorous, intense, and lengthy science-based education, I realize that a blockade had been erected, in effect obliterating any worthy thought or discussion regarding one's soul—or anyone else's for that matter. One could not prove it. Therefore it did not exist. End of discussion. It has been only recently that I have dismantled this blockade. Now I see why the education I received in medical school and residency felt so incomplete. What was missing?

The soul. There was much to learn regarding the body, with its complicated array of organ systems, much to learn about physiology and pathophysiology, and much to learn about treating and preventing disease. I also had to learn how to act like a doctor, think like a doctor, and look like a doctor. (I was not born knowing this.) So much to learn in eight years. Yet it remained unsatisfactory and vaguely unsettling. The picture was not complete. Someone forgot to teach us the importance of considering that the body has a soul. I do not know many physicians who practice medicine with this in mind. As far as I am concerned, however, belief in this concept of the soul adds a much needed breath of fresh air to the practice of medicine.

I believe that my patients have souls. I am assuming that the soul has been in the body since birth, at the very least. I can imagine the soul making daily rounds throughout the body—checking each organ system; analyzing the muscles, bones, and joints; checking the blood flow, the pulse rate, and all of those wonderful autonomic and vital systems that we take for granted. It makes sense to me, then, that the soul would be the first to know when something is wrong. It would then see to it that the body presents itself to the doctor. If the physician can be viewed as possessing a highly trained "listening" soul, we have established the ideal physician-patient interaction: one soul telling a story about the problem in the body, the second soul listening and believing. When this happens, the patient experiences great relief, and the problem can be identified and attended to. I know that the dialogue has been complete and satisfactory when I hear the following:

"Thank you for listening to me. I feel so much better now."

"I feel as though I really connected with you today, Doctor."

I do not believe that it was only my particular array of organ systems, red blood cells, bone marrow, integument, and cerebral cortex that "listened" and "connected" with them. No, it was my soul. It listened and paid attention. I can recall three instances of lifesaving behavior carried out by the soul.

The first concerns Irene. A few years ago, she came to me for a second opinion. She had found a lump in her breast. She felt that it did not "belong there." She had been seen recently by another gynecologist and had been evaluated with an exam and a mammogram and been told that everything was fine. This assessment left Irene feeling uneasy and dissatisfied (the night watchwoman on rounds not backing down). Everything was not fine. She then came to see me. I listened to her. It was a lengthy interview, for she had a great deal to tell me. I believed her story (my soul respecting hers). A definite abnormality was not found on examination. I found only a vague area of somewhat increased density.

Nonetheless, we proceeded with the workup. She obtained a repeat mammogram. The results remained within normal limits. I sent her to a general surgeon for a second opinion. The surgeon listened to Irene and believed her. She performed a biopsy of the "vague area in question" and established the diagnosis of early breast cancer. Her treatment consisted of a mastectomy, and her life was saved. Due to the early stage of the cancer, Irene did not require radiation or chemotherapy.

To this day, Irene and her family thank me for saving her life. I do not deserve sole credit for this. I must share it with her soul—who precipitated the visit to the doctor, would not settle for no, and insisted on obtaining the second opinion. My soul takes credit only for listening.

A second story also revolves around breast cancer. As in the first case, Frances was new to my practice. At the outset, she was in the office ostensibly for a routine peri-menopausal checkup. Things were going fine. No acute problems were identified. It was a relatively uneventful interview—that is, until she mentioned her recent concern about a vague "difference" in her left breast. Physical examination was within normal limits. I could not find any abnormality. However, to address her concern adequately, I advised that she obtain a mammogram. She complied. The mammogram demonstrated findings in that location that were suspicious for breast cancer. This was confirmed by biopsy. Frances underwent a mastectomy for early breast cancer. Again, she did not require radiation or chemotherapy.

These two stories are examples of what occurs when the physician actually listens to the patient with all of his or her heart and soul and believes what is said. It also demonstrates what a good guardian or night watchwoman the soul can be if allowed to play this role. The third example illustrates what happens when this is not the case.

My good friend Colleen is a typical Silicon Valley businesswoman (i.e., highly intelligent, verbally proficient, and well educated). She awakened one day not feeling very well. While she had had a cough for a few days, as well as the occasional mild temperature, this day things were much worse. The cough felt as though it were coming from much "deeper" in her chest. She was experiencing difficulty with breathing and was particularly concerned with the development of left-sided chest pain. It actually hurt to take a breath. She felt an "urgent" need to get to the doctor. (The soul's message: Hurry!) She went that day and was seen by her primary care physician. After listening to her story, he informed her that this was just a bad cold and that she was suffering from a little anxiety. He expected that her problem would get better in a few days without any additional treatment. Diagnostic studies were not deemed to be necessary. Colleen received this assessment in a state of disbelief. This was followed by anger. Why didn't he believe her? she wanted to know. She tried to convince him that her symptoms were real and were causing great concern, but to no avail. She then left the office angry, frustrated (the soul above all else wants respect), and worried. Her next visit was to her allergist, because she knew that she needed medical attention. (The soul is persistent.) Fortunately, the allergist listened to her story, ordered the appropriate diagnostic tests, and informed Colleen that she had walking pneumonia. With appropriate care and after several weeks of convalescence, Colleen enjoyed a full and complete recovery.

These stories are just examples that illustrate the power of a simple belief: There is a soul in the patient's body, and it is capable of telling the physician what is wrong. The physician and his or her soul just need to listen . . . and believe.

Trick or Treat? The Soul Within the Child and the Postoperative Response

It was one year ago that my son Stephen underwent a relatively minor and apparently uneventful outpatient surgery. There were no complications and no unexpected medical findings. It was such a routine procedure that it qualified to receive the narration that physicians most like to relay to those anxious parents in the waiting room: "All went extremely well. There were no problems."

I was a grateful recipient of this sentiment. My thoughts concurred with the surgeon's regarding the ordinary quality of the event. That is, until I witnessed Stephen's behavior in the recovery room. It was almost indescribable, and I required several hours to digest and synthesize it into a frame of reference that I could understand. As it turned out, I was required to widen my perspective and acknowledge that something significant and underappreciated was at work that day. Something that prior to that day I had never considered. It was such a profound insight that I have not felt the same about persons in the recovery room since, particularly children.

The nature of my son's surgery was simple. An extra, undesired tooth was discovered between the two front teeth. The recommendation was for removal. Due to its location, outpatient surgery was scheduled. It was such a simple and straightforward procedure that I knew upon leaving the consultation room that all would go well. I need not worry.

On the night before surgery, I talked to Stephen about his tooth. He had an extra one, I said. The doctor would remove it and give it to the tooth fairy. She would be so grateful upon receiving it that a present would be waiting for him under his pillow upon his return. At the age of five, his understanding was incomplete. I thought at the time that this would be a blessing. I would later have this assumption proved wrong.

The anesthesiologist called later that evening, as is customary. We discussed the usual particulars and I was ready to end the conversation when she surprised me with her ending comments.

"I feel that it is very important to warn you of something that I have observed repeatedly over the years. It is normal for children to awaken from anesthesia crying, agitated, belligerent, or angry. Usually, once they are sitting in Mommy's lap they calm down. Sometimes their reaction can be quite intense. I feel that you should know this so that you can be adequately prepared."

I thanked her for the advice and was then left to mull over the conversation. I found it curious that she felt the need to warn me—a seasoned veteran of the operating room. I have witnessed dramatic scenes in that theater. I have had to participate in life-or-death surgery on the labor-and-delivery suite. At this point in my career, I felt that there was little with regard to emotional outlay that I was unprepared to manage. If my son was angry, I would be able to handle it. I had seen some whopper temper tantrums. This was my frame of reference. It could not be as worrisome as the anesthesiologist suggested. I then did not think about it again.

We awakened bright and early for the morning surgery and arrived at the surgery center. Stephen was admitted. I knew the staff well, and they treated my son as if he were their child as well. They could not have been kinder. He enjoyed loving care and attention. In the moments just before the surgery, he was given a yummy sweet-tasting drink that soon caused him to giggle and laugh. I noticed soon after a glazed appearance to his eyes. As he sat there in the gurney hugging his two teddy bears, I was reminded of how small and vulnerable he was. I held back my tears as I gave him a kiss and watched as they wheeled him away to the operating room. Only my supreme confidence in the surgeon and the anesthesiologist allowed me to sit still in the waiting room, awaiting their return, anticipating those longed-for words of reassurance.

I did not have to wait long. "Everything went fine. Here is the tooth!" The surgeon entered the room with the energy, enthusiasm, and confidence that accompanies doctors when a procedure goes well and according to their own preconceived expectations.

I was relieved and expressed a sigh of relief as he, without further ceremony, handed me the little plastic container that held the errant tooth. He was gone after a moment, leaving to prepare for his next case without any further discussion or explanation. I did not need any. He had already told me what I needed to hear. I only had to await the anesthesiologist, who would give me permission to enter the recovery room. She came and repeated these reassuring words.

"All went well. There were no complications. Your son is in the recovery room. He is awake. I feel that I must warn you again that he is behaving like most other children in this circumstance. He is very angry. I want you to be prepared to see it."

I left my comfortable seat in the hushed, subdued atmosphere of the waiting room and opened the door leading to the narrow hallway that led to the recovery room. As soon as I opened the door I could hear him. Screaming.

I was assaulted by the scene before my eyes. I could sense the deep disturbance emanating from within my son, and I witnessed his desperate actions. Blood was splattered across his cheek. His urgent and compelling need to investigate the sutures and the pain in his mouth had caused it. He was trying most certainly to remove these offending agents with the repetitive movement of his finger going inside his mouth and trying most determinedly to extract them. The nurse had her hands full trying to prevent him from accomplishing his aim. He saw me, began to cry, and reached out to me.

"Take it out! Take it out! Take it out!" He screamed at the top of his voice, pointing to the IV access that had been placed in his foot. As I now held my fifty-pound son in my arms, I could sense his desperation.

He was writhing in my arms, fighting off the sedatives with a force of will that I found almost incomprehensible. It was all I could do to restrain his desire to remove the stitches from his mouth and distract his hand from its goal of personally removing the IV from its offensive site. As he lay writhing in my arms, he was insistent. Why didn't I listen to him? He repeated, screaming at the top of his lungs: "Take it out, take it out, TAKE IT OUT!"

This was *not* mere anger. That was a pitiful understatement. No, I was assaulted here by emotions that were more a cross between fury and blind panic. Powerful and unrelenting. I was caught in this passionate outpouring of grievous feelings that no amount of maternal love and consolation could counter.

His speech was beginning to slur, and it acquired a garbled tone due to the built-up secretions in his throat. He continued in his repetitive activities of checking his mouth, then returning to the IV site. Even while fighting against the influence of the strong sedatives, he was able to clearly express his desire for removal of the IV and his profound unhappiness at finding those strange "fishing wires" in his mouth. I wondered how much longer his body could sustain such an unrestricted and unfiltered outlay of emotional energy and determination. The nurses came to offer their words of consolation: "They all act like this in the recovery room. It will pass. Try not to worry."

I was running out of energy trying to manage this. I was so grateful when the anesthesiologist granted permission for removal of the IV. The deed was done. Stephen fastidiously inspected the two-millimeter pink circle on his skin—the only visual reminder of the memory of that most offensive site. An attempt was made to apply a pretty bandage, but this was refused. Stephen did not want it covered up. He wanted to keep looking at it—maintaining a state of watchful vigilance, I suppose, lest the offensive object return. It was only at this point that he at last collapsed into a fitful sleep that lasted all of about thirty minutes. He awakened from his sleep and repeated his all-too-familiar ritual. He checked his mouth and woefully verified that the sutures were still present. He then carefully inspected the small pink circle on his foot. At least no additional injuries or unwelcome surprises had been discovered. He fell asleep again. This time he relaxed far more comfortably and awakened at last having slept off most of the effects of the anesthetic agents. He began to look more like his old self again.

"Let's go home, Mommy." His quiet little determined voice spoke to me. I could not have agreed more.

With the approval of the anesthesiologist, we were allowed to change him into his familiar clothes and prepare to be escorted to our car. He was offered a cute little "I was a Brave Boy" sticker. He refused it. Far too much had gone on that day, of such a grievous nature, for a little sticker to erase. As we were leaving, I was brought up short by the anguished cries of another youngster just entering the recovery room. I witnessed the overwhelming concern on his mother's face as she hurried toward his side. I could see the nurses sighing, then mentally preparing to deal with the anguish, the fury, the panic. I had acquired a newfound respect for their profession. We were happy to be leaving.

Stephen was subdued on the ride home. He did not want to talk about what had occurred. We arrived home, and I could see that, though very tired, he was happy to be back in familiar surroundings. He was quickly on his way to forgetting the entire episode. I was fixated on the entire sequence of events. Such profound, powerful emotions emanating from a five-year-old boy! Emotions that far exceeded the capacity of his mere body and mind to produce. Not only to produce but to sustain far beyond what would have been expected given the endurance and stamina of a mere five-year-old child. An outlay that clearly taxed him dearly as he lay sleeping beside me on the couch—at last in a peaceful slumber, at home safe and sound. What could be the source of such an overwhelming display? Of course . . . *the soul within.*

I then ruminated on the possibility of viewing this episode from the perspective of the soul residing within my son's body. Confined by the limited reasoning capacity as referenced to the cognitive development of a five-year-old child, I could imagine that the preoperative discussion would have given no cause for concern. Since the child primarily senses the environment, the feeling tone exhibited by the parent would have been most important. As his parent was very comfortable with the entirety of the arrangements, confidence would have been relayed to the child. There would be nothing to worry about on this new and different adventure.

Upon arrival at the surgery center, the soul would have been enchanted with the smiles and encouragement relayed by the staff, particularly since there was an evident familiarity with the parent. The addition of the teddy bears was delightful. This was followed by that yummy treat of a sweet substance that soon made the soul and body feel such happiness and erased any traces of concern and doubt. At this point, the experience would have had all the appearances of an extremely pleasant field trip to the surgery center. Then off to the operating room accompanied by additional nice, well-meaning adults. Then it was nap time.

All went very well until awakening. With the achievement of consciousness and thus the reactivation of the soul, the mind and soul would have been alerted to the searing pain present in the palate. What was this!? And that funny gauze pack in the mouth that was not there at the last awareness. What was it doing there? It most certainly did not belong! As increasing cognitive functioning was returning, increasing anxiety, anger, and concern would mount. What had happened here!? What had happened to the body? In this place, with such nice grownups? Why the searing pain? Why the gauze in the mouth? The internal scream of agony and betrayal would be emitted. What a most grievous trick!

Increasingly, the soul would mount its furious response and exhibit the symptoms associated with blind panic, as it now would be compelled to race around the body checking the inventory. What else of an offensive nature had happened to the body? And then it was found. That plastic tubing lodged in the foot! What was it, and who put it there? It became the visual fixation point for the soul in its determination to try to make sense of all that had occurred. It became the site to which to direct all its intentions. Most particularly its desire to set things right again. It would not let the mind or body rest until the offensive sight was removed. The fury of the soul had been released unchecked and unfiltered and remained focused on the one element in all of this that could conceivably be addressed and rectified.

Its wishes were eventually honored. Only then would it mercifully allow the child to rest. Only after the soul had been satisfied. Then there would have been repeated checks. Was there nothing else that had been done to this body? No other gross violations? Satisfied with the passage of time that no other insults were occurring, the soul relented and retreated back inside the body. It slowly relaxed its protective guard and tentatively began to trust that perhaps the worst was over. At this point the mind and body were allowed to rest completely. The soul had been reassured.

What was the precise nature of the trigger that unleashed such a torrential outburst from the soul?

I can imagine that the soul in my son's body had been very busy. Among other activities, I believe that it was involved in making "practice rounds" throughout the body, learning to check on this organ system, monitoring the function of another, and so on. This would have been done in preparation for assumption of its role as the night watchman, a role that would play increasing importance as the body aged and matured. These "practice rounds" would have been taken very seriously.

Somehow, some way, while the soul was asleep "on the watch," someone had inexplicably slipped through the gates.

Art . . . and Finesse

Listening and paying attention to patients and to what they say almost make differential diagnosis appear like child's play. That is, once one develops the talent, patients virtually tell the physician what is wrong.

The finesse comes in when patients do not even realize that they are doing it. I surmise that this is because they subconsciously suspect the serious nature of the underlying problem and are in denial. Perhaps this is because the consequences of admitting it and facing treatment seem overwhelming or undesirable.

The task of the physician in this circumstance is to listen to what is being said, identify the problem, and present the conclusion in such a way as to gently remove the veil of denial and in its place insert the hope that the treatment will correct the problem. Such was the case today when I examined Kate, who had undergone a cesarean section one week ago.

She called the office to make an appointment, because she had been bothered by a temperature over the weekend. She just "did not feel well." The temperature was not severe, and she did not have shaking chills or any overt signs of infection. Her presenting complaints were subtle.

My first interest was in learning her present temperature: 99.6 degrees Fahrenheit. Mildly elevated. Not too unusual. The next step involved obtaining an overall impression: How does she look? She actually looked OK. Definitely not in acute distress.

On the surface of this calm, deceptive lake, nothing apparently was wrong. Nothing reaching out to me, no obvious clues. They were sequestered. My task was to start the detective mission. Thus begins a physician's version of twenty questions.

"How do you feel?"

"Oh . . . so-so."

"Do you have a sore throat?"

"No."

"Do you have a cough or difficulty breathing?"

"No."

"Do you have any pain with voiding?"

"No."

"Any abdominal pain?"

"Not really."

"Incisional pain or redness?"

"No."

"Is there anything at all that you can tell me that feels unusual with respect to this recovery compared to your previous cesarean section and that recovery?"

"Nothing definite."

I am having to work extra hard today. The soul has brought the body in for inspection, but the mind is engaged in subterfuge. The clues remain tightly hidden away. Like a child who holds fast to the security that a favorite teddy bear brings.

"Something made you come in today. What was the reason?"

"I had a temperature over the weekend. I knew that this was not normal."

"I see. Well, I suspect you realize that it is necessary to perform a complete physical exam as well as a pelvic exam."

She grimaced, and I could read her fully displayed reluctance.

"Are you afraid to have a pelvic exam?" *(Here is the first glimpse through the well-fortified veil of denial. Acting on the hunch that I had actually located the source of the problem, I was curious as to why she would not want to acknowledge this.)*

Hesitation . . . "No. It's just that I think that it will be painful."

The quest is in reach. "So, you have been bothered with uterine pain? Perhaps some unusual cramps?"

"Maybe." There it is. The reluctant admission. The mind gives way in face of the imperative soul.

I then performed the physical exam, during which I found irrefutable evidence of a pelvic infection. I gently explained this to Kate and discussed that it would require readmission to the hospital and IV antibiotic treatment. It was then that she began to cry.

The motives of the mind crystallize before me. She does not want to be readmitted to the hospital and probably suspected this all along. No mother with a seven-day-old baby wants to go back to the hospital. It is the last place on earth that she wants to be.

With soft, soothing tones I explained that the infection was in its early stages and definitely treatable. I anticipated that a full and complete recovery would be hers in a few days' time. Furthermore, arrangements would be made so that the baby would be able to stay with her in the hospital. Thus, breast-feeding would not be interrupted. It would only be a short stay, I promised. Then all would be better. This was helpful to her, and she was grateful.

I then had to explain all of this to her waiting husband, who had his hands full with a four-year-old nearing the completion of the most topsy-turvy week of her young life and a newborn who was hungry. The news did not engender any happy feelings on his part. After having just settled everyone in the household down again after mother's three-day absence the previous week, it appeared as though all was thrown up into the air again. Intellectually, of course, he could appreciate the reasons given and the value of this admission, but a husband after such an unsettled week is not in a premier state for intellectual reasoning. The deeper, primitive emotions rule during such a time as this.

The four-year-old let loose with her absolutely honest assessment—not having the accumulated aging experience that teaches grown-ups to repress their truest feelings.

"No, Mommy. No! Do not go back to the hospital! Please." She wailed as she wrapped herself around her mother's legs, as if by her sheer will she could prevent such a thing.

I was surrounded by this family scene. A mother knowing that she was not well and suspecting that she needed treatment. A weary mother who found herself torn between treating herself adequately, satisfying the demands of a newborn, and trying to settle down a distraught four-year-old who, having just become accustomed to the new order, did not want any additional rearranging. And the kind, caring husband who, in his state of fatigue, was trying to make it all work out.

Little wonder, then, that Kate did not really want to acknowledge the serious nature of her problem. To be taken away from home at this most vulnerable and sensitive time was something any mother would avoid. Perhaps at any cost.

With this realization came double the effort at reassuring all of them—all four affected so adversely by this readmission.

To the husband: "She will become well. She will be back at home soon."

To the four-year-old: "You will be your mommy's helper in the hospital. You may stay all day long if you like."

To Kate with baby in arms: "You knew that there was something wrong. That is why you called. We have found the problem, and because we have caught it so early you will recover very quickly. You will be back at home before you know it. *Everything will be all right.*"

Art and Divinity on Labor and Delivery

It seems that virtually every hospital with a labor-and-delivery suite is advertising in this valley. The ads attempt to convince women that their particular unit is the best, the kindest, and the friendliest, with state-of-the-art equipment thrown in to boot.

Why spend all this money? This is done to attract women in order that they will give birth at these hospitals. There is money to be made in obstetrics. It has always been a money-maker for hospitals. It still is, but perhaps somewhat less so under managed care. In order to make up for decreased revenue, volume must increase. Hence the advertising campaigns.

Though a certain amount of business acumen is needed in this competitive managed care environment, it seems as though it has gone too far. What occurs on the labor-and-delivery suite is a manifestation of the powerful mystery of one human being giving birth to another, a culmination of life-giving events set in place nine months earlier. It is far from ordinary commerce.

While many hospitals give lip service to the idea that they understand this, their actions do not match their words. In opposition to the streamlined, busy, profit-oriented labor-and-delivery unit, I present another view for consideration—a view that encompasses what I perceive occurs. What occurs on the unit is not commerce. It is powerful. It is mysterious. It is a dance between Art and Divinity.

Art . . . and Fear

Art on the labor and delivery unit involves direct patient contact. Eye-to-eye contact, to be precise. Preferably by experienced eyes. More than one set is always appreciated and sometimes absolutely critical.

As I look into a patient's eyes, I often see pain, and I often see anxiety. This is expected and easily dealt with. What I am really looking for is fear. There are two types.

The most common type of fear is that associated with the dawning realization that the patient is involved in a process that she cannot control. She senses the powerful, unstoppable force entering her body. It is a frightening moment when she realizes that she cannot modify, prevent, or direct this force. It is all the more disturbing when she is not even prepared for it. This fear can be abated by careful, calm reassurance, by comforting words and reassuring physical presence. It passes once the patient gives in and relinquishes all feeble attempts at control.

The other type of fear is a horse of a completely different color. It is the fear of the unspeakable. Having seen this rarity, it is seared onto the memory banks as though branded there. It is never possible to forget it.

I ask the patient in labor in a careful, casual tone, "So, how are things going?" What I am really asking is "How are things going to be?" *The soul knows.*

If I ever see the look that accompanies primordial fear, I do not leave. I remain on the unit because extreme vigilance is required. Sometime soon I will be called upon to save the life of the mother or the baby or both.

The Guardian Angel

Our labor-and-delivery unit has a friend. A very dear friend. She arrived on the scene several months ago. The recollection of the precise moment of her arrival has been dimmed, having been overshadowed by the gratitude that accompanied it.

She came of her own accord—as the story goes. I have yet to meet her in person, but I have heard plenty about her. I am aware of her presence.

She brings many gifts. She has purchased artwork to adorn the hallways of the unit. Usually this is seasonal, and it has varied—such as the Christmas and Easter decorations that were placed. She has brought food for the nurses to eat in their break room during those hurried moments that pretend to be lunch. On Mother's Day, she brought three dozen small gifts of stationery to be given out to those giving birth, as well as to the nurses who were working.

She brings many gifts. The most important of all are her compassion, kindness, and consideration—things that the nurses give out in abundance throughout their long, tiring shifts but that they themselves have not received from their superiors in a long time.

This friend arrives like a breath of spring air, carrying hope, carrying love, bringing comfort. Her visits are eagerly anticipated, gratefully appreciated, and followed by the longing for the next one.

The nurses hold only the fondest feelings for this woman. She is their guardian angel.

Divinity

Divinity is present on the labor-and-delivery suite. She comes in many forms. She is chameleon-like and unpredictable and does not welcome any intent of control. She is to be respected above all else. She is to be revered as the directress of all that occurs.

She is present at all births. Her presence throughout the entire labor experience is apparent, though usually subtle in the beginning.

Upon entering the labor room, I inquire about the presence of the Divine. She is present. I am aware of this, but she is not visible. I walk into the labor room with my moistened finger held up to test the wind. Which direction is it blowing? It is an inquiry about the feel, the mood, of the labor process. It is an attempt to obtain some clue about what may yet transpire. Is there an underlying pulse of discord? Is there a reassuring calm, soothing balm being applied to the patient? Sometimes she is just barely present, having withdrawn herself from immediate engagement, withdrawn from the query, having decided not to reveal any clues too soon. She can be repressive.

Many times I feel that Divinity has come to engage the patient in early labor. She has come to test her mettle. She observes from a distance, I think, especially the first-time mothers. They do not know the force or strength of her power. They do not know yet what they are in for.

She starts off with subtlety, this testing in early labor. The gradual onset of increasingly powerful contractions gives the barest outline of what is to come. Women realize, at this point, that something is going on in their body. Some other essence is tapping firmly on their shoulder, inquiring gently but succinctly, *"Are you ready? I am with you."*

As the intensity, force, and strength of the contractions increase, the women quickly realize that they are involved in a process beyond their true comprehension. Beyond comparison to any prior event in their lives. As they are caught up in the eddying currents, they can sense that the journey down the roiling rapids awaits. It cannot be postponed, delayed, or denied. Divinity is gathering the current. She is beckoning and alternately commanding, *"Come, it is your turn. You must come . . . now!"*

At some point, while waiting in the eddying and pooling foam, women can be divided into three categories.

There are those who acquiesce and enter easily, confident that they will survive and all will go well.

Then there are those who are afraid to enter, afraid to give up control, afraid of the power, afraid of the swift current, who eventually enter. In the process they learn to face and conquer their greatest fear.

The third group is terrified of entering, carrying the knowledge in their subconscious, the fear that some of the sharp, pointed rocks and imprisoning sandbars are waiting for them. It is their fate that awaits, and in their terror they resist. These women should take solace in the fact that, while they cannot escape their fate, because it is now the beginning of the twenty-first century they will emerge relatively unscathed.

Those who acquiesce quickly are pulled into the powerful current and find themselves pushed and pulled and almost torn apart by the time they have completed this experience. But Divinity is with them always. They are aware of this on a peripheral level. They are comforted by this knowledge.

The very end of the journey is the most climactic and most unbelievable. Mercifully, it is at this stage that the women realize it is within their power to finish this. It is also in their own best interest to do so. They engage in the pushing effort as if their whole life depended upon it—which in times past it did. They long for completion and release. They want the security of the knowledge that they have survived this journey. A dim memory that eludes precise definition surfaces at this point, reminding them that, in times past, no such assurance was ever given.

Caught up in the maelstrom just prior to delivery, they are oblivious to everyone else in the room. Vision is dimmed. Focus is missing. All effort is concentrated internally, all effort primordial. They are in another time and space. They are with the Divine. They are not really in the room.

Then the moment of birth occurs—an excruciating moment, a moment full of apprehension and unbelievable pain. After being fully convinced that their pelvic girdle is being split in two, they feel the bliss of release, followed by relief, accompanied by the cry of the newborn babe. The overpowering awareness hits that this is their baby, that it came out of their body.

It is real. It is alive. They are alive. Tears stream down their face.

The entire event essentially is composed of the necessary ingredients for a miraculous human experience, marked by an overabundance of blood, sweat, and tears. Divinity is present.

Mercy

I was awakened from a deep sleep by a jarring telephone call. The shrill ring echoed in the pitch-black darkness of the call room at the hospital. The telephone call was a complete surprise, as my patient had been doing very well the last time that I checked.

"You are needed in room three immediately! We are having trouble finding the fetal heartbeat!" *The baby is in distress!*

Many thoughts crossed my mind as I hurriedly laced my shoes and brushed the fog from my brain. What was going on? I was fully awake by the time I entered the room. I was grateful for the many years of training that had fine-tuned the switching mechanism in my brain that can take it from zero to sixty in a space of a few dozen seconds.

Once in the room, however, sixty was not fast enough. The initial collection of information took no longer than one minute. The fetal heart rate was low. The mother was exhibiting signs of the most heinous of obstetrical emergencies—a placental abruption. (This is a nasty accident of Mother Nature in which the placenta separates from its attachment to the uterine wall before the baby is born—something that is not supposed to happen. It is a critical problem, because the baby initially is deprived of oxygen and nutrients and, in severe cases, will be deprived of life-sustaining blood.)

I had walked right into an extremely advanced case of this—something that I had not witnessed in a long time. The baby and the mother's life were at stake. Each low, labored beat of the baby's heart was audible on the monitor. It was an agonizing sound, a sound of distress, an SOS signal: *going down for the last time.*

Immediate surgery was required—immediate being now. I am moving way beyond sixty. I am off the speedometer rating. My brain is racing because I have only a few minutes left before it will be too late.

I bark orders at the nurses. "Let's get going to the operating room! Assemble the team!" I rush out to place a call for a surgical assistant, and after the briefest of curt conversations I am back in the room. I realize that I cannot wait for the assistant. I cannot wait for anybody.

Back in the room, it is suddenly and painfully clear that the nurses do not seem to recognize the absolute emergency of this situation. *They are moving too slowly!*

"Look!" I implore them. "We have to work fast! Let's go!"

It's then that I recognize from the looks of inexperience and confusion on their young faces that they do not know exactly what it is they need to do. Due to their inexperience, they have never seen this before.

I am the conductor of an orchestra that does not know its parts. Some do not even know what instruments to play.

I then begin frantically to hand out the parts, imploring them to play. I have to play the first few bars for some of them before they catch on. Some have to have their instrument thrust into their hesitant arms. Some, mercifully, catch on right away.

It is a chaotic, frenzied, symphonic rush to the operating room.

Eventually, the orchestra is tuned up and the last essential player arrives—the anesthesiologist. He is the second physician called from a dead sleep in order to save someone's life. This is one of anesthesiologists' most challenging moments—to be required to put a fully conscious, frightened patient to sleep in sixty seconds. It is a fast track to the unconscious and one fraught with peril. One false step, and dire consequences ensue. That they do this well is a tribute to the finely honed steel-trap mind that has mentally rehearsed just such a scenario countless times and has put it to practical use a few dozen times previously.

I wait now for my order to begin surgery. After completing the overseeing of everyone else's duties, it is my turn. I wait with the knife poised over the belly. *Hold on, I pray to the baby. We are almost there. I can sense the blood draining from the baby's body as if it were my own. I need to fly. Time is running out. I know this instinctively.*

"Cut!"

I respond. The scalpel in my hand flies through tissue, and there is the sense that it is parting before me. All goes well and quickly. I am going fast. Faster than I have ever gone before. I am the only surgeon in the room. My assistant is the scrub tech. She is somewhat helpful—mainly by staying out of the way. Although by all outward appearances I am alone, inwardly I know better. All is going too smoothly. I am quickly cutting the tissue layers necessary and am able to avoid those structures that should not be cut. To do all of this at this speed is beyond my mere cognitive capabilities. I realize that I am not processing. I am just doing. I am a participating vessel. I have assistance.

Divinity, having been present in a capricious manner from the very beginning of this accidental journey, having been present during the chaotic rush to the operating room, having assisted the anesthesiologist to do his job perfectly, has finally settled around my shoulders for this short period of time. She is helping and I am aware of this. I am not alone.

In less than two minutes the baby is delivered—limp, pale, and not breathing. I see this child suspended over the precipice that separates life from death and have come running up to the edge to snatch the child furiously away. I hand this precious bundle over to the resuscitation nurse, who makes the same assessment and runs with the baby to the resuscitation room—where the neonatologist becomes the third physician in succession to be awakened from sleep in order to save someone's life.

My hands are trembling at this point—fine-muscle tremors due to acute overexertion. I stretch my back and neck to relieve the ache and tension. I refocus on the task at hand. I still have work to do.

The symphony is quiet now, stunned by the activity just witnessed. Many of them are seeing this for the first time. It will be an event that they will never forget.

The silence from the resuscitation room is deep, profound, and foreboding. It drifts into the operating room and pervades our conscious awareness. The silence is broken only by the softly spoken staccato. Suture . . . Scissors . . . Lap tape . . .

Each stitch taken to repair the wounded uterus is a stitch taken to repair the wounded hearts of those in the operating room. We think that we were too late.

Those with any experience at all in the labor-and-delivery suite have shed their innocence a long time ago. We know full well that, although Divinity is present, it does not mean everything will turn out all right.

Eight minutes into the resuscitation effort, a heartbeat is detected. The baby is taken to the NICU. We hear this as whispered commentary from the back of the room. What does this mean? We will have to live with this question for a few days. It could mean many things.

I complete the surgery and assist with moving the dazed and confused young mother to the recovery room. As the effects of doctor-administered sleep wear off, the questions come rushing to her trembling lips. Many questions. All the important ones. I explain the entire situation and all the possible ramifications to the family. We will have to wait and see how the baby does. We have done all that is humanly possible.

I am incredibly fatigued for the next three days. I cannot bring myself to visit the baby in the NICU. I do not have the energy to assimilate all that goes on there.

I have been involved in these life-and-death emergencies only a few times during my career. It seems that a transfer of an essential essence from deep down inside of me occurs in this process. Somewhere during the incredible expenditure of energy that is necessary to counteract a momentous natural process gone terribly awry a toll is extracted from the physician.

A part of me is missing. I realize that I have given it up for the baby. Perhaps this portion comes from the inner core of healing essence that I possess—this inner core that guided me to select this profession in the first place.

Many times during the day I dole out portions of healing essence to my patients in the normal discharge of my professional duties. That is a replenishable source from which I draw. These extraordinary circumstances do not draw from such a source. This is a *permanent* withdrawal of principal. I am left to stagger around as I learn to live off the subsequent reduced interest. These withdrawals are cumulative, and each time it takes longer to readjust. After this particular incident, it is several days before I feel like myself again.

A few days later I am greeted outside the NICU by the neonatologist who was called to the delivery.

Smiling, she says, "You must come see the baby. It is amazing!"

I stare at her incredulously, not ready to believe what she has just told me.

I accompany her into the nursery, and my eyes are captivated by the beautiful sight before them. A perfectly normal, perfectly lovely newborn baby. The soft, downy hair encircles the cherubic face. The skin glistens with that healthy newborn glow, and the movement of the perfectly formed fingers is a mesmerizing dance as they begin to tentatively explore the world.

The neonatologist gently interrupts my reverie. "All is going well. We have started discharge planning."

This is an almost unbelievable pronouncement, and I can see that the neonatologist can hardly believe she is saying it. As is often the case, physicians will "rerun the tapes" from the emergency that have been stored in the memory banks. We both do this at this time and make a vain attempt to splice them together. We attempt to create a logical sequence of events from then until now. However we try in various configurations, it cannot be done.

Divinity had stepped in—from her vantage point, having witnessed the struggles of the human beings involved. The sweat, the stress, the fervent passion, the commitment, the integrity. Having convinced herself that the human beings involved had done all within their power to assist that child and had held nothing back, Divinity stepped in at the very last possible moment, after we had exhausted our entire repertoire of human interventions. A portion of all of us resides within that newborn babe. Divinity was merciful.

"Only those who regard healing as the ultimate goal of their efforts can, therefore, be designated as physicians."
— *Rudolf Virchow (1821–1902)*
"Standpoints in Scientific Medicine," Disease,
Life, and Man (tr. by Jacques Barzun)

Healing Essence

A physician's practice requires nurturing. It is in many ways similar to gardening. One needs to view it slowly from afar, taking in the wide variety that Mother Nature has created and appreciating the beautiful diversity. One then needs to move in for closer inspection and admire the individual rows. One can appreciate the faithful and predictable varieties—those that come up year after year, demonstrating their solid steadiness and predictable constancy. This is in contrast to the hybrid varieties that will constantly surprise one—which color will the flower be this year? Then there are those exotic plants that stand out for immediate appraisal. They announce themselves with the self-evident assurance of something completely different. Then one needs to attend to the somewhat barren part of the garden, where the plants were not started in "good soil." How are these struggling, compromised seedlings doing? They have had the misfortune of having been planted in less than optimal soil—perhaps lacking sufficient nutrients, fortification, or water. It's humbling to see their staid persistence and witness their gritty will to keep growing in spite of it all.

All of this is appreciated from various perspectives. Sometimes it appears as a chaotic jumble of color. Sometimes it is appreciated by inspecting each individual and unique plant carefully, one after the other. Any mildew on the leaves? Any evidence of root damage? Any premature ripening of the fruit? What fortification or supplements might be needed?

Yes, a physician's practice is in many ways just like gardening. I find it interesting that really serious gardeners mention their secret tricks—those that make their garden really wonderful. Some gardeners talk to their plants, some sing. Some believe that hugging trees makes them grow faster. This is an acknowledgment of the belief that we all—humans, plants, animals—are endowed with energy. Furthermore, if we purposefully give energy boosts to those things we love, those grateful recipients blossom. With all of these tricks of the trade comes the true constant—that time is necessary to make the garden blossom.

Time to wander, time to inspect, time to sit back and appreciate the changes from year to year. Time to ponder the next needed adjustment, time to connect with and appreciate the intense beauty of it all.

The physician's office practice, done well, has all of these characteristics. The most important seems to be the necessary time to connect. To stop and really take note of the patients. How are they this year? What has changed? How is their environment? Is it healthy? Stressful?

To engage in easy, open dialogue is the goal. For in this state of "open-ended" connection it is possible to truly assess the patient. Hidden problems become visible, and the opportunity to address them is at hand. The patient in this dialogue also has the opportunity to assess the physician. Is the physician really paying attention? Is he or she listening? Are my concerns being addressed?

This level of two-way communication is not necessarily easy to establish. It requires that a certain level of trust be achieved. This takes time to fully establish. It might be possible in one lengthy office visit, but it often requires supplementation by additional visits. Then the required element of sufficient time to allow for the establishment of familiarity, comfort, and trust has been reached. It is as though the "frequency" of the interaction has been learned by both parties. There is a memory component involved as well. It happens when the patient and physician know each other well enough. Then, after initial polite conversation comes to an end, the serious business of health issues is addressed. . . .

"So tell me, how are you doing?" The frequency is locked in, and transmission of information proceeds almost effortlessly. The sender and receiver are tuned in. The patient sends out the pertinent information, sometimes with amplification as needed, and the physician takes it all in. It is processed, and then the communication channel and energy flow are reversed.

The physician sends all of the pertinent medical information back, *but it is not just words that come across the channel.* Words are accompanied by feelings such as concern, empathy, compassion, and hope. Energy is transmitted back to patients, and it is at this point that they begin to notice that they feel better. They have just received something of great value. They have received *healing essence.* While additional medical tests or procedures may still be needed to fully address the problem, they have already received the most important element and subconsciously are aware of this. They recognize a sense of relaxation and the beginning of "well-being." They are very grateful.

In this state of gratitude, the channels are reversed again. The patient communicates this new feeling back—invariably amplified. Often, the capacity of the channel is pushed to its limits. The physician may be surprised at the intensity of the incoming message, so he or she needs to be prepared to receive it. Sometimes the message is so intense that the incoming circuitry is overloaded. It is important to realize that the message needs to come back to the physician. It is coming from a special, warm place within the patient and wants to connect with the same place within the physician. When a message comes back in such a manner to the physician, it is appreciated as a heartwarming experience. The physician also begins to feel better.

This is the essence of the physician-patient relationship. A good, solid relationship based on the foundations of time, trust, and familiarity.

Once a physician learns this, it becomes unsatisfying to practice medicine any other way. This is because the "other ways" seem empty and meaningless—as if one is practicing within a vacuum.

Once patients find such physicians, they will never leave them. Such a level of gratitude inspires tenacious loyalty.

Left alone to this special reciprocating relationship, the healing physician and the patient would be able to get along quite well. Oftentimes, magnificently. If only an awareness of this ideal were sought out by both parties.

All that is needed is time—and plenty of it.

Consequences of Inadequate Healing Essence

Physicians are unable to spend enough time with their patients anymore. We can thank managed care for this. It has created great unhappiness among the patients, who are feeling less restrained in venting their feelings in this regard.

Increasingly, they complain that the visits to their doctor seem "empty," devoid of something. Some patients will actually describe their visits as meaningless and unhelpful. As more and more physicians adapt to the "service model" of medicine as dictated by the insurance industry, a correlation can be seen in the increase in anger and resentment on the patients' part. They are being deprived of something that they cannot quite put their finger on. Something important. Something that used to be more readily available. Something that they took for granted and that the insurance industry seems perilously unaware even exists. These patients are being deprived of healing essence.

It is not only in their interaction with their physician that this is lacking. As the business model is applied almost universally across the medical care field, all persons employed in the role of taking care of patients have had their job descriptions drastically curtailed. A single characteristic that stands out for commentary in all of these new job descriptions is less time spent with the patient—less direct patient care.

Ironically, almost all of those persons who have chosen a career in the health care field did so because they wanted to take care of people. To help people recover their health. To assist in the healing process. That is why they became nurses; occupational, physical, and respiratory therapists; nurse's aides; operating room technicians; orderlies; and so on. It is within them all to do this. They possess their own type of healing essence, and by their nature they would like to transmit this. They are increasingly hampered in their ability to do so.

Their own frustration is echoed by that of the patients, who, again, find themselves deprived of an essential ingredient needed in their recovery effort.

One can speculate that with the masses of ill people now seeking medical care under this new system, which makes no allowance for the value of time—the prerequisite for transference of healing essence—the persons will find their entire experience with this new system extremely unsatisfying.

If patient satisfaction was all there was to worry about, it might possibly be justified under the present economic argument. The old way was just too expensive. We have had to cut costs, after all. However, other considerations need to be carefully examined. It would seem that with the larger numbers of patients being treated in this way, deprived of an essential ingredient by their health care system (by accident, perhaps, not by design), these patients are "left alone" to recover from their illness, their surgery, or their chemotherapy. With no one able to infuse the necessary "booster dose" of healing essence, it quite possibly will take these individuals much longer to recover from these adverse events. Length of time for recovery increases with fatigue and isolation, the unwanted companions.

Carrying all of this one step further, one can imagine that we could start to see increasing complication rates as well—as a result of insufficient healing essence. This would happen to those persons who are "inherently low" on their own healing energy—perhaps because they are tired or worn out from their illness. These individuals are in need of the essence to the greatest degree. If deprived of it, they find that the emptiness of the transaction does nothing for them and might possibly harm them.

It comes as no surprise to me that interest in and use of alternative practitioners have skyrocketed over the past few years. While I believe that there are diverse reasons for the increasing interest in complementary or integrative medicine, I also believe that the proliferation of managed care has only fueled the flames. My patients who utilize alternative practitioners usually describe their experiences with "I had such a wonderful feeling when I left the office. He spent so much time with me. It was terrific!"

It seems ironic that the alternative medicine healers, unhampered by insurance industry regulations, are free to practice their healing craft as they see fit—with the reality that the patients are very happy with their services and keep coming back for more. Compare this to those healers trapped within the current health care delivery system, who find themselves deprived of the single most important function of their calling.

This situation has not gone unnoticed by the general public. The patients are voting with their feet.

Refugees

They arrive with uncertainty in their eyes, fatigue, or, worse, smoldering irritation. They want to know . . . What will this experience be like? Will they have time to make sure their questions are answered? How long will they have to wait before being seen? Will they be seen by the doctor or the assistant? Will their questions be answered to their satisfaction?

They are in pain and they need help. Will they be listened to?

Many have already had one or more undesirable experiences with other professionals. They have learned to be wary. Some demonstrate outright suspicion.

They come seeking comfort, solace, and relief from pain, fear, and anxiety.

When they find comfort, they almost weep for joy—such a rare occurrence it seems to them. Their gratitude wells up from the bottom of their hearts. Why did it take so long to find someone who seems to care, who listens?

These are refugees from managed care, and they are seeking safe harbor. Their numbers are increasing exponentially, and the safe harbors are becoming inundated as word of mouth spreads the news.

"I have found a nice doctor." Or "This is a nice office. Try them."

But the masses of refugees overwhelm the safe harbors, and they eventually close their doors—not unlike a country that decides that, due to limited resources, it cannot feed the entire world.

Do these refugees want something unreasonable or expensive? No. What they desire is pitifully simple. They are seeking a physician who will sit down and listen to them. A physician who will give them time and attention. A physician who understands the essence of the healing arts and who has learned to practice it well.

Why are there seemingly so few of them left?

Perhaps the physicians have forgotten something terribly important.

Safe Houses

Small groups of physicians have begun meeting. They are trying to find their way among the muck and debris that litter this country. They are busy trying to establish (reinvent?) a way of practicing medicine that is consistent with their inner beliefs and values, their ethics and morals. In essence, in a manner that is consistent with their soul. They are looking for a way to practice medicine that gives honor to their calling and not discomfort or, worse, shame.

They have decided to establish a network outside of any PPO listing, HMO book, or other official, arbitrary division of physicians.

These doctors have decided to give old-fashioned, high-quality, strictly fee-for-service medicine a try. Something that seemed all but lost, ironically, is rising up from the rubble of managed care.

These physicians will establish offices that honor the physician-patient relationship. The physicians in this loosely affiliated and fledgling network have this as their top priority: They will treat the patients with honesty, integrity, and compassion. They will listen to the patients and attend to their needs to the best of their ability.

In return, the physicians ask only that the patients release them from third-party interference. It appears that it is not just the HMOs who are proving oppressive and tiresome—the PPOs are learning from their HMO colleagues. It is almost as if the participating doctors will put up with just about anything to collect a paycheck.

These newly released physicians cannot stomach being paid minions any longer. They will go out on their own and practice medicine the way they know it should be done: one to one. One patient at a time and plenty of time allotted to honor this sacred dialogue.

When patients arrive at these offices, they will feel the difference immediately. They will have to adjust to owning something that they thought they had lost—power.

You see, by making the relationship financially simple, things change. When the patient pays the physician directly, it behooves the physician to be absolutely certain that the patient's needs are clearly being met. Otherwise, the patient will not return. And he or she will not refer friends or neighbors.

Imagine the changing dynamic. Instead of payments being made by an interfering and unwelcome third party, the patient pays the physician. These physicians then have to act only one way, that is, to do all in their power to honor their professional commitment.

Patients treated in this manner and with this degree of respect will express loyalty. A loyalty based on deep mutual regard.

Both patient and physician will benefit. To practice this way is very freeing. The possibilities are exciting to contemplate.

For instance, the physicians will network with one another. If a particular patient needs the professional services of another, this will be accomplished in a quick phone call. Faxing of the medical record and a timely appointment are guaranteed.

Patients will be sent reverently and securely from office to office. The patient will know implicitly that the integrity and the intentions are true.

The soul of the physician will sing in these offices, and the melody will reverberate throughout.

At these preliminary meetings, the discussions have energy, commitment, and passion. It is almost as though the physicians are grasping at something apparently long lost but now beginning to come sharply into focus. This is the right step. It seems so natural, so logical, so pure. This idea to establish an office practice where patients can feel secure, comforted, honored, and respected. And the physician's soul can sing.

Sacred Documents

In a courteous manner, mixed with studied deliberation, Martha handed the file to me during that first office visit.

The manila folder was two shades darker than what is used at present. The edges were ever so slightly tattered, this having been done by the hands of her previous physician— who, over the course of the years, had opened that file countless times.

Stamped on the front and forming the margin along one entire side were the years that Martha had been under the care of the physician who had had previous ownership of the well-used manila folder. The first year was stamped 1957. All of the subsequent years were stamped in faithful chronological order—marching along the entire length of that side of the chart. The years ran out of room and had to be doubled back. Thus, a new row had been started parallel to the first. This row ended in 1996.

"Retirement letter sent" was stamped in black ink at the top. After thirty-nine years in the care of one physician, she had come seeking another.

She hoped that the chart would be helpful. She assumed that it would be. It held her entire adult medical history.

I received it in a state of reverent curiosity. In a sequestered bit of leisure time and in accordance with my professional responsibilities, I perused the inviting pages.

Tucked into the very back were records preceding the last physician's. They had apparently been passed on, thus honoring the rights of succession from that one to her most recent. I realized I had become the latest heir to the office of "Keeper of the Medical Record."

The earliest entry was dated 1946. Just after the war. At that time Santa Clara Valley was a sleepy agricultural community. The twenty-five-year-old and her husband were living on a small ranch. They had a fruit orchard, as did many of their neighbors. Almost everyone either owned a fruit orchard or was involved in the work associated with one. It seemed so, anyway.

She had come because she was pregnant.

The fountain-pen-inked entries under the categories "Past Medical History" and "Present Illness" were legible fifty years after first being penned.

She was the mother of an energetic twenty-month-old at home. Baby number two was on the way. Her "status" was listed as "housewife." Her husband was employed as a superintendent at a local cannery. Her health was generally good. She was noted to have only an occasional headache and minor backache.

The fountain pen was traded for a pencil to narrate the progress of her pregnancy. It continued, thankfully uneventfully, marked only by the little boy at home coming down with German measles. All went well subsequently, and the delivery of a little girl was marked in ink on September 30, 1946.

Life had suddenly become much busier for our twenty-six-year-old. Subsequent visits spoke of some minor health problems, broken up by a vacation visit to Kings Canyon in 1949.

By 1951, ready-made standardized typed charting had replaced the fountain-pen narrative. The physician attending her for her third pregnancy had the luxury of merely filling in the corresponding boxes to complete the long column describing the progress of the pregnancy. It was easier to follow, and progress was more easily delineated. At least from the physician's perspective. Our now twenty-nine-year-old found this pregnancy much different from her previous two. The first two months found her under strict bed rest as she had to deal with the scary circumstances of threatened miscarriage. Between her mother-in-law and her husband, the children were taken care of. She lay there day after day—hoping and praying. Eventually all was well. The pregnancy would keep. She was relieved. All went back to normal, and all that concerned her were increasing back pain and an aching hip discomfort that would feel much like arthritis as the pregnancy progressed. However, she was busy with the full-time care of her children.

The seven-year-old was enrolled in school, and the five-year-old was asking every day why she couldn't go, too. The pregnancy went relatively unnoticed by her during the busy days. It was just at night, when she was finally able to put her feet up, that the hip discomfort and back pain would demand attention. Added to these considerations was the pregnancy-induced insomnia that was little appreciated, especially knowing that much activity was necessary first thing in the morning. But these occupied just a few of her reflections.

It had been the nature of her upbringing to cherish children. They were to be rejoiced in above everything else. Therefore, all of these bodily complaints receded to the background of her consciousness. She did not dwell upon them excessively. It was not encouraged by her upbringing. It was not encouraged by society. She did not dwell upon much regarding the pregnancy except this: the occasional prayers that all would turn out well. For she was twenty-nine now, not twenty-three as with her first pregnancy. She had lived a little now. She had known women who had suffered tragedies. She was no longer naive. She would hope and pray for the best. These thoughts were her guide. All else was truly trivial. She would be just fine.

From the physician's point of view, the pregnancy was defined in much simpler and purely scientific terms (as much as could have been done in 1951). From week six to thirty-nine, the weight gain, blood pressure, and size of the uterus, along with documentation of the baby's heartbeat, were faithfully recorded. A few scrawled green-ink entries noted the hormone injections given in the hopes of preventing miscarriage.

She can still remember the day that she went into labor. They had just built their home, and she was up on a ladder painting. It was a magnificent day! The sky was crystal clear, the orchard was in full bloom, and the blossoms were absolutely breathtaking. She could sense it, breathe it, inhale the succulent beauty. She was awestruck—the moment frozen in the crystalline recesses of her mind.

She knew why it was called the valley of the heart's delight. She could taste it that day.

Her third baby was a daughter, born March 30, 1952. The labor was fast—three hours—and the delivery was without complications.

During the remainder of the 1950s, stamped-ink date marks appeared, replacing the carefully penned handwritten dates. The stamp of the forward march of technology was evident in the clearly blocked out date Feb 11, 1955, marking this first visit of the new era.

Visits now described a woman in her thirties—occupied with three children at home. She was bothered by some minor gynecological problems, but ever-faithful visits were recorded. On average, two to four visits were made per year during the decade of the 1950s, when a slight variation in menses cycle was noted during a visit in 1958. This proved a short-lived puzzle to this thirty-five-year-old and her gynecologist. Now, with three children ages thirteen, eleven, and five, what was the reason for the delay in menses? Child number four, a boy, born June 13, 1958.

Life was indescribably busy now for this Santa Clara housewife. Between the orchard, her husband's career, the children, and the new baby, time ceased to exist linearly. It seemed simply to cease to exist—at least by the usual measuring standards. Days blended into nights, weeks into months, and months into years. All seemed to merge almost simultaneously. She was brought back to the reality of linear time by the birthday parties, as those four sharply defined dates would not stand for convergence into simultaneous time. No, they would stand out for linear time acknowledgment. Accordance was given to these days, so important was this to the recipients of these happy celebrations. So bewildering at times to the organizer, baker, and chief party giver, who found herself wondering more than once: How is it that they can be that *old*? It seems like only yesterday. . . .

Faithful visits to the gynecologist continued. Menses became increasingly bothersome, and a hysterectomy was performed in 1960. All was uneventful. Faithful annual visits continued thereafter.

Periodic family vacations entered the medical record along with other minor medical problems. The children were growing up, and she was growing older.

At age forty-four, menopausal symptoms began. Hormone therapy was initiated that brought welcome relief to this woman whose children were now twenty-two, twenty, fourteen, and eight.

Menopausal symptoms persisted, and this transition was not easy. It proved to be one of the most tiresome periods of her life. Treatment was adjusted, and faithful visits continued. Taped lab reports now appeared, covering the physician's scrawl. By now she was in the hands of my predecessor—her previous gynecologist—who would have her care for thirty-nine years.

One such lab report was held tenuously in place, as the stickiness of the adhesive was all but gone twenty-five years after having been placed. Beneath this was an entry stating that one son was now married and enrolled in dental school.

Three years later, a prominently scribbled note, standing out for recognition among the others, stated "She is going to be a grandmother." This was followed by mention of a longed-for trip to Germany.

Back pain continued and perhaps was a little worse after menopause. Treatment was sought and given. Life went on. The problem receded into the past. The only remembrance of it now lies in the inked, scrawled lines of the physician's entry dated October 14, 1971.

The decade of the seventies passed with some intermittent abdominal pain that turned out not to be anything serious. This was followed by a benign breast biopsy. Benign, thank God! Because it was now that Martha would again look around her, as her friends and acquaintances began to experience medical problems of a serious nature—breast cancer being one of these. She was again reminded of feelings closeted since that third pregnancy, now so long ago. *But for the grace of God, there go I.* She could not remember who had taught her that phrase. It seemed fitting now as she looked around her. She had brought meals to friends who were dying. There was, indeed, much to be thankful for in receiving the news of a benign breast biopsy.

They planned a vacation to Mexico in 1974. She had been married thirty-plus years. The children, almost unbelievably, were all grown up, with her youngest turning twenty in 1978.

Her husband was occasionally mentioned as continuing to enjoy his employment. His health, thankfully, had been good.

The 1980s began with her husband, now of thirty-eight years, having a heart attack. He survived. Their lives were changed.

The decade continued with a visit to the dermatologist for a skin condition. Additionally, persistent abdominal pain now caused increasing concern.

Found under taped entries was the vacation in 1981 to New Zealand, Australia, and Fiji. These vacations—always delightful—now assumed increasing importance in her life. They were longed for. It seemed as if time was becoming precious, indeed. They needed to travel while they both still could. It was beginning to become apparent. Looking at their circle of friends and acquaintances, it was not prudent to take much for granted.

The follow-up visit six weeks later mentioned that she had had a wonderful time!

The first recorded mammogram report appeared in 1986. A visit to a rheumatologist in 1988 described the development of arthritis in this "delightful 65 year old woman." Yes, she was delightful—and gracious, too. For imprinted in her memory and most likely not directly accessible to her was the knowledge of how to grow old gracefully. This is what she had learned from her elder role models when she was a young girl and woman. They unknowingly and unconsciously implanted this knowledge in her then. Not that she needed it back then, before the war. But it now came unbidden, as if it were coded "delivered upon demand." This business of how to act, how to speak, how to relate, how to interpret circumstances, how to do it all with grace. This is what she had learned. It was now becoming evident that she had learned it well.

Treatment for the arthritis was begun, and there was some improvement.

She was still bothered by abdominal discomfort that persisted throughout the decade of the 1980s. Remedies and regimens were discussed and dutifully followed. Some remedies were more skeptically received than others.

Full-page printed lab results, replacing abbreviated orange and yellow three-by-five-inch versions and taped fastidiously to the visit entry, appeared in 1988. This coincided with the increase in the width of the progress note.

A second gynecological operation occurred in 1989. It was performed without difficulty. A satisfactory and complete recovery was noted.

Preceding the dictated operative report appeared the letter from the Medicare Provider Review Monitoring Department.

This discussed proper disclosure to beneficiaries regarding elective surgeries and claim documentation requirements, as well as a charge determination worksheet. A sample beneficiary letter was included to assist the physicians with communication of these instructions to their patients, as if assistance would be needed. Assistance needed? By 1989, this woman had been in the care of this physician for thirty-two years. He had more intimate knowledge of her entire life than anyone else—with the exception of her husband. What could be the basis for proper disclosure other than this secure and trusted thirty-two-year relationship? This irony was not lost on the physician. Neither knew quite what to do with these forms—presumably generated on the patient's behalf—except to go through with the required motions of the mandated compliance.

The decade of the 1990s arrived with the incident of her having dropped a frozen duck on her left foot. She made this incident known to her gynecologist, who acted accordingly by ordering X rays to look for a fracture. Fortunately, there was none. She recovered from this event, left with the remembrance of not quite understanding how it had happened but vowing most assuredly that it would not happen again.

Old habits die hard, as surely evidenced by other lab results still being carefully taped onto the progress notes. Their shape, as well as the placement of the tape, had changed, making it easier to read underneath. This simply required lifting the results straight up to peer at what lay hidden.

Abdominal problems continued. Persistent mammogram reports were done annually and faithfully—all documenting normal results.

The year 1992 required her to undergo a colonoscopy. She was thankful for having endured the pain of childbirth, as this discomfort was placed into proper perspective. She also found the grit to complete it. It remained, however, nothing that she wanted to undergo again. Particularly at seventy years old.

The very last entry was dated March 5, 1996. She was seventy-four years old, was in basically good health, and had been in the care of the physician thirty-nine years.

Thus concludes the physician's review of the medical record.

A review covering fifty years of this woman's life. Details noted about the children, her husband, her medical problems, their treatment, the outcomes, the follow-up, and the names of all the other physicians involved in her care. All of this was professionally done. Carefully done. Done with reverence and deep respect, arising from a place within the physician that mandates assumption of the ordained role of "Keeper of the Medical Record."

A scribe in a monastery could not have been more faithful or more committed.

Are these documents none other than a testimonial to this delightful, gracious woman? Indeed, they serve as a confirmation of her life, the ups and downs, the difficulties, the worries, the fears, the relief, the reality.

These are intimate details intended long ago for the eyes of the physician only. For the physician to review with a sense of awe at the discovery of what lay hidden between the confines of that tattered manila folder. For what lay hidden is an affidavit to this woman's life. As such, these documents must be considered none other than sacred. This requires that they receive their due: to be treated with nothing less than profound regard and reverence.

With due respect for technology, we rush as if pursued by demons into the future. Technology's impact on the medical field, as well as on every other aspect of our lives, has been felt. There is a need for *pause* with respect to the rapid push and clamor for medical records to go "online," to be computerized, to be readily available.

Let us not forget this: *The confidentiality of these sacred documents must be assured.*

The Medical Savings Account:
The First Step in the Right Direction

I make no claim of attempting to correct the entire health care crisis. I harbor no such delusions of grandeur.

It is the physician-patient relationship that concerns me. It is sacrosanct—or needs to be considered as such. It has been warped, rearranged, and almost, but not quite, distorted beyond recognition.

This is where the Medical Savings Account (MSA) comes in. I would dearly love to meet the genius (or geniuses) who created this gem. It certainly is a first step in the right direction. By its nature, it places the responsibility on the relationship between the physician and the patient. It is necessary to reestablish the supremacy of this relationship in the practice of medicine. It is the relationship around which all else revolves.

Third parties have intruded into this relationship much like unwelcome guests at dinner. It is time to ask them to leave. Firmly. Politely. Adamantly.

It seems safe to say that they no longer have either party's best interest at heart. It is time for that to change. The Medical Savings Account works in the following manner. (A list of references has been included at the end of this essay.)

MSAs are tax-advantaged, personal savings accounts intended for medical expenses. They were created to go hand in hand with a high-deductible health care plan so that individuals could pay less in monthly premiums and put the savings into a tax-exempt MSA. People can use tax-free dollars from an MSA to cover routine and minor medical expenses as they are satisfying their deductibles. MSAs were introduced by the Health Insurance Portability and Accountability Act of 1996 and have been available since 1997. They are similar to flexible spending accounts presently offered by employers. The key difference is that the money left over in the account can be rolled over into the following year.

The MSA is presently available as a nationwide federal pilot program. Eligible persons at present include self-employed individuals and companies with fewer than fifty employees.

If you bear with the facts and figures, the examples that follow are not too hard to understand, especially when your good health is at stake.

One example is Blue Shield of California MSA. For an individual plan with a $2,250 deductible per person, the maximum annual contribution for a single person's MSA is $1,462.50. This money is then used to pay directly for health services as one satisfies the deductible. This money can also be used for health care expenses not covered by the plan but deductible for federal income tax purposes. Such expenses include dental, chiropractic, acupuncture, vision, psychological, and long-term care; and health plan premiums paid while receiving unemployment compensation.

A second example is Medical Saving Insurance Company of Anaheim, California. This company offers a premium charge of $452.50 per month for a family. That consists of $265 per month in premiums for a high-deductible policy with a $3,000 family deductible, plus $187.50 per month in contributions to the MSA. The family can put 75 percent of the insurance deductible into the tax-exempt account. In this example the family has chosen a $3,000 deductible, so the family can put $2,250 into the medical savings account. That is, $2,250 for this family to spend anywhere they want, selecting any doctor they choose. They would also have the ability to resume some control over where their ancillary work is being done.

A woman would have the power to insist that her pap smear go to the best lab—the one that her physician thinks is best. She would have the option to take herself to the best mammogram facility, not just the one that has contracted with her HMO. Men and women would have the ability to insist that all pathology specimens go to the preferred lab—the one deemed best by their physician, not an outfit that has landed a "good" deal. Most important, they would be able to receive health care from any physician they choose. So if they are kept waiting for one hour in the waiting room with no valid explanation given, they can go elsewhere. Similarly, if patients are referred to a specialist and the information or the manner in which it is given is not to their liking, they have the ability to keep looking. Another very important benefit of the MSA is that it will give patients the ability to negotiate the cost of their care in regard to laboratory testing, diagnostic testing, or suggested procedures.

You need to realize that you do not have health insurance for the purpose of staying healthy. You need it solely to protect you from personal bankruptcy in the event you have the misfortune to become afflicted with a serious illness or accident.

What would be the expenditures for a healthy family of four per year? Let's use this example, because 80 percent of the population is basically healthy and needs to access health care services only for well visits. At present, all of the premium dollars go to HMOs or other health insurance companies. The fate of these dollars, as well as management and impact, has been clearly laid out in the preceding pages. Imagine this new redistribution.

Our family has $2,250 to spend wherever they like. Mother is forty-two years old. She needs a gynecological checkup. The approximate cost for this would be $150. Father needs a checkup this year. (He does not need to go every year, but assume this is his designated year.) This would cost $180. Each of their two children, ages four and seven, needs an annual checkup. The approximate charge per child for a physical is $80. Mother needs a mammogram. This would cost an additional $150. Assume that Dad needs comprehensive lab work. This would cost $340. So far, our family has spent $980 out of $2,250 on their preventive health care. Most important, they have gone to their physician of choice—where they have been treated well. The money has simply traveled from their MSA at the local bank to the physician via a convenient debit card. No authorizations, no permission slips, no "Mother May I's," no unacceptable delays in the waiting room, no haggard doctor seeing too many patients. *(No longer is there a need to impose upon our good friends in India for processing.)*

Simplicity is the design; gratitude is the reward.

Our family then has $1,270 left to cover, say, a flu shot or periodic vaccinations that the children may need, or the occasional visit for an ear infection or visits for other problems. They could also choose to spend this money for acupuncture, chiropractic, or other health expenses. Or, best yet, they could choose to save this money for a rainy day, as it will accumulate tax-free and roll over from this year to the next. It is theirs to save for the day—knock on wood—when one family member might fall seriously ill. In that case, it is imperative to have the option to go to the best doctor. The money that has been accumulating in the Medical Savings Account will allow this to happen.

I reiterate that my advocacy for the MSA lies in the restorative potential that it will have on the physician-patient relationship. I am aware that it has its detractors, as well as its advocates. Again, please see the references included after this discussion for additional information. Readers may reach their own conclusions.

It is my belief that the MSA would reinstate the integrity of the physician-patient relationship. The patient is empowered with spending money and given the freedom, *as well as the responsibility*, to choose his or her own physician and hospital facility and make informed decisions.

At last, the covered life is no longer a pawn of insurance brokers and negotiators. The covered life actually has a voice. Let the covered life speak!

Contrary to some prevailing opinions, I place great faith in patients' ability to make good judgments. I feel that patients do know when they are in the hands of a good physician. Such a physician will demonstrate care and compassion.

Integrity is a quality that will extend outward from the physician like a welcoming aura.

Keep in mind that the majority of physicians choose their profession because it is a *calling*. Now assume that perhaps, *just perhaps*, your particular illness or affliction is not as random as you have been led to believe. *Neither should your choices of a physician and other health care professionals be considered so.*

Picture yourself ill, in considerable pain, and in need of solace. You have spent anxious moments in the waiting room, filling out the requisite medical history forms while balancing the clipboard on your knee. After riffling through your wallet a few times for the health insurance card, you start nervously as the nurse calls your name.

You take a deep breath and steady yourself for the interview. Your heart pounds a little harder and your palms moisten as you walk through the waiting-room door and into the inner office.

After the obligatory stop at the scale, the nurse takes your blood pressure.

"How is it?" you ask suddenly.

"A little high today." She smiles softly. "Are you nervous?"

You do not have time to answer as the physician walks in. The nurse hands over the chart and, with a look of reassurance, leaves quietly.

Now you inhale deeply, followed by heavy exhalation. You look intensely at this person before you. Who is so *very, very* important to you. Someone to whom you will turn over your life. Someone whom you have not even spoken to yet.

The doctor smiles his reassurance and sits down—equally looking at you in his turn. Looking at all of you. Looking through you and beyond you. He takes a deep breath, is centered, and is ready.

"How are you today?"

You mumble something slightly incoherent, trying to block the pain that suddenly reminds you of the reason you have come.

He notices, heightens his attention, and in all readiness to perceive your reply inquires gently, "How can I help you?"

This is said with such calm, comforting reassurance that you stare at the doctor. You find yourself looking resolutely at him. At his face. Looking into his eyes, you find yourself talking about the pain: when it started, what you have already tried so far, what helps, what doesn't. You shift your position in an attempt to become comfortable. You continue talking.

It hits you then that this doctor is *really* listening. *Really* paying attention. Moreover, you distinctly discern that he is rapidly gaining an understanding of what is wrong with you. You pause as this awareness rushes over you in a warmly felt cascade of reassurance.

You want to continue the dialogue but are overwhelmed by an unbidden intuitive flash that will not be repressed. . . . It is the strangest feeling. . . . There is a familiarity about this interview that strikes you as some type of replay, but how can that be? It is not—your conscious mind tells you that it is not—yet there is this feeling . . . so hard to explain, this feeling demanding your acknowledgment. Good God! The impression is overpowering! Somehow, it is as if . . . yes, exactly as if, in a very strange way, this doctor has been *waiting* for you!

For those interested in reading further, here are some references regarding Medical Savings Accounts:

Author unknown. "American College of Physicians position paper on medical savings accounts." *Annals of Internal Medicine* (August 15, 1996):333–40.

Author unknown. *Blue Shield of California: Beginner's Guide to Medical Savings Accounts.*

Author unknown. "Congress: MSA pilot disappointing." *Managed Healthcare* (February 1998):10.

Author unknown. "Medical savings accounts are proving a tough sell." *Wall Street Journal* (May 22, 1997).

Bond, Michael. "Can MSAs help reduce healthcare costs?" *Healthcare Financial Management* (April 1996):34.

Gardner, Jonathan. "Medical savings accounts make waves." *Modern Healthcare* (February 27, 1995):57.

Gilbert, Evelyn. "Pundits split on medical savings account benefits." *National Underwriter Property & Casualty—Risk and Benefits Management* (March 18, 1996):21.

Goltry, Vernon L. "MSAs—what's good for Idaho is good for America." *Medical Sentinel* (Winter 1997):35.

Grimaldi, Paul L. "Is a medical savings account in your future?" *Nursing Management* (May 1996):14–16.

Halva, Kimberly. "Are medical savings accounts an effective insurance alternative?" *Minnesota Medicine* (June 1997):52–53.

Hansen, Erling. "1995 in the states: Refinement of reform." *Medical Interface* (December 1995):98–102.

Jampel, Henry D. "The case for medical savings accounts." *Arch. Ophthalmol.* (September 1997):1185–88.

Jennings, Carole P. "Corner on issues: The controversial medical savings account: What needs to be known." *Journal of the American Academy of Nurse Practitioners* (September 1996):427–28.

Keeler, Emmett B., et al. "Can medical savings accounts for the nonelderly reduce health care costs?" *Journal of the American Medical Association* (June 5, 1996):1666–71.

Kosterlitz, Julie. "Rise of the medical savings account." *National Journal* (June 22, 1996):1395.

Meyer, Harris. "Bank on it: Thrift, theft or confusion? Medical savings accounts may bring all three." *Hospitals & Health Networks* (February 5,1997):26, 28.

Ozanne, L. "How will medical savings accounts affect medical spending?" *Inquiry* (Fall 1996):225–36.

Pallarito, Karen. "MSA interest rising." *Modern Healthcare* (May 5,1997):108, 110.

Pulec, Jack L. "Medical savings account: Available at last." *Ear, Nose & Throat Journal* (May 1997):286.

Schweitzer, Maurice, and David A. Asch, "The role of employee flexible spending accounts in health care financing." *American Journal of Public Health* (August 1996):1079–1081.

Schweitzer, Maurice, et al. "Individual choice in spending accounts: Can we rely on employees to choose well?" *Medical Care*, vol. 34, no. 6:583–93.

How to Heal Hospitals?
Adopt the Planetree Philosophy

There is a special place in my heart for the Planetree philosophy of care giving and patient empowerment. It would be wonderful to live in a city that had a hospital devoted to this philosophy, as some cities do. That is surely the hospital where I would go myself, should the need arise, and also the place where I would send my family and friends, as well as my patients. If a hospital decided to adopt the Planetree model, it would not need to advertise—think of all the money that could be saved and put to better use. Patients and the community would *know* this was the best place to be.

I learned about the Planetree philosophy through my involvement with our local Planetree Health Resource Center in San Jose, California.

Planetree is a nonprofit health care organization dedicated to creating health care environments that are nurturing, healing, and educational. Its philosophy of care came about after a frustrated, angry health care consumer and her family lived through hospital experiences that she found lacking in many ways. Out of these experiences, Angelica Thieriot worked with farsighted health care administrators, physicians, nurses, business leaders, and community activists to found, in 1978, a radically different type of health care organization. Thieriot looked to medical history for a symbolic name for the organization. Many centuries ago in Greece, Hippocrates, the father of modern medicine, often taught his students under the shade of a plane tree (also known as a sycamore tree). In the same spirit of creating a healing, learning, and natural environment, Thieriot and her colleagues created a hospital model to personalize, humanize, and demystify the health care experience for patients and their families.

Planetree recognizes that healing takes place on many levels: physical, mental, emotional, and spiritual. In essence,

Planetree is a set of philosophies and values that refocus attention on the patient and his or her needs. This is emphasized by its focus on humanizing the hospital and health care experience as well as the importance it places on empowering the patient through information—both in the hospital and in the community setting, through health advocacy and education classes and extensive consumer health libraries. Planetree offers a unique perspective on a person's illness in that it views the hospital and health care experience as an opportunity for healthy life-style changes, personal growth, and spiritual transformation.

Planetree hospitals and health care systems often sponsor Planetree Health Resource Centers, excellent libraries that offer a tremendous breadth and depth of health and medical information—from easy-to-understand materials to the latest research. These libraries serve patients and their families, as well as the general community.

We are lucky in San Jose to have such a facility where many, many patients and their families have been grateful recipients of the information located inside welcoming walls. There are ten other Planetree libraries located throughout the United States. If you ever need hospital services, then you would certainly want to be admitted to a hospital that incorporates the Planetree principles. There, in as healing an environment as a hospital could have, you and your loved ones would benefit from services such as the Bedside Health Information Service, patient/family libraries in hospital units, and the Care Partner program. Planetree's open chart policy is another element that encourages individuals to inform themselves about their medical concerns and health issues and to participate actively in decisions relating to their treatment and care.

Hospitals that have implemented the Planetree philosophy have consistently reported increased patient satisfaction, including better coordination of care, better education, and more patient/family participation. Decreased turnover and increased satisfaction among nursing and allied staff and employees are also typical. Planetree hospitals have also reported fewer postoperative infections and an increase in the number of patients making life-style changes that support better overall health and wellness.

If hospitals are serious about enhancing the experience of the patients entrusted to them at the most vulnerable time of their lives, then they need to answer the question of why they are not adopting a truly patient-centered philosophy.

"What Planetree is all about," says a longtime Planetree nurse, "is bringing the personal touch back to health care and rediscovering our human values, which we've tended to lose sight of in the midst of so much technology." The personal touch is particularly critical during the experience of illness, to patients as well as care givers.

In addition to the best of conventional medicine, Planetree hospitals often offer complementary therapies for patients and staff, including aromatherapy, yoga, meditation, therapeutic massage, acupuncture, and art and music programs. There are currently over thirty-four hospitals and health centers around the country that count themselves as members of the Planetree Alliance. *Only thirty-four? What are all the other hospitals waiting for?*

A Planetree administrator recently stated, "Many studies clearly support consumers' desire to get clear answers to their questions, have more say in their treatment, and have access to more treatment options. In the past, health care consumers have been largely passive participants in their health care. But the explosion of health information, coupled with the changes associated with managed care, has enabled and emboldened consumers to demand a larger role in their health care process."

Another segment of the Planetree philosophy focuses on the needs of hospital employees, improving relationships and enhancing their work environment. By encouraging staff to care for one another and themselves, the Planetree model nurtures respect for each individual. When staff feel better cared for, they will take better care of their most precious short-term guests—members of the community. And all—patients, families, hospital staff, and physicians—will benefit.

For information about the Planetree national organization and hospital/health organization affiliates, contact:

Planetree, 130 Division Street, Derby, CT 06418. Telephone 203–732–7569; website *www.planetree.org*.

For information about Planetree Health Resource Centers and other consumer health libraries around the country, contact:

Planetree Health Resource Center, 98 North 17th Street, San Jose, CA 95112. Telephone 408–977–4549; website *www.planetreesanjose.org*.

Epilogue

After completing a final year of participation in managed health care, I made the painful, frightening, and unnerving decision to leave my secure job, my wonderful physician partners, and the only professional life I had known for nine and a half years. I am not a risk taker by nature (as confirmed by a career counselor whose advice I sought during this tumultuous time of transition).

However, even non–risk takers will jump from a window ledge to escape a burning room when they realize there is no other way out. So I jumped and hoped and prayed that there would be a safety net. After taking two months off for recovery from the trauma sustained as a result of this turmoil and upheaval, I opened my own quiet private office with the goal of practicing medicine the only way that was professionally acceptable—that is, practicing old-fashioned, strictly fee-for-service medicine. The worst thing that could happen to me, I considered, was that I would go bankrupt. If that came to pass, I would switch careers. There was no going back.

I severed all connections to every insurance plan in this state—or so it seemed. It was a glorious feeling to cut the chains of bondage! To my relief and joy, I discovered that it was still possible—*and only in this way possible*—to practice medicine, honor my commitment, and be able to live with myself at the end of the day. At the time of this writing, I have been in my new practice eighteen months. I have not felt this happy or content in a very long time.

A mutually nurturing, healing environment has been created. It is an environment suitable for fostering the health of my patients, my employees, and myself. It is an office where the spirit of the healing arts is respected and the art of medicine is allowed to flourish.

It is an oasis providing medical refreshment. The intent is that all should leave feeling better than when they arrived. This includes the patients, naturally, but it also extends to the employees, the couriers, the postal workers, and curious visitors.

Yes, there has been a steady stream of curious visitors, all wanting to know: How is it going? How is it working? Is it working?

In this oasis the patient comes first. I am allowed to practice the art of medicine without interference. And my employees leave every day not fatigued, but refreshed. For it has been a good day's work for everyone.

It feels good to go home. But the office is a place to which everyone longs to return. And that is a very good thing. I am pleased.

And, oh yes, I am sleeping peacefully at long last.

Acknowledgments

I am very grateful for all the help that I have had from so many individuals along the journey taken to write this book. All have been excellent, appearing in their own time—at the right time—to encourage, advise, educate and support.

From the earliest days I have had my faithful believers. Without their early critical support and advice, I am certain that this book would not have materialized. I am indebted to my talented authoress-friend Joan Ohanneson, my authoress-to-be friend Karla Callahan and her husband, Del Mank, as well as to the world's most excellent medical librarian, Candace Ford Gray, and all the top-notch staff at Planetree Health Resource Center. I thank Eva Diamond, Michael Myers, M.D., and Steve Jackson, M.D., who read early editions of the manuscript and said, "Keep going." With love I thank my husband, Michael, for his tremendous and unwavering support during the three years taken to complete this manuscript. Without this alone, it would not have been possible to complete this tremendous undertaking.

I also extend special gratitude to the Reverend Timothy Raasch for his inspiring sermons.

Midway along the journey, I was the grateful recipient of excellent counsel, support, and advice from the impeccable Ed Davis, Jr. Esq.

Several other folks also stepped forward during a temporary lull, and their words of encouragement at this time restored forward momentum: They include Mark Steinberg, Ph.D.; Drew Pierson, Ph.D.; Christi Welter; Cindy Ling; Catherine Pandori; and Stephanie Peterson.

I am very grateful to the excellent staff at Copyland, San Jose, CA, who were asked to make the first few precious copies of this manuscript and later were gracious enough to comply with "I need ten copies by this afternoon" without missing a beat.

I thank Mary Roybal for superb editing and proof-reading and Teresa Villalvazo for transcription assistance.

I am grateful to Calder Lowe, editor of *The Montserrat Review*, who saw the promise in the writing and published three essays in the 1998 autumn edition.

I thank Tina Farrell for invaluable feedback, enlightening input on structure and layout, and overall editorial advice. She also assisted with design and typesetting, helping to bring this book to its final form.

For the finishing touches, I am grateful for the advice and help of Ron Bronow, M.D. and Tom Lagrelius, M.D.; and I extend many thanks to Jack Strayer and Dr. John C. Goodman at the National Center for Policy Analysis and J. Patrick Rooney at Golden Rule Insurance Company.

And last, but not least, I am grateful to my editor Pam Jacobs, and my publisher, Bob Reed, at Robert D. Reed Publishers for their easy manner, and straightforward and honest approach that, combined with their expertise, have made going through this last incredibly hectic stage as good as it could possibly be. Every first-time author should be as fortunate as I have been.

About the Author

Margaret A. Mahony, M.D., is a practicing physician in San Jose, California, where she lives with her husband and two children.

She was born and raised in Illinois and received her medical education at Washington University School of Medicine in St. Louis, Missouri. She received her training in obstetrics and gynecology at Los Angeles County Medical Center.

She has had a full-time private practice in San Jose for eleven years. Her present practice is devoted to women's health issues and is focused on prevention and wellness in the mid-life transition and optimizing health choices for the menopause. She is also the director of the Women's Health Program at the Center for Integrative Medicine at O'Connor Hospital in San Jose.